Essentials of Software Engineering

Essentials of
Software Engineering

Edited by Theodore Hammond

LANRYE
INTERNATIONAL
www.clanryeinternational.com

Clanrye International,
750 Third Avenue, 9th Floor,
New York, NY 10017, USA

ISBN: 978-1-63240-704-7

Cataloging-in-Publication Data

Essentials of software engineering / edited by Theodore Hammond.
    p. cm.
Includes bibliographical references and index.
ISBN 978-1-63240-704-7
1. Software engineering. I. Hammond, Theodore.
QA76.758 .E87 2018
005.1--dc23

For information on all Clanrye International publications
visit our website at www.clanryeinternational.com

Contents

Preface

Software engineering refers to the process of applying engineering principles to develop software in a systematic method. It includes developing, designing, researching, operating and compiling system-level software. The field is further divided into many sub-fields like software testing, software quality, software construction, software design, etc. This book outlines the processes and applications of software engineering in detail. The topics included in it are of utmost significance and bound to provide incredible insights to readers. As the field of software engineering is emerging at a rapid pace, the contents of this book will help the readers understand the modern concepts and applications of the subject. The textbook is appropriate for those seeking detailed information in this area.

A foreword of all chapters of the book is provided below:

Chapter 1 - Software engineering is a field of engineering that is devoted to the development of software by writing and designing programs. Software engineering goes through many steps. Firstly, the requirements are taken into account and then the design is created. After this, the software is coded, and then, testing is carried out. This chapter is an overview of the subject matter incorporating all the major aspects of software engineering; **Chapter 2 -** Software design is the process by which the idea of a software is converted into a computer-friendly language. The process normally includes planning a software solution and problem solving. One of its major components is software requirement analysis, which tables the required specification for the software concerned. Software design is best understood in confluence with the major topics listed in the following section; **Chapter 3 -** Programming paradigm is a method to sort languages on the basis of their features. Various types of programming paradigms include structured programming, procedural programming, declarative programming, imperative programming, object-oriented programming, functional programming etc. The major components of programming paradigm are discussed in this chapter; **Chapter 4 -** User interface is the area where interactions between humans and machines take place. Ease of use, ease of access and error prevention are some of the essential features of user interface design. User interface design helps create a design that keeps these aspects in focus while maximizing user-friendliness. The chapter closely examines the key concepts of user interface and its design to provide an extensive understanding of the subject.

At the end, I would like to thank all the people associated with this book devoting their precious time and providing their valuable contributions to this book. I would also like to express my gratitude to my fellow colleagues who encouraged me throughout the process.

Editor

Software Engineering: An Integrated Study

Software engineering is a field of engineering that is devoted to the development of software by writing and designing programs. Software engineering goes through many steps. Firstly, the requirements are taken into account and then the design is created. After this, the software is coded, and then, testing is carried out. This chapter is an overview of the subject matter incorporating all the major aspects of software engineering.

Software Engineering

Software engineering is an engineering approach for software development. We can alternatively view it as a systematic collection of past experience. The experience is arranged in the form of methodologies and guidelines. A small program can be written without using software engineering principles. But if one wants to develop a large software product, then software engineering principles are indispensable to achieve a good quality software cost effectively. These definitions can be elaborated with the help of a building construction analogy.

Suppose you have a friend who asked you to build a small wall as shown in fig. You would be able to do that using your common sense. You will get building materials like bricks; cement etc. and you will then build the wall.

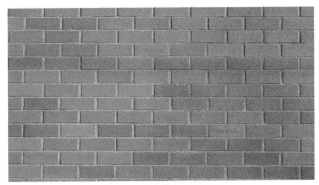

A Small Wall

But what would happen if the same friend asked you to build a large multistoried building as shown in figure below?

A Multistoried Building

You don't have a very good idea about building such a huge complex. It would be very difficult to extend your idea about a small wall construction into constructing a large building. Even if you tried to build a large building, it would collapse because you would not have the requisite knowledge about the strength of materials, testing, planning, architectural design, etc. Building a small wall and building a large building are entirely different ball games. You can use your intuition and still be successful in building a small wall, but building a large building requires knowledge of civil, architectural and other engineering principles.

Without using software engineering principles it would be difficult to develop large programs. In industry it is usually needed to develop large programs to accommodate multiple functions. A problem with developing such large commercial programs is that the complexity and difficulty levels of the programs increase exponentially with their sizes as shown in fig. For example, a program of size 1,000 lines of code has some complexity. But a program with 10,000 LOC is not just 10 times more difficult to develop, but may as well turn out to be 100 times more difficult unless software engineering principles are used. In such situations software engineering techniques come to rescue. Software engineering helps to reduce the programming complexity. Software engineering principles use two important techniques to reduce problem complexity: abstraction and decomposition.

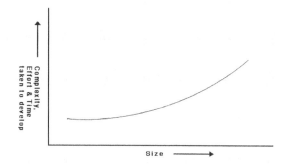
Increase in development time and effort with problem size

The principle of abstraction (in fig) implies that a problem can be simplified by omitting irrelevant details. In other words, the main purpose of abstraction is to consider only those aspects of the problem that are relevant for certain purpose and suppress other aspects that are not relevant for the given purpose. Once the simpler problem is solved, then the omitted details can be taken into consideration to solve the next lower level abstraction, and so on. Abstraction is a powerful way of reducing the complexity of the problem.

The other approach to tackle problem complexity is decomposition. In this technique, a complex problem is divided into several smaller problems and then the smaller problems are solved one by one. However, in this technique any random decomposition of a problem into smaller parts will not help. The problem has to be decomposed such that each component of the decomposed problem can be solved independently and then the solution of the different components can be combined to get the full solution. A good decomposition of a problem as shown in fig. should minimize interactions among various components. If the different subcomponents are interrelated, then the different components cannot be solved separately and the desired reduction in complexity will not be realized.

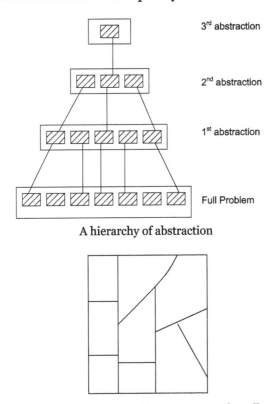

A hierarchy of abstraction

Fig: Decomposition of a large problem into a set of smaller problems.

Causes of and Solutions for Software Crisis

Software engineering appears to be among the few options available to tackle the present software crisis.

To explain the present software crisis in simple words, consider the following. The expenses that organizations all around the world are incurring on software purchases compared to those on hardware purchases have been showing a worrying trend over the years.

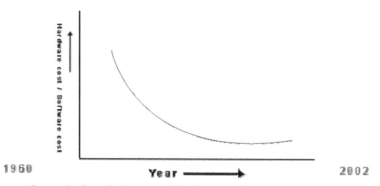

Change in the relative cost of hardware and software over time

Organizations are spending larger and larger portions of their budget on software. Not only are the software products turning out to be more expensive than hardware, but they also present a host of other problems to the customers: software products are difficult to alter, debug, and enhance; use resources non- optimally; often fail to meet the user requirements; are far from being reliable; frequently crash; and are often delivered late. Among these, the trend of increasing software costs is probably the most important symptom of the present software crisis. Remember that the cost we are talking of here is not on account of increased features, but due to ineffective development of the product characterized by inefficient resource usage, and time and cost over-runs.

There are many factors that have contributed to the making of the present software crisis. Factors are larger problem sizes, lack of adequate training in software engineering, increasing skill shortage, and low productivity improvements.

It is believed that the only satisfactory solution to the present software crisis can possibly come from a spread of software engineering practices among the engineers, coupled with further advancements to the software engineering discipline itself.

A software engineer programming

Software engineering (SWE) is the application of engineering to the development of software in a systematic method.

Definitions

Typical formal definitions of software engineering include:

- "Research, design, develop, and test operating systems-level software, compilers, and network distribution software for medical, industrial, military, communications, aerospace, business, scientific, and general computing applications"—Bureau of Labor Statistics

- "The systematic application of scientific and technological knowledge, methods, and experience to the design, implementation, testing, and documentation of software"—The Bureau of Labor Statistics—IEEE *Systems and software engineering - Vocabulary*

- "The application of a systematic, disciplined, quantifiable approach to the development, operation, and maintenance of software"—IEEE *Standard Glossary of Software Engineering Terminology*

- "An engineering discipline that is concerned with all aspects of software production"— Ian Sommerville

- "The establishment and use of sound engineering principles in order to economically obtain software that is reliable and works efficiently on real machines"—Fritz Bauer

History

When the first digital computers appeared in the early 1940s, the instructions to make them operate were wired into the machine. Practitioners quickly realized that this design was not flexible and came up with the "stored program architecture" or von Neumann architecture. Thus the division between "hardware" and "software" began with abstraction being used to deal with the complexity of computing.

Programming languages started to appear in the early 1950s and this was also another major step in abstraction. Major languages such as Fortran, ALGOL, and COBOL were released in the late 1950s to deal with scientific, algorithmic, and business problems respectively. Edsger W. Dijkstra wrote his seminal paper, "Go To Statement Considered Harmful", in 1968 and David Parnas introduced the key concept of modularity and information hiding in 1972 to help programmers deal with the ever increasing complexity of software systems.

The origins of the term "software engineering" have been attributed to different sources, but it was used in 1968 as a title for the World's first conference on software engineering, sponsored and facilitated by NATO. The conference was attended by international experts on software who agreed on defining best practices for software grounded in the application of engineering. The result of the conference is a report that defines how software should be developed. The original report is publicly available.

The discipline of software engineering was created to address poor quality of software, get projects exceeding time and budget under control, and ensure that software is built systematically, rigorously, measurably, on time, on budget, and within specification. Engineering already addresses all these issues, hence the same principles used in engineering can be applied to software. The widespread lack of best practices for software at the time was perceived as a "software crisis".

Barry W. Boehm documented several key advances to the field in his 1981 book, 'Software Engineering Economics'. These include his Constructive Cost Model (COCOMO), which relates software development effort for a program, in man-years T, to *source lines of code* (SLOC). $T = k * (SLOC)^{(1+x)}$ The book analyzes sixty-three software projects and concludes the cost of fixing errors escalates as the project moves toward field use. The book also asserts that the key driver of software cost is the capability of the software development team.

In 1984, the Software Engineering Institute (SEI) was established as a federally funded research and development center headquartered on the campus of Carnegie Mellon University in Pittsburgh, Pennsylvania, United States. Watts Humphrey founded the SEI Software Process Program, aimed at understanding and managing the software engineering process. His 1989 book, Managing the Software Process, asserts that the Software Development Process can and should be controlled, measured, and improved. The Process Maturity Levels introduced would become the Capability Maturity Model Integration for Development(CMMi-DEV), which has defined how the US Government evaluates the abilities of a software development team.

Modern, generally accepted best-practices for software engineering have been collected by the ISO/IEC JTC 1/SC 7 subcommittee and published as the Software Engineering Body of Knowledge (SWEBOK).

Subdisciplines

Software engineering can be divided into 15 sub-disciplines. They are:

- Software requirements (or Requirements engineering): The elicitation, analysis, specification, and validation of requirements for software.

- Software design: The process of defining the architecture, components, interfaces, and other characteristics of a system or component. It is also defined as the result of that process.

- Software construction: The detailed creation of working, meaningful software through a combination of coding, verification, unit testing, integration testing, and debugging.

- Software testing: An empirical, technical investigation conducted to provide stakeholders with information about the quality of the product or service under test.

- Software maintenance: The totality of activities required to provide cost-effective support to software.

- Software configuration management: The identification of the configuration of a system at distinct points in time for the purpose of systematically controlling changes to the configuration, and maintaining the integrity and traceability of the configuration throughout the system life cycle.

- Software engineering management: The application of management activities—planning, coordinating, measuring, monitoring, controlling, and reporting—to ensure that the development and maintenance of software is systematic, disciplined, and quantified.

- Software development process: The definition, implementation, assessment, measurement, management, change, and improvement of the software life cycle process itself.

- Software engineering models and methods impose structure on software engineering with the goal of making that activity systematic, repeatable, and ultimately more success-oriented.

- Software quality

- Software engineering professional practice is concerned with the knowledge, skills, and attitudes that software engineers must possess to practice software engineering in a professional, responsible, and ethical manner.

- Software engineering economics is about making decisions related to software engineering in a business context.

- Computing foundations

- Mathematical foundations

- Engineering foundations

Education

Knowledge of computer programming is a prerequisite for becoming a software engineer. In 2004 the IEEE Computer Society produced the SWEBOK, which has been published as ISO/IEC Technical Report 1979:2004, describing the body of knowledge that they recommend to be mastered by a graduate software engineer with four years of experience. Many software engineers enter the profession by obtaining a university degree or training at a vocational school. One standard international curriculum for undergraduate software engineering degrees was defined by the CCSE, and updated in 2004. A number of universities have Software Engineering degree programs; as of 2010, there were 244 Campus Bachelor of Software Engineering programs, 70 Online programs, 230 Masters-level programs, 41 Doctorate-level programs, and 69 Certificate-level programs in the United States.

For practitioners who wish to become proficient and recognized as professional software engineers, the IEEE offers two certifications that extend knowledge above the level achieved by an academic degree: *Certified Software Development Associate* and *Certified Software Development Professional*.

In addition to university education, many companies sponsor internships for students wishing to pursue careers in information technology. These internships can introduce the student to interesting real-world tasks that typical software engineers encounter every day. Similar experience can be gained through military service in software engineering.

Profession

Legal requirements for the licensing or certification of professional software engineers vary around the World. In the UK, the British Computer Society licenses software engineers and members of the society can also become Chartered Engineers (CEng), while in some areas of Canada, such as Alberta, British Columbia, Ontario, and Quebec, software engineers can hold the Professional Engineer (P.Eng) designation and/or the Information Systems Professional (I.S.P.) designation. In Canada, there is a legal requirement to have P.Eng when one wants to use the title "engineer" or practice "software engineering". In Europe, Software Engineers can obtain the European Engineer (EUR ING) professional title.

The United States, starting from 2013 offers an *NCEES Professional Engineer* exam for Software Engineering, thereby allowing Software Engineers to be licensed and recognized. Mandatory licensing is currently still largely debated, and perceived as controversial. In some parts of the US such as Texas, the use of the term Engineer is regulated by law and reserved only for use by individuals who have a Professional Engineer license. The IEEE informs the professional engineer license is not required unless the individual would work for public where health of others could be at risk if the engineer was not fully qualified to required standards by the particular state. Professional engineer licenses are specific to the state that has awarded them, and have to be regularly retaken.

The IEEE Computer Society and the ACM, the two main US-based professional organizations of software engineering, publish guides to the profession of software engineering.

The IEEE's *Guide to the Software Engineering Body of Knowledge - 2004 Version,* or SWEBOK, defines the field and describes the knowledge the IEEE expects a practicing software engineer to have. The most current SWEBOK v3 is an updated version and was released in 2014. The IEEE also promulgates a "Software Engineering Code of Ethics".

Employment

In November 2004, the U. S. Bureau of Labor Statistics counted 760,840 software engineers holding jobs in the U.S.; in the same time period there were some 1.4 million practitioners employed in the U.S. in all other engineering disciplines combined. Due to its relative newness as a field of study, formal education in software engineering is often taught as part of a computer science curriculum, and many software engineers hold computer science degrees and have no engineering background whatsoever.

Many software engineers work as employees or contractors. Software engineers work with businesses, government agencies (civilian or military), and non-profit organizations. Some software engineers work for themselves as freelancers. Some organizations have specialists to perform each of the tasks in the software development process. Other organizations require software engineers to do many or all of them. In large projects, people may specialize in only one role. In small projects, people may fill several or all roles at the same time. Specializations include: in industry (analysts, architects, developers, testers, technical support, middleware analysts, managers) and in academia (educators, researchers).

Most software engineers and programmers work 40 hours a week, but about 15 percent of software engineers and 11 percent of programmers worked more than 50 hours a week in 2008. Injuries in these occupations are rare. However, like other workers who spend long periods in front of a computer terminal typing at a keyboard, engineers and programmers are susceptible to eyestrain, back discomfort, and hand and wrist problems such as carpal tunnel syndrome.

The field's future looks bright according to Money Magazine and Salary.com, which rated Software Engineer as the best job in the United States in 2006. In 2012, software engineering was again ranked as the best job in the United States, this time by Career-Cast.com.

Certification

The Software Engineering Institute offers certifications on specific topics like security, process improvement and software architecture. Apple, IBM, Microsoft and other companies also sponsor their own certification examinations. Many IT certification programs are oriented toward specific technologies, and managed by the vendors of these technologies. These certification programs are tailored to the institutions that would employ people who use these technologies.

Broader certification of general software engineering skills is available through various professional societies. As of 2006, the IEEE had certified over 575 software professionals as a Certified Software Development Professional (CSDP). In 2008 they added an entry-level certification known as the Certified Software Development Associate (CSDA). The ACM had a professional certification program in the early 1980s, which was discontinued due to lack of interest. The ACM examined the possibility of professional certification of software engineers in the late 1990s, but eventually decided that such certification was inappropriate for the professional industrial practice of software engineering.

In the U.K. the British Computer Society has developed a legally recognized professional certification called *Chartered IT Professional (CITP)*, available to fully qualified members (*MBCS*). Software engineers may be eligible for membership of the Institution of Engineering and Technology and so qualify for Chartered Engineer status. In Canada the Canadian Information Processing Society has developed a legally recognized professional certification called *Information Systems Professional (ISP)*. In Ontario, Canada, Software Engineers who graduate from a *Canadian Engineering Accreditation Board (CEAB)* accredited program, successfully complete PEO's (*Professional Engineers Ontario*) Professional Practice Examination (PPE) and have at least 48 months of acceptable engineering experience are eligible to be licensed through the *Professional Engineers Ontario* and can become Professional Engineers P.Eng. The PEO does not recognize any online or distance education however; and does not consider Computer Science programs to be equivalent to software engineering programs despite the tremendous overlap between the two. This has sparked controversy and a certification war. It has also held the number of P.Eng holders for the profession exceptionally low. The vast majority of working professionals in the field hold a degree in CS, not SE. Given the difficult certification path for holders of non-SE degrees, most never bother to pursue the license.

Impact of Globalization

The initial impact of outsourcing, and the relatively lower cost of international human resources in developing third world countries led to a massive migration of software development activities from corporations in North America and Europe to India and later: China, Russia, and other developing countries. This approach had some flaws, mainly the distance / timezone difference that prevented human interaction between clients and developers and the massive job transfer. This had a negative impact on many aspects of the software engineering profession. For example, some students in the developed world avoid education related to software engineering because of the fear of offshore outsourcing (importing software products or services from other countries) and of being displaced by foreign visa workers. Although statistics do not currently show a threat to software engineering itself; a related career, computer programming does appear to have been affected. Nevertheless, the ability to smartly leverage offshore and near-shore resources via the follow-the-sun workflow has improved the overall operational capability of many organizations. When North Americans are leaving work, Asians are just arriving to work.

When Asians are leaving work, Europeans are arriving to work. This provides a continuous ability to have human oversight on business-critical processes 24 hours per day, without paying overtime compensation or disrupting a key human resource, sleep patterns.

While global outsourcing has several advantages, global - and generally distributed - development can run into serious difficulties resulting from the distance between developers. This is due to the key elements of this type of distance that have been identified as geographical, temporal, cultural and communication (that includes the use of different languages and dialects of English in different locations). Research has been carried out in the area of global software development over the last 15 years and an extensive body of relevant work published that highlights the benefits and problems associated with the complex activity. As with other aspects of software engineering research is ongoing in this and related areas.

Related Fields

Software engineering is a direct sub-field of engineering and has an overlap with computer science and management science. It is also considered a part of overall systems engineering.

Controversy

Over Definition

Typical formal definitions of software engineering are:

- "The application of a systematic, disciplined, quantifiable approach to the development, operation, and maintenance of software".

- "An engineering discipline that is concerned with all aspects of software production".

- "The establishment and use of sound engineering principles in order to economically obtain software that is reliable and works efficiently on real machines".

The term has been used less formally:

- As the informal contemporary term for the broad range of activities that were formerly called computer programming and systems analysis;

- As the broad term for all aspects of the *practice* of computer programming, as opposed to the *theory* of computer programming, which is called computer science;

- As the term embodying the *advocacy* of a specific approach to computer programming, one that urges that it be treated as an engineering discipline rather than an art or a craft, and advocates the codification of recommended practices.

Criticism

Software engineering sees its practitioners as individuals who follow well-defined engineering approaches to problem-solving. These approaches are specified in various software engineering books and research papers, always with the connotations of predictability, precision, mitigated risk and professionalism. This perspective has led to calls for licensing, certification and codified bodies of knowledge as mechanisms for spreading the engineering knowledge and maturing the field.

Software craftsmanship has been proposed by a body of software developers as an alternative that emphasizes the coding skills and accountability of the software developers themselves without professionalism or any prescribed curriculum leading to ad-hoc problem-solving (craftmanship) without engineering (lack of predictability, precision, missing risk mitigation, methods are informal and poorly defined). The Software Craftsmanship Manifesto extends the Agile Software Manifesto and draws a metaphor between modern software development and the apprenticeship model of medieval Europe.

Software engineering extends engineering and draws on the engineering model, i.e. engineering process, engineering project management, engineering requirements, engineering design, engineering construction, and engineering validation. The concept is so new that it is rarely understood, and it is widely misinterpreted, including in software engineering textbooks, papers, and among the communities of programmers and crafters.

One of the core issues in software engineering is that its approaches are not empirical enough because a real-world validation of approaches is usually absent, or very limited and hence software engineering is often misinterpreted as feasible only in a "theoretical environment."

Dijkstra who developed computer languages in the last century refuted the concepts of "software engineering" that was prevalent thirty years ago in the 1980s, arguing that those terms were poor analogies for what he called the "radical novelty" of computer science:

A number of these phenomena have been bundled under the name "Software Engineering". As economics is known as "The Miserable Science", software engineering should be known as "The Doomed Discipline", doomed because it cannot even approach its goal since its goal is self-contradictory. Software engineering, of course, presents itself as another worthy cause, but that is eyewash: if you carefully read its literature and analyse what its devotees actually do, you will discover that software engineering has accepted as its charter "How to program if you cannot."

Software Requirements

Software requirements is a field within software engineering that deals with establishing the needs of stakeholders that are to be solved by software. The IEEE Standard

Glossary of Software Engineering Terminology defines a requirement as:

1. A condition or capability needed by a user to solve a problem or achieve an objective.

2. A condition or capability that must be met or possessed by a system or system component to satisfy a contract, standard, specification, or other formally imposed document.

3. A documented representation of a condition or capability as in 1 or 2.

The activities related to working with software requirements can broadly be broken down into elicitation, analysis, specification, and management.

Elicitation

Elicitation is the gathering and discovery of requirements from stakeholders and other sources. A variety of techniques can be used such as joint application design (JAD) sessions, interviews, document analysis, focus groups, etc. Elicitation is the first step of requirements development.

Analysis

Analysis is the logical breakdown that proceeds from elicitation. Analysis involves reaching a richer and more precise understanding of each requirement and representing sets of requirements in multiple, complementary ways.

Specification

Specification involves representing and storing the collected requirements knowledge in a persistent and well-organized fashion that facilitates effective communication and change management. Use cases, user stories, functional requirements, and visual analysis models are popular choices for requirements specification.

Validation

Validation involves techniques to confirm that the correct set of requirements has been specified to build a solution that satisfies the project's business objectives.

Management

Requirements change during projects and there are often many of them. Management of this change becomes paramount to ensuring that the correct software is built for the stakeholders.

Tool Support for Requirements Engineering

Specialized commercial tools for requirements engineering are 3SL Cradle, IRise, Gatherspace, Rational RequisitePro, Doors, CaliberRM or QFDCapture, but also free tools like FreeMind and Concordion can be used. Issue trackers implementing the Volere requirements template have been used successfully in distributed environments.

Software Project Planning

Once a project is found to be feasible, software project managers undertake project planning. Project planning is undertaken and completed even before any development activity starts. Project planning consists of the following essential activities:

- Estimating the following attributes of the project:

Project size: What will be problem complexity in terms of the effort and time required to develop the product?

Cost: How much is it going to cost to develop the project? Duration: How long is it going to take to complete development? Effort: How much effort would be required?

The effectiveness of the subsequent planning activities is based on the accuracy of these estimations.

- Scheduling manpower and other resources

- Staff organization and staffing plans

- Risk identification, analysis, and abatement planning

- Miscellaneous plans such as quality assurance plan, configuration management plan, etc.

Precedence Ordering Among Project Planning Activities

Different project related estimates done by a project manager have already been discussed. Figure shows the order in which important project planning activities may be undertaken. From figure it can be easily observed that size estimation is the first activity. It is also the most fundamental parameter based on which all other planning activities are carried out. Other estimations such as estimation of effort, cost, resource, and project duration are also very important components of project planning.

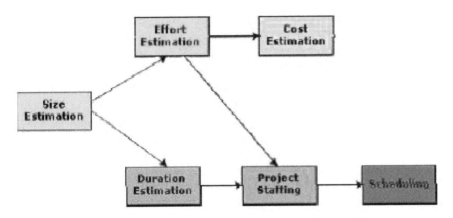

Precedence ordering among planning activities

Sliding Window Planning

Project planning requires utmost care and attention since commitment to unrealistic time and resource estimates result in schedule slippage. Schedule delays can cause customer dissatisfaction and adversely affect team morale. It can even cause project failure. However, project planning is a very challenging activity. Especially for large projects, it is very much difficult to make accurate plans. A part of this difficulty is due to the fact that the proper parameters, scope of the project, project staff, etc. may change during the span of the project. In order to overcome this problem, sometimes project managers undertake project planning in stages. Planning a project over a number of stages protects managers from making big commitments too early. This technique of staggered planning is known as Sliding Window Planning. In the sliding window technique, starting with an initial plan, the project is planned more accurately in successive development stages. At the start of a project, project managers have incomplete knowledge about the details of the project. Their information base gradually improves as the project progresses through different phases. After the completion of every phase, the project managers can plan each subsequent phase more accurately and with increasing levels of confidence.

Software Project Management Plan (SPMP)

Once project planning is complete, project managers document their plans in a Software Project Management Plan (SPMP) document. The SPMP document should discuss a list of different items that have been discussed below. This list can be used as a possible organization of the SPMP document.

Organization of the Software Project Management Plan (SPMP) Document

1. Introduction

    (a)   Objectives

(b)   Major Functions

(c)   Performance Issues

(d)   Management and Technical Constraints

2. Project Estimates

(a)   Historical Data Used

(b)   Estimation Techniques Used

(c)   Effort, Resource, Cost, and Project Duration Estimates

3. Schedule

(a)   Work Breakdown Structure

(b)   Task Network Representation

(c)   Gantt Chart Representation

(d)   PERT Chart Representation

4. Project Resources

(a)   People

(b)   Hardware and Software

(c)   Special Resources

5. Staff Organization

(a)   Team Structure

(b)   Management Reporting

6. Risk Management Plan

(a)   Risk Analysis

(b)   Risk Identification

(c)   Risk Estimation

(d)   Risk Abatement Procedures

7. Project Tracking and Control Plan

8. Miscellaneous Plans

(a)   Process Tailoring

(b)   Quality Assurance Plan

(c)   Configuration Management Plan

(d)   Validation and Verification

(e)   System Testing Plan

(f)   Delivery, Installation, and Maintenance Plan

Metrics for Software Project Size Estimation

Accurate estimation of the problem size is fundamental to satisfactory estimation of effort, time duration and cost of a software project. In order to be able to accurately estimate the project size, some important metrics should be defined in terms of which the project size can be expressed. The size of a problem is obviously not the number of bytes that the source code occupies. It is neither the byte size of the executable code. The project size is a measure of the problem complexity in terms of the effort and time required to develop the product.

Currently two metrics are popularly being used widely to estimate size: lines of code (LOC) and function point (FP). The usage of each of these metrics in project size estimation has its own advantages and disadvantages.

Lines of Code (LOC)

LOC is the simplest among all metrics available to estimate project size. This metric is very popular because it is the simplest to use. Using this metric, the project size is estimated by counting the number of source instructions in the developed program. Obviously, while counting the number of source instructions, lines used for commenting the code and the header lines should be ignored.

Determining the LOC count at the end of a project is a very simple job. However, accurate estimation of the LOC count at the beginning of a project is very difficult. In order to estimate the LOC count at the beginning of a project, project managers usually divide the problem into modules, and each module into submodules and so on, until the sizes of the different leaf-level modules can be approximately predicted. To be able to do this, past experience in developing similar products is helpful. By using the estimation of the lowest level modules, project managers arrive at the total size estimation.

Function Point (FP)

Function point metric was proposed by Albrecht [1983]. This metric overcomes many of the shortcomings of the LOC metric. Since its inception in late 1970s, function point metric has been slowly gaining popularity. One of the important advantages of using the function point metric is that it can be used to easily estimate the size of a software product directly from the problem specification. This is in contrast to the LOC metric, where the size can be accurately determined only after the product has fully been developed.

The conceptual idea behind the function point metric is that the size of a software product is directly dependent on the number of different functions or features it supports. A software product supporting many features would certainly be of larger size than a product with less number of features. Each function when invoked reads some input data and transforms it to the corresponding output data. For example, the issue book feature of a Library Automation Software takes the name of the book as input and displays its location and the number of copies available. Thus, a computation of the number of input and the output data values to a system gives some indication of the number of functions supported by the system. Albrecht postulated that in addition to the number of basic functions that a software performs, the size is also dependent on the number of files and the number of interfaces.

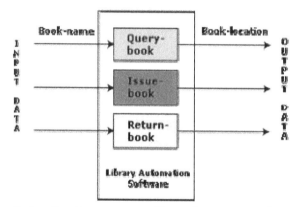

System function as a map of input data to output data

Besides using the number of input and output data values, function point metric computes the size of a software product (in units of functions points or FPs) using three other characteristics of the product as shown in the following expression. The size of a product in function points (FP) can be expressed as the weighted sum of these five problem characteristics. The weights associated with the five characteristics were proposed empirically and validated by the observations over many projects. Function point is computed in two steps. The first step is to compute the unadjusted function point (UFP).

UFP = (Number of inputs)*4 + (Number of outputs)*5 +

(Number of inquiries)*4 + (Number of files)*10 +

(Number of interfaces)*10

Number of inputs: Each data item input by the user is counted. Data inputs should be distinguished from user inquiries. Inquiries are user commands such as print-account-balance. Inquiries are counted separately. It must be noted that individual data items input by the user are not considered in the calculation of the number of inputs, but a group of related inputs are considered as a single input.

For example, while entering the data concerning an employee to employee pay roll software; the data items name, age, sex, address, phone number, etc. are together considered as a single input. All these data items can be considered to be related, since they pertain to a single employee.

Number of outputs: The outputs considered refer to reports printed, screen outputs, error messages produced, etc. While outputting the number of outputs the individual data items within a report are not considered, but a set of related data items is counted as one input.

Number of inquiries: Number of inquiries is the number of distinct interactive queries which can be made by the users. These inquiries are the user commands which require specific action by the system.

Number of files: Each logical file is counted. A logical file means groups of logically related data. Thus, logical files can be data structures or physical files.

Number of interfaces: Here the interfaces considered are the interfaces used to exchange information with other systems. Examples of such interfaces are data files on tapes, disks, communication links with other systems etc.

Once the unadjusted function point (UFP) is computed, the technical complexity factor (TCF) is computed next. TCF refines the UFP measure by considering fourteen other factors such as high transaction rates, throughput, and response time requirements, etc. Each of these 14 factors is assigned from 0 (not present or no influence) to 6 (strong influence). The resulting numbers are summed, yielding the total degree of influence (DI). Now, TCF is computed as (0.65+0.01*DI). As DI can vary from 0 to 70, TCF can vary from 0.65 to 1.35. Finally, FP=UFP*TCF.

Shortcomings of Function Point (FP) Metric

LOC as a measure of problem size has several shortcomings:

- LOC gives a numerical value of problem size that can vary widely with individual coding style – different programmers lay out their code in different ways. For example, one programmer might write several source instructions on a single line whereas another might split a single instruction across several lines. Of course, this problem can be easily overcome by counting the language tokens in the program rather than the lines of code. However, a more intricate problem arises because the length of a program depends on the choice of instructions used in writing the program. Therefore, even for the same problem, different programmers might come up with programs having different LOC counts. This situation does not improve even if language tokens are counted instead of lines of code.

- A good problem size measure should consider the overall complexity of the problem and the effort needed to solve it. That is, it should consider the local effort needed to specify, design, code, test, etc. and not just the coding effort. LOC, however, focuses on the coding activity alone; it merely computes the number of source lines in the final program. We have already seen that coding is only a small part of the overall software development activities. It is also wrong to argue that the overall product development effort is proportional to the effort required in writing the program code. This is because even though the design might be very complex, the code might be straightforward and vice versa. In such cases, code size is a grossly improper indicator of the problem size.

- LOC measure correlates poorly with the quality and efficiency of the code. Larger code size does not necessarily imply better quality or higher efficiency. Some programmers produce lengthy and complicated code as they do not make effective use of the available instruction set. In fact, it is very likely that a poor and sloppily written piece of code might have larger number of source instructions than a piece that is neat and efficient.

- LOC metric penalizes use of higher-level programming languages, code reuse, etc. The paradox is that if a programmer consciously uses several library routines, then the LOC count will be lower. This would show up as smaller program size. Thus, if managers use the LOC count as a measure of the effort put in the different engineers (that is, productivity), they would be discouraging code reuse by engineers.

- LOC metric measures the lexical complexity of a program and does not address the more important but subtle issues of logical or structural complexities. Between two programs with equal LOC count, a program having complex logic would require much more effort to develop than a program with very simple logic. To realize why this is so, consider the effort required to develop a program having multiple nested loop and decision constructs with another program having only sequential control flow.

- It is very difficult to accurately estimate LOC in the final product from the problem specification. The LOC count can be accurately computed only after the code has been fully developed. Therefore, the LOC metric is little use to the project managers during project planning, since project planning is carried out even before any development activity has started. This possibly is the biggest shortcoming of the LOC metric from the project manager's perspective.

Feature Point Metric

A major shortcoming of the function point measure is that it does not take into account the algorithmic complexity of a software. That is, the function point metric implicitly assumes that the effort required to design and develop any two functionalities of the system is the same. But, we know that this is normally not true, the effort required to develop any two functionalities may vary widely. It only takes the number of functions that the system supports into consideration without distinguishing the difficulty level of developing the various functionalities. To overcome this problem, an extension of the function point metric called feature point metric is proposed.

Feature point metric incorporates an extra parameter algorithm complexity. This parameter ensures that the computed size using the feature point metric reflects the fact that the more is the complexity of a function, the greater is the effort required to develop it and therefore its size should be larger compared to simpler functions.

Project Estimation Techniques

Estimation of various project parameters is a basic project planning activity. The important project parameters that are estimated include: project size, effort required to develop the software, project duration, and cost. These estimates not only help in quoting the project cost to the customer, but are also useful in resource planning and scheduling. There are three broad categories of estimation techniques:

- Empirical estimation techniques

- Heuristic techniques

- Analytical estimation techniques

Empirical Estimation Techniques

Empirical estimation techniques are based on making an educated guess of the project parameters. While using this technique, prior experience with development of similar products is helpful. Although empirical estimation techniques are based on common sense, different activities involved in estimation have been formalized over the years. Two popular empirical estimation techniques are: Expert judgment technique and Delphi cost estimation.

Expert Judgment Technique

Expert judgment is one of the most widely used estimation techniques. In this approach, an expert makes an educated guess of the problem size after analyzing the problem thoroughly. Usually, the expert estimates the cost of the different components (i.e. modules or subsystems) of the system and then combines them to arrive at the overall estimate. However, this technique is subject to human errors and individual bias. Also, it is possible that the expert may overlook some factors inadvertently. Further, an expert making an estimate may not have experience and knowledge of all aspects of a project. For example, he may be conversant with the database and user interface parts but may not be very knowledgeable about the computer communication part.

A more refined form of expert judgment is the estimation made by group of experts. Estimation by a group of experts minimizes factors such as individual oversight, lack of familiarity with a particular aspect of a project, personal bias, and the desire to win contract through overly optimistic estimates. However, the estimate made by a group of experts may still exhibit bias on issues where the entire group of experts may be biased due to reasons such as political considerations. Also, the decision made by the group may be dominated by overly assertive members.

Delphi Cost Estimation

Delphi cost estimation approach tries to overcome some of the shortcomings of the expert judgment approach. Delphi estimation is carried out by a team comprising of a group of experts and a coordinator. In this approach, the coordinator provides each estimator with a copy of the software requirements specification (SRS) document and a form for recording his cost estimate. Estimators complete their individual estimates anonymously and submit to the coordinator. In their estimates, the estimators mention any unusual characteristic of the product which has influenced his estimation. The coordinator prepares and distributes the summary of the responses of all the estimators, and includes any unusual rationale noted by any of the estimators. Based on this summary, the estimators re-estimate. This process is iterated for several rounds. However, no discussion among the estimators is allowed during the entire estimation process. The idea behind this is that if any discussion is allowed among the estimators, then many estimators may easily get influenced by the rationale of an estimator who may be more experienced or senior. After the completion of several iterations of estimations, the coordinator takes the responsibility of compiling the results and preparing the final estimate.

Heuristic Techniques

Heuristic techniques assume that the relationships among the different project parameters can be modeled using suitable mathematical expressions. Once the basic (independent) parameters are known, the other (dependent) parameters can be easily determined by substituting the value of the basic parameters in the mathematical expression. Different heuristic estimation models can be divided into the following two classes: single variable model and the multi variable model.

Single variable estimation models provide a means to estimate the desired characteristics of a problem, using some previously estimated basic (independent) characteristic of the software product such as its size. A single variable estimation model takes the following form:

$$\text{Estimated Parameter} = c_1 * e^{d_1}$$

In the above expression, e is the characteristic of the software which has already been estimated (independent variable). Estimated Parameter is the dependent parameter to be estimated. The dependent parameter to be estimated could be effort, project duration, staff size, etc. c_1 and d_1 are constants. The values of the constants c_1 and d_1 are usually determined using data collected from past projects (historical data). The basic COCOMO model is an example of single variable cost estimation model.

A multivariable cost estimation model takes the following form:

$$\text{Estimated Resource} = c_1 * e^{d_1} + c_2 * e^{d_2} + \dots$$

Where e_1, e_2,... are the basic (independent) characteristics of the software already estimated, and c_1, c_2, d_1, d_2,... are constants. Multivariable estimation models are expected to give more accurate estimates compared to the single variable models, since a project parameter is typically influenced by several independent parameters. The independent parameters influence the dependent parameter to different extents. This is modeled by the constants c_1, c_2, d_1, d_2,.... . Values of these constants are usually determined from historical data. The intermediate COCOMO model can be considered to be an example of a multivariable estimation model.

Analytical Estimation Techniques

Analytical estimation techniques derive the required results starting with basic assumptions regarding the project. Thus, unlike empirical and heuristic techniques, analytical techniques do have scientific basis. Halstead's software science is an example of an analytical technique. Halstead's software science can be used to derive some interesting results starting with a few simple assumptions. Halstead's software science is especially useful for estimating software maintenance efforts. In fact, it outperforms both empirical and heuristic techniques when used for predicting software maintenance efforts.

Halstead's Software Science – An Analytical Technique

Halstead's software science is an analytical technique to measure size, development effort, and development cost of software products. Halstead used a few primitive program parameters to develop the expressions for over all program length, potential minimum value, actual volume, effort, and development time.

For a given program, let:

- η_1 be the number of unique operators used in the program,

- η_2 be the number of unique operands used in the program,

- N_1 be the total number of operators used in the program,

- N_2 be the total number of operands used in the program.

Length and Vocabulary

The length of a program as defined by Halstead, quantifies total usage of all operators and operands in the program. Thus, length $N = N_1 + N_2$. Halstead's definition of the length of the program as the total number of operators and operands roughly agrees with the intuitive notation of the program length as the total number of tokens used in the program.

The program vocabulary is the number of unique operators and operands used in the program. Thus, program vocabulary $\eta = \eta_1 + \eta_2$.

Program Volume

The length of a program (i.e. the total number of operators and operands used in the code) depends on the choice of the operators and operands used. In other words, for the same programming problem, the length would depend on the programming style. This type of dependency would produce different measures of length for essentially the same problem when different programming languages are used. Thus, while expressing program size, the programming language used must be taken into consideration:

$$V = N \log_2 \eta$$

Here the program volume V is the minimum number of bits needed to encode the program. In fact, to represent η different identifiers uniquely, at least $\log_2 \eta$ bits (where η is the program vocabulary) will be needed. In this scheme, $N \log_2 \eta$ bits will be needed to store a program of length N. Therefore, the volume V represents the size of the program by approximately compensating for the effect of the programming language used.

Potential Minimum Volume

The potential minimum volume V* is defined as the volume of most succinct program in which a problem can be coded. The minimum volume is obtained when the program can be expressed using a single source code instruction., say a function call like foo( ) ;. In other words, the volume is bound from below due to the fact that a program would have at least two operators and no less than the requisite number of operands.

Thus, if an algorithm operates on input and output data $d_1, d_2, \dots d_n$, the most succinct program would be $f(d_1, d_2, \dots d_n)$; for which $\eta_1 = 2$, $\eta_2 = n$. Therefore, $V^* = (2 + \eta_2) \log_2 (2 + \eta_2)$

The program level L is given by L = V*/V. The concept of program level L is introduced in an attempt to measure the level of abstraction provided by the programming language. Using this definition, languages can be ranked into levels that also appear intuitively correct.

The above result implies that the higher the level of a language, the less effort it takes to develop a program using that language. This result agrees with the intuitive notion that it takes more effort to develop a program in assembly language than to develop a program in a high-level language to solve a problem.

Effort and Time

The effort required to develop a program can be obtained by dividing the program volume with the level of the programming language used to develop the code. Thus, effort $E = V/L$, where E is the number of mental discriminations required to implement the program and also the effort required to read and understand the program. Thus, the programming effort $E = V^2/V^*$ (since $L = V^*/V$) varies as the square of the volume. Experience shows that E is well correlated to the effort needed for maintenance of an existing program.

The programmer's time $T = E/S$, where S the speed of mental discriminations. The value of S has been empirically developed from psychological reasoning, and its recommended value for programming applications is 18.

Length Estimation

Even though the length of a program can be found by calculating the total number of operators and operands in a program, Halstead suggests a way to determine the length of a program using the number of unique operators and operands used in the program. Using this method, the program parameters such as length, volume, cost, effort, etc. can be determined even before the start of any programming activity. His method is summarized below.

Halstead assumed that it is quite unlikely that a program has several identical parts– in formal language terminology identical substrings – of length greater than η (η being the program vocabulary). In fact, once a piece of code occurs identically at several places, it is made into a procedure or a function. Thus, it can be assumed that any program of length N consists of N/η unique strings of length η. Now, it is standard combinatorial result that for any given alphabet of size K, there are exactly K^r different strings of length r.

Thus

$$N/\eta \leq \eta^\eta \ \text{Or} \ N \leq \eta^{\eta+1}$$

Since operators and operands usually alternate in a program, the upper bound can be further refined into $N \leq \eta \eta_1^{\eta_1} \eta_2^{\eta_2}$. Also, N must include not only the ordered set of n elements, but it should also include all possible subsets of that ordered sets, i.e. the power set of N strings (This particular reasoning of Halstead is not very convincing!!!).

Therefore,

$$2^N = \eta \eta_1^{\eta_1} \eta_2^{\eta_2}$$

Or, taking logarithm on both sides,

$$N = \log_2 \eta + \log_2 \left(\eta_1^{\eta_1} \eta_2^{\eta_2} \right)$$

So we get,

$$N = \log_2 \left(\eta_1^{\eta_1} \eta_2^{\eta_2} \right)$$

(approximately, by ignoring $\log_2 \eta$)

Or

$$N = \log_2 \eta_1^{\eta_1} + \log_2 \eta_2^{\eta_2}$$
$$= \eta_1 \log_2 \eta_1 + \eta_2 \log_2 \log_2 \eta_2$$

Experimental evidence gathered from the analysis of larger number of programs suggests that the computed and actual lengths match very closely. However, the results may be inaccurate when small programs when considered individually.

In conclusion, Halstead's theory tries to provide a formal definition and quantification of such qualitative attributes as program complexity, ease of understanding, and the level of abstraction based on some low-level parameters such as the number of operands, and operators appearing in the program. Halstead's software science provides gross estimation of properties of a large collection of software, but extends to individual cases rather inaccurately.

Example:

Let us consider the following C program:

```
main( )
{
        int a, b, c, avg;


        scanf("%d %d %d", &a, &b, &c);
```

```
        avg = (a+b+c)/3;

        printf("avg = %d", avg);

}
```

The unique operators are:

main,(),{},int,scanf,&,",",";",=,+,/, printf

The unique operands are:

a, b, c, &a, &b, &c, a+b+c, avg, 3,

"%d %d %d", "avg = %d"

Therefore,

$$\eta_1 = 12, \eta_2 = 11$$

Estimated Length   = (12*log12 + 11*log11)

               = (12*3.58 + 11*3.45)

               = (43+38) = 81

Volume   = Length*log(23)

             = 81*4.52

             = 366

COCOMO

The Constructive Cost Model (COCOMO) is a procedural software cost estimation model developed by Barry W. Boehm. The model parameters are derived from fitting a regression formula using data from historical projects (61 projects for COCOMO 81 and 163 projects for COCOMO II).

History

The constructive cost model was developed by Barry W.Boehm in the late 1970s and published in Boehm's 1981 book *Software Engineering Economics* as a model for estimating effort, cost, and schedule for software projects. It drew on a study of 63 projects at TRW Aerospace where Boehm was Director of Software Research and Technology. The study examined projects ranging in size from 2,000 to 100,000 lines of code, and programming languages ranging from assembly to PL/I. These projects were based on the waterfall model of software development which was the prevalent software development process in 1981.

References to this model typically call it *COCOMO 81*. In 1995 *COCOMO II* was developed and finally published in 2000 in the book *Software Cost Estimation with COCOMO II*. COCOMO II is the successor of COCOMO 81 and is claimed to be better suited for estimating modern software development projects; providing support for more recent software development processes and was tuned using a larger database of 161 projects. The need for the new model came as software development technology moved from mainframe and overnight batch processing to desktop development, code reusability, and the use of off-the-shelf software components.

COCOMO consists of a hierarchy of three increasingly detailed and accurate forms. The first level, *Basic COCOMO* is good for quick, early, rough order of magnitude estimates of software costs, but its accuracy is limited due to its lack of factors to account for difference in project attributes (*Cost Drivers*). *Intermediate COCOMO* takes these Cost Drivers into account and *Detailed COCOMO* additionally accounts for the influence of individual project phases.

Basic COCOMO

Basic COCOMO compute software development effort (and cost) as a function of program size. Program size is expressed in estimated thousands of source lines of code (SLOC, KLOC).

COCOMO applies to three classes of software projects:

- Organic projects - "small" teams with "good" experience working with "less than rigid" requirements

- Semi-detached projects - "medium" teams with mixed experience working with a mix of rigid and less than rigid requirements

- Embedded projects - developed within a set of "tight" constraints. It is also combination of organic and semi-detached projects.(hardware, software, operational, ...)

The basic COCOMO equations take the form

$$\text{Effort Applied (E)} = a_b \left(\text{KLOC} \right)^{b_b} \text{ [man-months]}$$

$$\text{Development Time (D)} = c_b \left(\text{Effort Applied} \right)^{d_b} \text{ [months]}$$

$$\text{People required (P)} = \text{Effort Applied / Development Time [count]}$$

where, KLOC is the estimated number of delivered lines (expressed in thousands) of code for project. The coefficients a_b, b_b, c_b and d_b are given in the following table (note: the values listed below are from the original analysis, with a modern reanalysis producing different values):

Software project	a_b	b_b	c_b	d_b
Organic	2.4	1.05	2.5	0.38
Semi-detached	3.0	1.12	2.5	0.35
Embedded	3.6	1.20	2.5	0.32

Basic COCOMO is good for quick estimate of software costs. However it does not account for differences in hardware constraints, personnel quality and experience, use of modern tools and techniques, and so on.

Intermediate COCOMOs

Intermediate COCOMO computes software development effort as function of program size and a set of "cost drivers" that include subjective assessment of product, hardware, personnel and project attributes. This extension considers a set of four "cost drivers", each with a number of subsidiary attributes:-

- Product attributes

  o Required software reliability

  o Size of application database

  o Complexity of the product

- Hardware attributes

  o Run-time performance constraints

  o Memory constraints

  o Volatility of the virtual machine environment

  o Required turnabout time

- Personnel attributes

  o Analyst capability

  o Software engineering capability

  o Applications experience

  o Virtual machine experience

    o Programming language experience

  • Project attributes

    o Use of software tools

    o Application of software engineering methods

    o Required development schedule

Each of the 15 attributes receives a rating on a six-point scale that ranges from "very low" to "extra high" (in importance or value). An effort multiplier from the table below applies to the rating. The product of all effort multipliers results in an *effort adjustment factor (EAF)*. Typical values for EAF range from 0.9 to 1.4.

Cost Drivers	Ratings					
	Very Low	Low	Nominal	High	Very High	Extra High
Product attributes						
Required software reliability	0.75	0.88	1.00	1.15	1.40	
Size of application database		0.94	1.00	1.08	1.16	
Complexity of the product	0.70	0.85	1.00	1.15	1.30	1.65
Hardware attributes						
Run-time performance constraints			1.00	1.11	1.30	1.66
Memory constraints			1.00	1.06	1.21	1.56
Volatility of the virtual machine environment		0.87	1.00	1.15	1.30	
Required turnabout time		0.87	1.00	1.07	1.15	
Personnel attributes						
Analyst capability	1.46	1.19	1.00	0.86	0.71	
Applications experience	1.29	1.13	1.00	0.91	0.82	
Software engineer capability	1.42	1.17	1.00	0.86	0.70	
Virtual machine experience	1.21	1.10	1.00	0.90		
Programming language experience	1.14	1.07	1.00	0.95		
Project attributes						
Application of software engineering methods	1.24	1.10	1.00	0.91	0.82	
Use of software tools	1.24	1.10	1.00	0.91	0.83	
Required development schedule	1.23	1.08	1.00	1.04	1.10	

The Intermediate Cocomo formula now takes the form:

$$E = a_i \left(KLoC \right)^{(b_i)} \left(EAF \right)$$

where E is the effort applied in person-months, **KLoC** is the estimated number of thousands of delivered lines of code for the project, and **EAF** is the factor calculated above. The coefficient a_i and the exponent b_i are given in the next table.

Software project	a_i	b_i
Organic	3.2	1.05
Semi-detached	3.0	1.12
Embedded	2.8	1.20

The Development time **D** calculation uses **E** in the same way as in the Basic COCOMO.

Detailed COCOMO

Detailed COCOMO incorporates all characteristics of the intermediate version with an assessment of the cost driver's impact on each step (analysis, design, etc.) of the software engineering process.

The detailed model uses different effort multipliers for each cost driver attribute. These Phase Sensitive effort multipliers are each to determine the amount of effort required to complete each phase. In detailed cocomo,the whole software is divided in different modules and then we apply COCOMO in different modules to estimate effort and then sum the effort

In detailed COCOMO, the effort is calculated as function of program size and a set of cost drivers given according to each phase of software life cycle.

A Detailed project schedule is never static.

The Six phases of detailed COCOMO are:-

- plan and requirement.

- system design.

- detailed design.

- module code and test.

- integration and test.

- Cost Constructive model

COCOMO (Constructive Cost Estimation Model) was proposed by Boehm [1981]. According to Boehm, software cost estimation should be done through three stages: Basic COCOMO, Intermediate COCOMO, and Complete COCOMO.

Basic COCOMO Model

The basic COCOMO model gives an approximate estimate of the project parameters. The basic COCOMO estimation model is given by the following expressions:

$$Effort = a_1 x \left(KLOC\right)^{a_2} PM$$

$$Tdev = b_1 x \left(KLOC\right)^{b_2} Months$$

Where

- KLOC is the estimated size of the software product expressed in Kilo Lines of Code,

- a_1, a_2, b_1, b_2 are constants for each category of software products,

- Tdev is the estimated time to develop the software, expressed in months,

- Effort is the total effort required to develop the software product, expressed in person months (PMs).

The effort estimation is expressed in units of person-months (PM). It is the area under the person-month plot. It should be carefully noted that an effort of 100 PM does not imply that 100 persons should work for 1 month nor does it imply that 1 person should be employed for 100 months, but it denotes the area under the person-month curve.

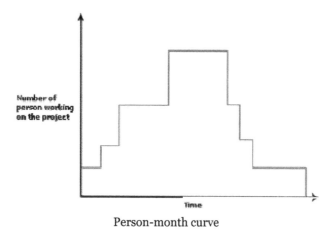

Person-month curve

According to Boehm, every line of source text should be calculated as one LOC irrespective of the actual number of instructions on that line. Thus, if a single instruction spans several lines (say n lines), it is considered to be nLOC. The values of a_1, a_2, b_1, b_2 for different categories of products (i.e. organic, semidetached, and embedded) as given by Boehm [1981] are summarized below. He derived the above expressions by examining historical data collected from a large number of actual projects.

Estimation of Development Effort

For the three classes of software products, the formulas for estimating the effort based on the code size are shown below:

Organic : Effort = $2.4(KLOC)^{1.05}$ PM

Semi-detached : Effort = $3.0(KLOC)^{1.12}$ PM

Embedded : Effort = $3.6(KLOC)^{1.20}$ PM

Estimation of Development Time

For the three classes of software products, the formulas for estimating the development time based on the effort are given below:

Organic : Tdev = $2.5(Effort)^{0.38}$ Months

Semi-detached : Tdev = $2.5(Effort)^{0.35}$ Months

Embedded : Tdev = $2.5(Effort)^{0.32}$ Months

some insight into the basic COCOMO model can be obtained by plotting the estimated characteristics for different software sizes. Figure shows a plot of estimated effort versus product size. From figure, we can observe that the effort is somewhat superlinear in the size of the software product. Thus, the effort required to develop a product increases very rapidly with project size.

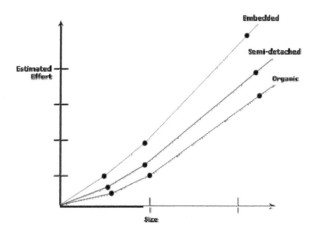

Effort versus product size

The development time versus the product size in KLOC is plotted in figure. From figure, it can be observed that the development time is a sublinear function of the size of the product, i.e. when the size of the product increases by two times, the time to develop the product does not double but rises moderately. This can be explained by the fact that for larger products, a larger number of activities which can be carried out concurrently can be identified. The parallel activities can be carried out simultaneously by the engineers. This reduces the time to complete the project. Further, from figure, it can be observed that the development time is roughly the same for all the three categories of products. For example, a 60 KLOC program can be developed in approximately 18 months, regardless of whether it is of organic, semidetached, or embedded type.

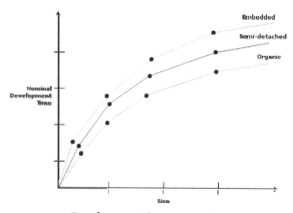

Development time versus size

From the effort estimation, the project cost can be obtained by multiplying the required effort by the manpower cost per month. But, implicit in this project cost computation is the assumption that the entire project cost is incurred on account of the manpower cost alone. In addition to manpower cost, a project would incur costs due to hardware and software required for the project and the company overheads for administration, office space, etc.

It is important to note that the effort and the duration estimations obtained using the COCOMO model are called as nominal effort estimate and nominal duration estimate. The term nominal implies that if anyone tries to complete the project in a time shorter than the estimated duration, then the cost will increase drastically. But, if anyone completes the project over a longer period of time than the estimated, then there is almost no decrease in the estimated cost value.

Example:

Assume that the size of an organic type software product has been estimated to be 32,000 lines of source code. Assume that the average salary of software engineers be Rs. 15,000/- per month. Determine the effort required to develop the software product and the nominal development time.

From the basic COCOMO estimation formula for organic software:

$$\text{Effort}=2.4\times(32)^{1.05}=91\text{PM}$$

$$\text{Nominal development time}=2.5\times(91)^{0.38}=14\,\text{months}$$

$$\text{Cost required to develop the product}=14\times15,000$$

$$=\text{Rs.}210,000$$

Intermediate COCOMO Model

The basic COCOMO model assumes that effort and development time are functions of the product size alone. However, a host of other project parameters besides the product size affect the effort required to develop the product as well as the development time. Therefore, in order to obtain an accurate estimation of the effort and project duration, the effect of all relevant parameters must be taken into account. The intermediate COCOMO model recognizes this fact and refines the initial estimate obtained using the basic COCOMO expressions by using a set of 15 cost drivers (multipliers) based on various attributes of software development. For example, if modern programming practices are used, the initial estimates are scaled downward by multiplication with a cost driver having a value less than 1. If there are stringent reliability requirements on the software product, this initial estimate is scaled upward. Boehm requires the project manager to rate these 15 different parameters for a particular project on a scale of one to three. Then, depending on these ratings, he suggests appropriate cost driver values which should be multiplied with the initial estimate obtained using the basic COCOMO. In general, the cost drivers can be classified as being attributes of the following items:

- Product: The characteristics of the product that are considered include the inherent complexity of the product, reliability requirements of the product, etc.

- Computer: Characteristics of the computer that are considered include the execution speed required, storage space required etc.

- Personnel: The attributes of development personnel that are considered include the experience level of personnel, programming capability, analysis capability, etc.

- Development Environment: Development environment attributes capture the development facilities available to the developers. An important parameter that is considered is the sophistication of the automation (CASE) tools used for software development.

Complete COCOMO Model

A major shortcoming of both the basic and intermediate COCOMO models is that they consider a software product as a single homogeneous entity. However, most large systems are made up several smaller sub-systems. These sub- systems may have widely different characteristics. For example, some sub- systems may be considered as organic type, some semidetached, and some embedded. Not only that the inherent development complexity of the subsystems may be different, but also for some subsystems the reliability requirements may be high, for some the development team might have no previous experience of similar development, and so on. The complete COCOMO model considers these differences in characteristics of the subsystems and estimates the effort and development time as the sum of the estimates for the individual subsystems. The cost of each subsystem is estimated separately. This approach reduces the margin of error in the final estimate.

The following development project can be considered as an example application of the complete COCOMO model. A distributed Management Information System (MIS) product for an organization having offices at several places across the country can have the following sub-components:

- Database part

- Graphical User Interface (GUI) part

- Communication part

Of these, the communication part can be considered as embedded software. The database part could be semi-detached software, and the GUI part organic software. The costs for these three components can be estimated separately, and summed up to give the overall cost of the system.

Software Maintenance

Software maintenance in software engineering is the modification of a software product after delivery to correct faults, to improve performance or other attributes.

A common perception of maintenance is that it merely involves fixing defects. However, one study indicated that over 80% of maintenance effort is used for non-corrective actions. This perception is perpetuated by users submitting problem reports that in reality are functionality enhancements to the system. More recent studies put the bug-fixing proportion closer to 21%.

History

Software maintenance and evolution of systems was first addressed by Meir M. Lehman in 1969. Over a period of twenty years, his research led to the formulation of Lehman's Laws (Lehman 1997). Key findings of his research include that maintenance is really evolutionary development and that maintenance decisions are aided by understanding what happens to systems (and software) over time. Lehman demonstrated that systems continue to evolve over time. As they evolve, they grow more complex unless some action such as code refactoring is taken to reduce the complexity.

In the late 1970s, a famous and widely cited survey study by Lientz and Swanson, exposed the very high fraction of life-cycle costs that were being expended on maintenance. They categorized maintenance activities into four classes:

- Adaptive – modifying the system to cope with changes in the software environment (DBMS, OS)

- Perfective – implementing new or changed user requirements which concern functional enhancements to the software

- Corrective – diagnosing and fixing errors, possibly ones found by users

- Preventive – increasing software maintainability or reliability to prevent problems in the future

The survey showed that around 75% of the maintenance effort was on the first two types, and error correction consumed about 21%. Many subsequent studies suggest a similar magnitude of the problem. Studies show that contribution of end user is crucial during the new requirement data gathering and analysis. And this is the main cause of any problem during software evolution and maintenance. So software maintenance is important because it consumes a large part of the overall lifecycle costs and also the inability to change software quickly and reliably means that business opportunities are lost.

Importance of Software Maintenance

The key software maintenance issues are both managerial and technical. Key management issues are: alignment with customer priorities, staffing, which organization does maintenance, estimating costs. Key technical issues are: limited understanding, impact analysis, testing, maintainability measurement.

Software maintenance is a very broad activity that includes error correction, enhancements of capabilities, deletion of obsolete capabilities, and optimization. Because change is inevitable, mechanisms must be developed for evaluation, controlling and making modifications.

So any work done to change the software after it is in operation is considered to be maintenance work. The purpose is to preserve the value of software over the time. The value can be enhanced by expanding the customer base, meeting additional requirements, becoming easier to use, more efficient and employing newer technology. Maintenance may span for 20 years, whereas development may be 1-2 years.

Software Maintenance Planning

An integral part of software is the maintenance one, which requires an accurate maintenance plan to be prepared during the software development. It should specify how users will request modifications or report problems. The budget should include resource and cost estimates. A new decision should be addressed for the developing of every new system feature and its quality objectives. The software maintenance, which can last for 5–6 years (or even decades) after the development process, calls for an effective plan which can address the scope of software maintenance, the tailoring of the post delivery/deployment process, the designation of who will provide maintenance, and an estimate of the life-cycle costs. The selection of proper enforcement of standards is the challenging task right from early stage of software engineering which has not got definite importance by the concerned stakeholders.

Software Maintenance Processes

This section describes the six software maintenance processes as:

1. The implementation process contains software preparation and transition activities, such as the conception and creation of the maintenance plan; the preparation for handling problems identified during development; and the follow-up on product configuration management.

2. The problem and modification analysis process, which is executed once the application has become the responsibility of the maintenance group. The maintenance programmer must analyze each request, confirm it (by reproducing the situation) and check its validity, investigate it and propose a solution, document the request and the solution proposal, and finally, obtain all the required authorizations to apply the modifications.

3. The process considering the implementation of the modification itself.

4. The process acceptance of the modification, by confirming the modified work with the individual who submitted the request in order to make sure the modification provided a solution.

5. The migration process (platform migration, for example) is exceptional, and is not part of daily maintenance tasks. If the software must be ported to another platform without any change in functionality, this process will be used and a maintenance project team is likely to be assigned to this task.

6. Finally, the last maintenance process, also an event which does not occur on a daily basis, is the retirement of a piece of software.

There are a number of processes, activities and practices that are unique to maintainers, for example:

- Transition: a controlled and coordinated sequence of activities during which a system is transferred progressively from the developer to the maintainer;

- Service Level Agreements (SLAs) and specialized (domain-specific) maintenance contracts negotiated by maintainers;

- Modification Request and Problem Report Help Desk: a problem-handling process used by maintainers to prioritize, documents and route the requests they receive;

Categories of Maintenance in ISO/IEC 14764

E.B. Swanson initially identified three categories of maintenance: corrective, adaptive, and perfective. These have since been updated and ISO/IEC 14764 presents:

- Corrective maintenance: Reactive modification of a software product performed after delivery to correct discovered problems.

- Adaptive maintenance: Modification of a software product performed after delivery to keep a software product usable in a changed or changing environment.

- Perfective maintenance: Modification of a software product after delivery to improve performance or maintainability.

- Preventive maintenance: Modification of a software product after delivery to detect and correct latent faults in the software product before they become effective faults.

There is also a notion of pre-delivery/pre-release maintenance which is all the good things you do to lower the total cost of ownership of the software. Things like compliance with coding standards that includes software maintainability goals. The management of coupling and cohesion of the software. The attainment of software supportability goals (SAE JA1004, JA1005 and JA1006 for example). Note also that some academic institutions are carrying out research to quantify the cost to ongoing software maintenance due to the lack of resources such as design documents and system/software comprehension training and resources (multiply costs by approx. 1.5-2.0 where there is no design data available).

Maintenance Factors

Impact of key adjustment factors on maintenance (sorted in order of maximum positive impact)

Maintenance Factors	Plus Range
Maintenance specialists	35%
High staff experience	34%
Table-driven variables and data	33%
Low complexity of base code	32%
Y2K and special search engines	30%
Code restructuring tools	29%
Re-engineering tools	27%
High level programming languages	25%
Reverse engineering tools	23%
Complexity analysis tools	20%
Defect tracking tools	20%
Y2K "mass update" specialists	20%

Automated change control tools	18%
Unpaid overtime	18%
Quality measurements	16%
Formal base code inspections	15%
Regression test libraries	15%
Excellent response time	12%
Annual training of > 10 days	12%
High management experience	12%
HELP desk automation	12%
No error prone modules	10%
On-line defect reporting	10%
Productivity measurements	8%
Excellent ease of use	7%
User satisfaction measurements	5%
High team morale	5%
Sum	**503%**

Not only are error-prone modules troublesome, but many other factors can degrade performance too. For example, very complex "spaghetti code" is quite difficult to maintain safely. A very common situation which often degrades performance is lack of suitable maintenance tools, such as defect tracking software, change management software, and test library software. Below describe some of the factors and the range of impact on software maintenance.

Impact of key adjustment factors on maintenance (sorted in order of maximum negative impact)

Maintenance Factors	Minus Range
Error prone modules	-50%
Embedded variables and data	-45%
Staff inexperience	-40%
High code complexity	-30%
No Y2K of special search engines	-28%
Manual change control methods	-27%
Low level programming languages	-25%
No defect tracking tools	-24%
No Y2K "mass update" specialists	-22%
Poor ease of use	-18%
No quality measurements	-18%
No maintenance specialists	-18%

Poor response time	-16%
No code inspections	-15%
No regression test libraries	-15%
No help desk automation	-15%
No on-line defect reporting	-12%
Management inexperience	-15%
No code restructuring tools	-10%
No annual training	-10%
No reengineering tools	-10%
No reverse-engineering tools	-10%
No complexity analysis tools	-10%
No productivity measurements	-7%
Poor team morale	-6%
No user satisfaction measurements	-4%
No unpaid overtime	0%
Sum	**-500%**

Necessity of Software Maintenance

Software maintenance is becoming an important activity of a large number of software organizations. This is no surprise, given the rate of hardware obsolescence, the immortality of a software product per se, and the demand of the user community to see the existing software products run on newer platforms, run in newer environments, and/ or with enhanced features. When the hardware platform is changed, and a software product performs some low-level functions, maintenance is necessary. Also, whenever the support environment of a software product changes, the software product requires rework to cope up with the newer interface. For instance, a software product may need to be maintained when the operating system changes. Thus, every software product continues to evolve after its development through maintenance efforts. Therefore it can be stated that software maintenance is needed to correct errors, enhance features, port the software to new platforms, etc.

Types of Software Maintenance

There are basically three types of software maintenance. These are:

- Corrective: Corrective maintenance of a software product is necessary to rectify the bugs observed while the system is in use.

- Adaptive: A software product might need maintenance when the customers need the product to run on new platforms, on new operating systems, or when they need the product to interface with new hardware or software.

- • Perfective: A software product needs maintenance to support the new features that users want it to support, to change different functionalities of the system according to customer demands, or to enhance the performance of the system.

Problems Associated with Software Maintenance

Software maintenance work typically is much more expensive than what it should be and takes more time than required. In software organizations, maintenance work is mostly carried out using ad hoc techniques. The primary reason being that software maintenance is one of the most neglected areas of software engineering. Even though software maintenance is fast becoming an important area of work for many companies as the software products of yester years age, still software maintenance is mostly being carried out as fire-fighting operations, rather than through systematic and planned activities.

Software maintenance has a very poor image in industry. Therefore, an organization often cannot employ bright engineers to carry out maintenance work. Even though maintenance suffers from a poor image, the work involved is often more challenging than development work. During maintenance it is necessary to thoroughly understand someone else's work and then carry out the required modifications and extensions.

Another problem associated with maintenance work is that the majority of software products needing maintenance are legacy products.

Software Reverse Engineering

Software reverse engineering is the process of recovering the design and the requirements specification of a product from an analysis of its code. The purpose of reverse engineering is to facilitate maintenance work by improving the understandability of a system and to produce the necessary documents for a legacy system. Reverse engineering is becoming important, since legacy software products lack proper documentation, and are highly unstructured. Even well-designed products become legacy software as their structure degrades through a series of maintenance efforts.

The first stage of reverse engineering usually focuses on carrying out cosmetic changes to the code to improve its readability, structure, and understandability, without changing of its functionalities. A process model for reverse engineering has been shown in figure. A program can be reformatted using any of the several available prettyprinter programs which layout the program neatly. Many legacy software products with complex control structure and unthoughtful variable names are difficult to comprehend. Assigning meaningful variable names is important because meaningful variable names are the most helpful thing in code documentation. All variables, data structures, and functions should be assigned meaningful names wherever possible. Complex nested conditionals in the program can be replaced by simpler conditional statements or whenever appropriate by case statements.

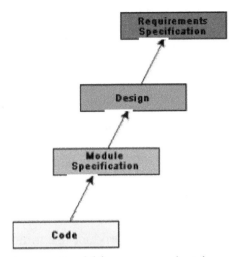

A process model for reverse engineering

After the cosmetic changes have been carried out on a legacy software, the process of extracting the code, design, and the requirements specification can begin. These activities are schematically shown in figure. In order to extract the design, a full understanding of the code is needed. Some automatic tools can be used to derive the data flow and control flow diagram from the code. The structure chart (module invocation sequence and data interchange among modules) should also be extracted. The SRS document can be written once the full code has been thoroughly understood and the design extracted.

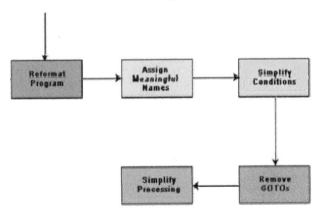

Cosmetic changes carried out before reverse engineering

Legacy Software Products

It is prudent to define a legacy system as any software system that is hard to maintain. The typical problems associated with legacy systems are poor documentation, unstructured (spaghetti code with ugly control structure), and lack of personnel knowledgeable in the product. Many of the legacy systems were developed long time back. But, it is possible that a recently developed system having poor design and documentation can be considered to be a legacy system.

Factors on which Software Maintenance Activities Depend

The activities involved in a software maintenance project are not unique and depend on several factors such as:

- The extent of modification to the product required.

- The resources available to the maintenance team.

- The conditions of the existing product (e.g., how structured it is, how well documented it is, etc.)

- The expected project risks, etc.

When the changes needed to a software product are minor and straightforward, the code can be directly modified and the changes appropriately reflected in all the documents. But more elaborate activities are required when the required changes are not so trivial. Usually, for complex maintenance projects for legacy systems, the software process can be represented by a reverse engineering cycle followed by a forward engineering cycle with an emphasis on as much reuse as possible from the existing code and other documents.

Software Maintenance Process Models

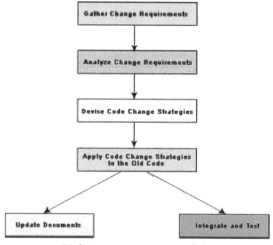

Maintenance process model 1

Two broad categories of process models for software maintenance can be proposed. The first model is preferred for projects involving small reworks where the code is changed directly and the changes are reflected in the relevant documents later. This maintenance process is graphically presented in figure. In this approach, the project starts by gathering the requirements for changes. The requirements are next analyzed to formulate the strategies to be adopted for code change. At this stage, the association of at least a few members of the original development team goes a long way in reducing the cycle team, especially for projects involving unstructured and inadequately documented code. The availability of a working old system to the maintenance engineers at the maintenance site greatly facilitates the task of the maintenance team as they get a good insight into the working of the old system and also can compare the working of their modified system with the old system. Also, debugging of the reengineered system becomes easier as the program traces of both the systems can be compared to localize the bugs.

The second process model for software maintenance is preferred for projects where the amount of rework required is significant. This approach can be represented by a reverse engineering cycle followed by a forward engineering cycle. Such an approach is also known as software reengineering. This process model is depicted in figure. The reverse engineering cycle is required for legacy products. During the reverse engineering, the old code is analyzed (abstracted) to extract the module specifications. The module specifications are then analyzed to produce the design. The design is analyzed (abstracted) to produce the original requirements specification. The change requests are then applied to this requirements specification to arrive at the new requirements specification. At the design, module specification, and coding a substantial reuse is made from the reverse engineered products. An important advantage of this approach is that it produces a more structured design compared to what the original product had, produces good documentation, and very often results in increased efficiency. The efficiency improvements are brought about by a more efficient design. However, this approach is more costly than the first approach. An empirical study indicates that process 1 is preferable when the amount of rework is no more than 15%. Besides the amount of rework, several other factors might affect the decision regarding using process model 1 over process model 2:

- Reengineering might be preferable for products which exhibit a high failure rate.

- Reengineering might also be preferable for legacy products having poor design and code structure.

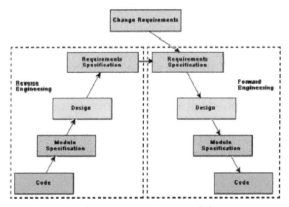

Maintenance process model 2

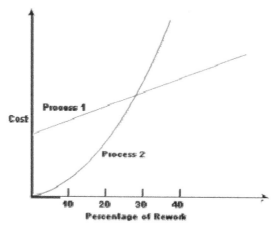

Empirical estimation of maintenance cost versus percentage rework

Software Reengineering

Software reengineering is a combination of two consecutive processes i.e. software reverse engineering and software forward engineering as shown in the figure.

Estimation of Approximate Maintenance Cost

It is well known that maintenance efforts require about 60% of the total life cycle cost for a typical software product. However, maintenance costs vary widely from one application domain to another. For embedded systems, the maintenance cost can be as much as 2 to 4 times the development cost.

Boehm [1981] proposed a formula for estimating maintenance costs as part of his CO-COMO cost estimation model. Boehm's maintenance cost estimation is made in terms of a quantity called the Annual Change Traffic (ACT). Boehm defined ACT as the fraction of a software product's source instructions which undergo change during a typical year either through addition or deletion.

$$ACT = \frac{KLOC_{added} + KLOC_{deleted}}{KLOC_{total}}$$

where, $KLOC_{total}$ is the total kilo lines of source code added during maintenance. $KLOC_{deleted}$ is the total KLOC deleted during maintenance. Thus, the code that is changed, should be counted in both the code added and the code deleted. The annual change traffic (ACT) is multiplied with the total development cost to arrive at the maintenance cost:

$$maintenance\ cost = ACT \times development\ cost$$

Most maintenance cost estimation models, however, yield only approximate results because they do not take into account several factors such as experience level of the engineers, and familiarity of the engineers with the product, hardware requirements, software complexity, etc.

CASE Tool

A CASE (Computer Aided Software Engineering) tool is a generic term used to denote any form of automated support for software engineering. In a more restrictive sense, a CASE tool means any tool used to automate some activity associated with software development. Many CASE tools are available. Some of these CASE tools assist in phase related tasks such as specification, structured analysis, design, coding, testing, etc.; and others to non-phase activities such as project management and configuration management.

Reasons for using CASE Tools

The primary reasons for using a CASE tool are:

- To increase productivity

- To help produce better quality software at lower cost

CASE Environment

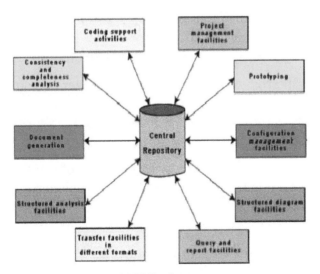

A CASE Environment

Although individual CASE tools are useful, the true power of a tool set can be realized only when these set of tools are integrated into a common framework or environment. CASE tools are characterized by the stage or stages of software development life cycle on which they focus. Since different tools covering different stages share common information, it is required that they integrate through some central repository to have a consistent view of information associated with the software development artifacts. This central repository is usually a data dictionary containing the definition of all composite and elementary data items. Through the central repository all the CASE tools in a CASE environment share common information among themselves. Thus a CASE environment facilities the automation of the step-by-step methodologies for software development. A schematic representation of a CASE environment is shown in figure.

CASE Environment Vs Programming Environment

A CASE environment facilitates the automation of the step-by-step methodologies for software development. In contrast to a CASE environment, a programming environment is an integrated collection of tools to support only the coding phase of software development.

Benefits of CASE

Several benefits accrue from the use of a CASE environment or even isolated CASE tools. Some of those benefits are:

- A key benefit arising out of the use of a CASE environment is cost saving through all development phases. Different studies carry out to measure the impact of CASE put the effort reduction between 30% to 40%.

- Use of CASE tools leads to considerable improvements to quality. This is mainly due to the facts that one can effortlessly iterate through the different phases of software development and the chances of human error are considerably reduced.

- CASE tools help produce high quality and consistent documents. Since the important data relating to a software product are maintained in a central repository, redundancy in the stored data is reduced and therefore chances of inconsistent documentation is reduced to a great extent.

- CASE tools take out most of the drudgery in a software engineer's work. For example, they need not check meticulously the balancing of the DFDs but can do it effortlessly through the press of a button.

- CASE tools have led to revolutionary cost saving in software maintenance efforts. This arises not only due to the tremendous value of a CASE environment in traceability and consistency checks, but also due to the systematic information capture during the various phases of software development as a result of adhering to a CASE environment.

- Introduction of a CASE environment has an impact on the style of working of a company, and makes it oriented towards the structured and orderly approach.

Requirements of a Prototyping CASE Tool

Prototyping is useful to understand the requirements of complex software products, to demonstrate a concept, to market new ideas, and so on. The important features of a prototyping CASE tool are as follows:

- Define user interaction
- Define the system control flow
- Store and retrieve data required by the system
- Incorporate some processing logic

Features of a Good Prototyping CASE Tool

There are several stand-alone prototyping tools. But a tool that integrates with the data dictionary can make use of the entries in the data dictionary, help in populating the data dictionary and ensure the consistency between the design data and the prototype. A good prototyping tool should support the following features:

- Since one of the main uses of a prototyping CASE tool is graphical user interface (GUI) development, prototyping CASE tool should support the user to create a GUI using a graphics editor. The user should be allowed to define all data entry forms, menus and controls.
- It should integrate with the data dictionary of a CASE environment.
- If possible, it should be able to integrate with external user defined modules written in C or some popular high level programming languages.
- The user should be able to define the sequence of states through which a created prototype can run. The user should also be allowed to control the running of the prototype.
- The run time system of prototype should support mock runs of the actual system and management of the input and output data.

Structured Analysis and Design with CASE Tools

Several diagramming techniques are used for structured analysis and structured design. The following supports might be available from CASE tools.

- A CASE tool should support one or more of the structured analysis and design techniques.
- It should support effortlessly drawing analysis and design diagrams.
- It should support drawing for fairly complex diagrams, preferably through a hierarchy of levels.

- The CASE tool should provide easy navigation through the different levels and through the design and analysis.

- The tool must support completeness and consistency checking across the design and analysis and through all levels of analysis hierarchy. Whenever it is possible, the system should disallow any inconsistent operation, but it may be very difficult to implement such a feature. Whenever there arises heavy computational load while consistency checking, it should be possible to temporarily disable consistency checking.

Code Generation and CASE Tools

As far as code generation is concerned, the general expectation of a CASE tool is quite low. A reasonable requirement is traceability from source file to design data. More pragmatic supports expected from a CASE tool during code generation phase are the following:

- The CASE tool should support generation of module skeletons or templates in one or more popular languages. It should be possible to include copyright message, brief description of the module, author name and the date of creation in some selectable format.

- The tool should generate records, structures, class definition automatically from the contents of the data dictionary in one or more popular languages.

- It should generate database tables for relational database management systems.

- The tool should generate code for user interface from prototype definition for X window and MS window based applications.

Test Case Generation CASE Tool

The CASE tool for test case generation should have the following features:

- It should support both design and requirement testing.

- It should generate test set reports in ASCII format which can be directly imported into the test plan document.

Hardware and Environmental Requirements

In most cases, it is the existing hardware that would place constraints upon the CASE tool selection. Thus, instead of defining hardware requirements for a CASE tool, the task at hand becomes to fit in an optimal configuration of CASE tool in the existing hardware capabilities. Therefore, it can be emphasized on selecting the most optimal CASE tool configuration for a given hardware configuration.

The heterogeneous network is one instance of distributed environment and this can be chosen for illustration as it is more popular due to its machine independent features.

The CASE tool implementation in heterogeneous network makes use of client-server paradigm. The multiple clients who run different modules access data dictionary through this server. The data dictionary server may support one or more projects. Though it is possible to run many servers for different projects but distributed implementation of data dictionary is not common.

The tool set is integrated through the data dictionary which supports multiple projects, multiple users working simultaneously and allows to share information between users and projects. The data dictionary provides consistent view of all project entities, e.g. a data record definition and its entity-relationship diagram be consistent. The server should depict the per-project logical view of the data dictionary. This means that it should allow back up/restore, copy, cleaning part of the data dictionary, etc.

The tool should work satisfactorily for maximum possible number of users working simultaneously. The tool should support multi-windowing environment for the users. This is important to enable the users to see more than one diagram at a time. It also facilitates navigation and switching from one part to the other.

Documentation Support

The deliverable documents should be organized graphically and should be able to incorporate text and diagrams from the central repository. This helps in producing up-to-date documentation. The CASE tool should integrate with one or more of the commercially available desktop publishing packages. It should be possible to export text, graphics, tables, data dictionary reports to the DTP package in standard forms such as PostScript.

Project Management Support

The CASE tool should support collecting, storing, and analyzing information on the software project's progress such as the estimated task duration, scheduled and actual task start, completion date, dates and results of the reviews, etc.

External Interface

The CASE tool should allow exchange of information for reusability of design. The information which is to be exported by the CASE tool should be preferably in ASCII format and support open architecture. Similarly, the data dictionary should provide a programming interface to access information. It is required for integration of custom utilities, building new techniques, or populating the data dictionary.

Reverse Engineering

The CASE tool should support generation of structure charts and data dictionaries from the existing source codes. It should populate the data dictionary from the source code. If the tool is used for re-engineering information systems, it should contain conversion tool from indexed sequential file structure, hierarchical and network database to relational database systems.

Data Dictionary Interface

The data dictionary interface should provide view and update access to the entities and relations stored in it. It should have print facility to obtain hard copy of the viewed screens. It should provide analysis reports like cross-referencing, impact analysis, etc. Ideally, it should support a query language to view its contents.

Second-generation CASE Tool

An important feature of the second-generation CASE tool is the direct support of any adapted methodology. This would necessitate the function of a CASE administrator organization who can tailor the CASE tool to a particular methodology. In addition, the second-generation CASE tools have following features:

- Intelligent diagramming support. The fact that diagramming techniques are useful for system analysis and design is well established. The future CASE tools would provide help to aesthetically and automatically lay out the diagrams.

- Integration with implementation environment. The CASE tools should provide integration between design and implementation.

- Data dictionary standards. The user should be allowed to integrate many development tools into one environment. It is highly unlikely that any one vendor will be able to deliver a total solution. Moreover, a preferred tool would require tuning up for a particular system. Thus the user would act as a system integrator. This is possibly only if some standard on data dictionary emerges.

- Customization support. The user should be allowed to define new types of objects and connections. This facility may be used to build some special methodologies. Ideally it should be possible to specify the rules of a methodology to a rule engine for carrying out the necessary consistency checks.

Architecture of a CASE Environment

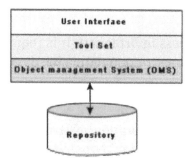

Architecture of a Modern CASE Environment

The architecture of a typical modern CASE environment is shown diagrammatically in figure. The important components of a modern CASE environment are user interface, tool set, object management system (OMS), and a repository.

User Interface

The user interface provides a consistent framework for accessing the different tools thus making it easier for the users to interact with the different tools and reducing the overhead of learning how the different tools are used.

Object Management System (OMS) and Repository

Different case tools represent the software product as a set of entities such as specification, design, text data, project plan, etc. The object management system maps these logical entities such into the underlying storage management system (repository). The commercial relational database management systems are geared towards supporting large volumes of information structured as simple relatively short records. There are a few types of entities but large number of instances. By contrast, CASE tools create a large number of entity and relation types with perhaps a few instances of each. Thus the object management system takes care of appropriately mapping into the underlying storage management system.

Data Modelling

Data modeling in software engineering is the process of creating a data model for an information system by applying certain formal techniques.

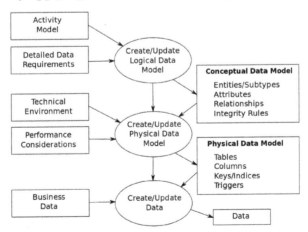

The data modeling process. The figure illustrates the way data models are developed and used today. A conceptual data model is developed based on the data requirements for the application that is being developed, perhaps in the context of an activity model. The data model will normally consist of entity types, attributes, relationships, integrity rules, and the definitions of those objects. This is then used as the start point for interface or database design.

Overview

Data modeling is a process used to define and analyze data requirements needed to support the business processes within the scope of corresponding information systems in organizations. Therefore, the process of data modeling involves professional data modelers working closely with business stakeholders, as well as potential users of the information system.

There are three different types of data models produced while progressing from requirements to the actual database to be used for the information system. The data requirements are initially recorded as a conceptual data model which is essentially a set of technology independent specifications about the data and is used to discuss initial requirements with the business stakeholders. The conceptual model is then translated into a logical data model, which documents structures of the data that can be implemented in databases. Implementation of one conceptual data model may require multiple logical data models. The last step in data modeling is transforming the logical data model to a physical data model that organizes the data into tables, and accounts for access, performance and storage details. Data modeling defines not just data elements, but also their structures and the relationships between them.

Data modeling techniques and methodologies are used to model data in a standard, consistent, predictable manner in order to manage it as a resource. The use of data modeling standards is strongly recommended for all projects requiring a standard means of defining and analyzing data within an organization, e.g., using data modeling:

- To assist business analysts, programmers, testers, manual writers, IT package selectors, engineers, managers, related organizations and clients to understand and use an agreed semi-formal model the concepts of the organization and how they relate to one another

- To manage data as a resource

- For the integration of information systems

- For designing databases/data warehouses (aka data repositories)

Data modeling may be performed during various types of projects and in multiple phases of projects. Data models are progressive; there is no such thing as the final data model for a business or application. Instead a data model should be considered a living document that will change in response to a changing business. The data models should ideally be stored in a repository so that they can be retrieved, expanded, and edited over time. Whitten et al. (2004) determined two types of data modeling:

- Strategic data modeling: This is part of the creation of an information systems strategy, which defines an overall vision and architecture for information systems is defined. Information engineering is a methodology that embraces this approach.

- Data modeling during systems analysis: In systems analysis logical data models are created as part of the development of new databases.

Data modeling is also used as a technique for detailing business requirements for specific databases. It is sometimes called *database modeling* because a data model is eventually implemented in a database.

Data Modeling Topics

Data Models

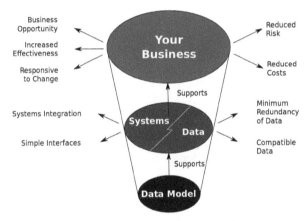

How data models deliver benefit.

Data models provide a structure for data used within information systems by providing specific definition and format. If a data model is used consistently across systems then compatibility of data can be achieved. If the same data structures are used to store and access data then different applications can share data seamlessly. The results of this are indicated in the diagram. However, systems and interfaces are often expensive to build, operate, and maintain. They may also constrain the business rather than support it. This may occur when the quality of the data models implemented in systems and interfaces is poor.

- Business rules, specific to how things are done in a particular place, are often fixed in the structure of a data model. This means that small changes in the way business is conducted lead to large changes in computer systems and interfaces. So, business rules need to be implemented in a flexible way that does not result in complicated dependencies, rather the data model should be flexible enough so that changes in the business can be implemented within the data model in a relatively quick and efficient way.

- Entity types are often not identified, or are identified incorrectly. This can lead to replication of data, data structure and functionality, together with the attendant costs of that duplication in development and maintenance.Therefore, data definitions should be made as explicit and easy to understand as possible to minimize misinterpretation and duplication.

- Data models for different systems are arbitrarily different. The result of this is that complex interfaces are required between systems that share data. These interfaces can account for between 25-70% of the cost of current systems. Required interfaces should be considered inherently while designing a data model, as a data model on its own would not be usable without interfaces within different systems.

- Data cannot be shared electronically with customers and suppliers, because the structure and meaning of data has not been standardised. To obtain optimal value from an implemented data model, it is very important to define standards that will ensure that data models will both meet business needs and be consistent.

Conceptual, Logical and Physical Schemas

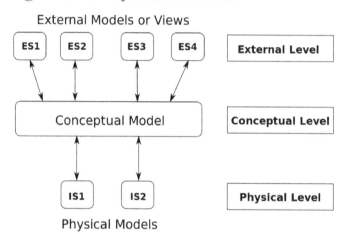

The ANSI/SPARC three level architecture. This shows that a data model can be an external model (or view), a conceptual model, or a physical model. This is not the only way to look at data models, but it is a useful way, particularly when comparing models.

In 1975 ANSI described three kinds of data-model *instance*:

- Conceptual schema: describes the semantics of a domain (the scope of the model). For example, it may be a model of the interest area of an organization or of an industry. This consists of entity classes, representing kinds of things of significance in the domain, and relationships assertions about associations between pairs of entity classes. A conceptual schema specifies the kinds of facts or propositions that can be expressed using the model. In that sense, it defines the allowed expressions in an artificial "language" with a scope that is limited by the scope of the model. Simply described, a conceptual schema is the first step in organizing the data requirements.

- Logical schema: describes the structure of some domain of information. This consists of descriptions of (for example) tables, columns, object-oriented classes, and XML tags. The logical schema and conceptual schema are sometimes implemented as one and the same.

- Physical schema: describes the physical means used to store data. This is concerned with partitions, CPUs, tablespaces, and the like.

According to ANSI, this approach allows the three perspectives to be relatively independent of each other. Storage technology can change without affecting either the logical or the conceptual schema. The table/column structure can change without (necessarily) affecting the conceptual schema. In each case, of course, the structures must remain consistent across all schemas of the same data model.

Data Modeling Process

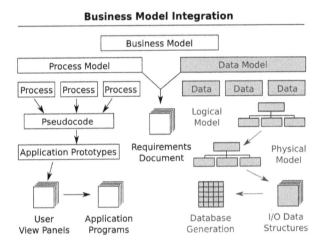

Data modeling in the context of Business Process Integration.

In the context of business process integration, data modeling complements business process modeling, and ultimately results in database generation.

The process of designing a database involves producing the previously described three types of schemas - conceptual, logical, and physical. The database design documented in these schemas are converted through a Data Definition Language, which can then be used to generate a database. A fully attributed data model contains detailed attributes (descriptions) for every entity within it. The term "database design" can describe many different parts of the design of an overall database system. Principally, and most correctly, it can be thought of as the logical design of the base data structures used to store the data. In the relational model these are the tables and views. In an object database the entities and relationships map directly to object classes and named relationships. However, the term "database design" could also be used to apply to the overall process of designing, not just the base data structures, but also the forms and queries used as part of the overall database application within the Database Management System or DBMS.

In the process, system interfaces account for 25% to 70% of the development and support costs of current systems. The primary reason for this cost is that these systems do not share a common data model. If data models are developed on a system by system basis, then not only is the same analysis repeated in overlapping areas, but further analysis must be performed to create the interfaces between them. Most systems within an organization contain the same basic data, redeveloped for a specific purpose. Therefore, an efficiently designed basic data model can minimize rework with minimal modifications for the purposes of different systems within the organization

Modeling Methodologies

Data models represent information areas of interest. While there are many ways to create data models, according to Len Silverston (1997) only two modeling methodologies stand out, top-down and bottom-up:

- Bottom-up models or View Integration models are often the result of a reengineering effort. They usually start with existing data structures forms, fields on application screens, or reports. These models are usually physical, application-specific, and incomplete from an enterprise perspective. They may not promote data sharing, especially if they are built without reference to other parts of the organization.

- Top-down logical data models, on the other hand, are created in an abstract way by getting information from people who know the subject area. A system may not implement all the entities in a logical model, but the model serves as a reference point or template.

Sometimes models are created in a mixture of the two methods: by considering the data needs and structure of an application and by consistently referencing a subject-area model. Unfortunately, in many environments the distinction between a logical data model and a physical data model is blurred. In addition, some CASE tools don't make a distinction between logical and physical data models.

Entity Relationship Diagrams

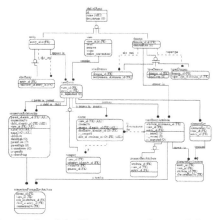

Example of an IDEF1X Entity relationship diagrams used to model IDEF1X itself. The name of the view is mm. The domain hierarchy and constraints are also given. The constraints are expressed as sentences in the formal theory of the meta model.

There are several notations for data modeling. The actual model is frequently called "Entity relationship model", because it depicts data in terms of the entities and relationships described in the data. An entity-relationship model (ERM) is an abstract conceptual representation of structured data. Entity-relationship modeling is a relational schema database modeling method, used in software engineering to produce a type of conceptual data model (or semantic data model) of a system, often a relational database, and its requirements in a top-down fashion.

These models are being used in the first stage of information system design during the requirements analysis to describe information needs or the type of information that is to be stored in a database. The data modeling technique can be used to describe any ontology (i.e. an overview and classifications of used terms and their relationships) for a certain universe of discourse i.e. area of interest.

Several techniques have been developed for the design of data models. While these methodologies guide data modelers in their work, two different people using the same methodology will often come up with very different results. Most notable are:

- Bachman diagrams

- Barker's notation

- Chen's Notation

- Data Vault Modeling

- Extended Backus–Naur form

- IDEF1X

- Object-relational mapping

- Object-Role Modeling

- Relational Model

- Relational Model/Tasmania

Generic Data Modeling

Generic data models are generalizations of conventional data models. They define standardized general relation types, together with the kinds of things that may be related by such a relation type. The definition of generic data model is similar to the definition of a natural language. For example, a generic data model may define relation types such as a 'classification relation', being a binary relation between an individual thing and a kind of thing (a class) and a 'part-whole relation', being a binary relation between two things, one with the role of part, the other with the role of whole, regardless the kind of things that are related.

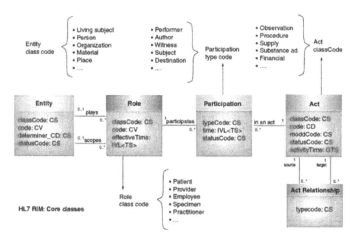

Example of a Generic data model.

Given an extensible list of classes, this allows the classification of any individual thing and to specify part-whole relations for any individual object. By standardization of an extensible list of relation types, a generic data model enables the expression of an un-limited number of kinds of facts and will approach the capabilities of natural languages. Conventional data models, on the other hand, have a fixed and limited domain scope, because the instantiation (usage) of such a model only allows expressions of kinds of facts that are predefined in the model.

Semantic Data Modeling

The logical data structure of a DBMS, whether hierarchical, network, or relational, can-not totally satisfy the requirements for a conceptual definition of data because it is limited in scope and biased toward the implementation strategy employed by the DBMS. That is unless the semantic data model is implemented in the database on purpose, a choice which may slightly impact performance but generally vastly improves productivity.

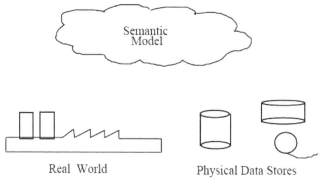

Semantic data models.

Therefore, the need to define data from a conceptual view has led to the development of semantic data modeling techniques. That is, techniques to define the meaning of data within the context of its interrelationships with other data. As illustrated in the figure the real world, in terms of resources, ideas, events, etc., are symbolically defined within physical data stores. A semantic data model is an abstraction which defines how the stored symbols relate to the real world. Thus, the model must be a true representation of the real world.

A semantic data model can be used to serve many purposes, such as:

- planning of data resources

- building of shareable databases

- evaluation of vendor software

- integration of existing databases

The overall goal of semantic data models is to capture more meaning of data by integrating relational concepts with more powerful abstraction concepts known from the Artificial Intelligence field. The idea is to provide high level modeling primitives as integral part of a data model in order to facilitate the representation of real world situations.

References

- "E. Burt Swanson, The dimensions of maintenance. Proceedings of the 2nd international conference on Software engineering, San Francisco, 1976, pp 492 − 497". Portal.acm.org. doi:10.1145/359511.359522. Retrieved 2013-12-02

- Abran, Alain; Moore, James W.; Bourque, Pierre; Dupuis, Robert; Tripp, Leonard L. (2004). Guide to the Software Engineering Body of Knowledge. IEEE. ISBN 0-7695-2330-7

- Prause, Christian; et al. (2008). "Managing the Iterative Requirements Process in a Multi-National Project using an Issue Tracker" (PDF). IEEE Computer Society. Retrieved February 5, 2013

- Sommerville, Ian (2008). Software Engineering (7 ed.). Pearson Education. ISBN 978-81-7758-530-8. Retrieved 10 January 2013

- "ISO/IEC 14764:2006 Software Engineering − Software Life Cycle Processes − Maintenance". Iso.org. 2011-12-17. Retrieved 2013-12-02

Understanding Software Design

Software design is the process by which the idea of a software is converted into a computer-friendly language. The process normally includes planning a software solution and problem solving. One of its major components is software requirement analysis, which tables the required specification for the software concerned. Software design is best understood in confluence with the major topics listed in the following section.

Software Design

Software design is the process by which an agent creates a specification of a software artifact, intended to accomplish goals, using a set of primitive components and subject to constraints. Software design may refer to either "all the activity involved in conceptualizing, framing, implementing, commissioning, and ultimately modifying complex systems" or "the activity following requirements specification and before programming, as ... [in] a stylized software engineering process."

Software design usually involves problem solving and planning a software solution. This includes both a low-level component and algorithm design and a high-level, architecture design.

Overview

Software design is the process of implementing software solutions to one or more sets of problems. One of the main components of software design is the software requirements analysis (SRA). SRA is a part of the software development process that lists specifications used in software engineering. If the software is "semi-automated" or user centered, software design may involve user experience design yielding a storyboard to help determine those specifications. If the software is completely automated (meaning no user or user interface), a software design may be as simple as a flow chart or text describing a planned sequence of events. There are also semi-standard methods like Unified Modeling Language and Fundamental modeling concepts. In either case, some documentation of the plan is usually the product of the design. Furthermore, a software design may be platform-independent or platform-specific, depending upon the availability of the technology used for the design.

The main difference between software analysis and design is that the output of a software analysis consists of smaller problems to solve. Additionally, the analysis should not be designed very differently across different team members or groups. In contrast, the design focuses on capabilities, and thus multiple designs for the same problem can and will exist. Depending on the environment, the design often varies, whether it is created from reliable frameworks or implemented with suitable design patterns. Design examples include operation systems, webpages, mobile devices or even the new cloud computing paradigm.

Software design is both a process and a model. The design process is a sequence of steps that enables the designer to describe all aspects of the software for building. Creative skill, past experience, a sense of what makes "good" software, and an overall commitment to quality are examples of critical success factors for a competent design. It is important to note, however, that the design process is not always a straightforward procedure; the design model can be compared to an architect's plans for a house. It begins by representing the totality of the thing that is to be built (e.g., a three-dimensional rendering of the house); slowly, the thing is refined to provide guidance for constructing each detail (e.g., the plumbing layout). Similarly, the design model that is created for software provides a variety of different views of the computer software. Basic design principles enable the software engineer to navigate the design process. Davis [DAV95] suggests a set of principles for software design, which have been adapted and extended in the following list:

- The design process should not suffer from "tunnel vision." A good designer should consider alternative approaches, judging each based on the requirements of the problem, the resources available to do the job.

- The design should be traceable to the analysis model. Because a single element of the design model can often be traced back to multiple requirements, it is necessary to have a means for tracking how requirements have been satisfied by the design model.

- The design should not reinvent the wheel. Systems are constructed using a set of design patterns, many of which have likely been encountered before. These patterns should always be chosen as an alternative to reinvention. Time is short and resources are limited; design time should be invested in representing truly new ideas and integrating patterns that already exist when applicable.

- The design should "minimize the intellectual distance" between the software and the problem as it exists in the real world. That is, the structure of the software design should, whenever possible, mimic the structure of the problem domain.

- The design should exhibit uniformity and integration. A design is uniform if it appears fully coherent. In order to achieve this outcome, rules of style and format should be defined for a design team before design work begins. A design is integrated if care is taken in defining interfaces between design components.

- The design should be structured to accommodate change. The design concepts discussed in the next section enable a design to achieve this principle.

- The design should be structured to degrade gently, even when aberrant data, events, or operating conditions are encountered. Well- designed software should never "bomb"; it should be designed to accommodate unusual circumstances, and if it must terminate processing, it should do so in a graceful manner.

- Design is not coding, coding is not design. Even when detailed procedural designs are created for program components, the level of abstraction of the design model is higher than the source code. The only design decisions made at the coding level should address the small implementation details that enable the procedural design to be coded.

- The design should be assessed for quality as it is being created, not after the fact. A variety of design concepts and design measures are available to assist the designer in assessing quality throughout the development process.

- The design should be reviewed to minimize conceptual (semantic) errors. There is sometimes a tendency to focus on minutiae when the design is reviewed, missing the forest for the trees. A design team should ensure that major conceptual elements of the design (omissions, ambiguity, inconsistency) have been addressed before worrying about the syntax of the design model.

Design Concepts

The design concepts provide the software designer with a foundation from which more sophisticated methods can be applied. A set of fundamental design concepts has evolved. They are as follows:

1. Abstraction - Abstraction is the process or result of generalization by reducing the information content of a concept or an observable phenomenon, typically in order to retain only information which is relevant for a particular purpose.

2. Refinement - It is the process of elaboration. A hierarchy is developed by decomposing a macroscopic statement of function in a step-wise fashion until programming language statements are reached. In each step, one or several instructions of a given program are decomposed into more detailed instructions. Abstraction and Refinement are complementary concepts.

3. Modularity - Software architecture is divided into components called modules.

4. Software Architecture - It refers to the overall structure of the software and the ways in which that structure provides conceptual integrity for a system. Good software architecture will yield a good return on investment with respect to the desired outcome of the project, e.g. in terms of performance, quality, schedule and cost.

5. Control Hierarchy - A program structure that represents the organization of a program component and implies a hierarchy of control.

6. Structural Partitioning - The program structure can be divided both horizontally and vertically. Horizontal partitions define separate branches of modular hierarchy for each major program function. Vertical partitioning suggests that control and work should be distributed top down in the program structure.

7. Data Structure - It is a representation of the logical relationship among individual elements of data.

8. Software Procedure - It focuses on the processing of each module individually.

9. Information Hiding - Modules should be specified and designed so that information contained within a module is inaccessible to other modules that have no need for such information.

In his object model, Grady Booch mentions Abstraction, Encapsulation, Modularisation, and Hierarchy as fundamental software design principles. The acronym PHAME (Principles of Hierarchy, Abstraction, Modularisation, and Encapsulation) is sometimes used to refer to these four fundamental principles.

Design Considerations

There are many aspects to consider in the design of a piece of software. The importance of each consideration should reflect the goals and expectations that the software is being created to meet. Some of these aspects are:

- Compatibility - The software is able to operate with other products that are designed for interoperability with another product. For example, a piece of software may be backward-compatible with an older version of itself.

- Extensibility - New capabilities can be added to the software without major changes to the underlying architecture.

- Modularity - the resulting software comprises well defined, independent components which leads to better maintainability. The components could be then implemented and tested in isolation before being integrated to form a desired software system. This allows division of work in a software development project.

- Fault-tolerance - The software is resistant to and able to recover from component failure.

- Maintainability - A measure of how easily bug fixes or functional modifications can be accomplished. High maintainability can be the product of modularity and extensibility.

- Reliability (Software durability) - The software is able to perform a required function under stated conditions for a specified period of time.

- Reusability - The ability to use some or all of the aspects of the preexisting software in other projects with little to no modification.

- Robustness - The software is able to operate under stress or tolerate unpredictable or invalid input. For example, it can be designed with resilience to low memory conditions.

- Security - The software is able to withstand and resist hostile acts and influences.

- Usability - The software user interface must be usable for its target user/audience. Default values for the parameters must be chosen so that they are a good choice for the majority of the users.

- Performance - The software performs its tasks within a time-frame that is acceptable for the user, and does not require too much memory.

- Portability - The software should be usable across a number of different conditions and environments.

- Scalability - The software adapts well to increasing data or number of users.

Modeling Language

A modeling language is any artificial language that can be used to express information, knowledge or systems in a structure that is defined by a consistent set of rules. These rules are used for interpretation of the components within the structure. A modeling language can be graphical or textual. Examples of graphical modeling languages for software design are:

- Architecture description language (ADL) is a language used to describe and represent the software architecture of a software system.

- Business Process Modeling Notation (BPMN) is an example of a Process Modeling language.

- EXPRESS and EXPRESS-G (ISO 10303-11) is an international standard general-purpose data modeling language.

- Extended Enterprise Modeling Language (EEML) is commonly used for business process modeling across a number of layers.

- Flowchart is a schematic representation of an algorithm or step-wise process.

- Fundamental Modeling Concepts (FMC) is modeling language for software-intensive systems.

- IDEF is a family of modeling languages, the most notable of which include IDEF0 for functional modeling, IDEF1X for information modeling, and IDEF5 for modeling ontologies.

- Jackson Structured Programming (JSP) is a method for structured programming based on correspondences between data stream structure and program structure.

- LePUS3 is an object-oriented visual Design Description Language and a formal specification language that is suitable primarily for modeling large object-oriented (Java, C++, C#) programs and design patterns.

- Unified Modeling Language (UML) is a general modeling language to describe software both structurally and behaviorally. It has a graphical notation and allows for extension with a Profile (UML).

- Alloy (specification language) is a general purpose specification language for expressing complex structural constraints and behavior in a software system. It provides a concise language base on first-order relational logic.

- Systems Modeling Language (SysML) is a new general-purpose modeling language for systems engineering.

- Service-oriented modeling framework (SOMF)

Design Patterns

A software designer or architect may identify a design problem which has been visited and perhaps even solved by others in the past. A template or pattern describing a solution to a common problem is known as a design pattern. The reuse of such patterns can help speed up the software development process.

Technique

The difficulty of using the term "design" in relation to software is that in some senses, the source code of a program *is* the design for the program that it produces. To the extent that this is true, "software design" refers to the design of the design. Edsger W. Dijkstra referred to this layering of semantic levels as the "radical novelty" of computer programming, and Donald Knuth used his experience writing TeX to describe the futility of attempting to design a program prior to implementing it:

> TEX would have been a complete failure if I had merely specified it and not participated fully in its initial implementation. The process of implementation constantly led me to unanticipated questions and to new insights about how the original specifications could be improved.

Usage

Software design documentation may be reviewed or presented to allow constraints, specifications and even requirements to be adjusted prior to computer programming. Redesign may occur after review of a programmed simulation or prototype. It is possible to design software in the process of programming, without a plan or requirement analysis, but for more complex projects this would not be considered feasible. A separate design prior to programming allows for multidisciplinary designers and Subject Matter Experts (SMEs) to collaborate with highly skilled programmers for software that is both useful and technically sound.

Software Design and its Activities

Software design deals with transforming the customer requirements, as described in the SRS document, into a form (a set of documents) that is suitable for implementation in a programming language. A good software design is seldom arrived by using a single step procedure but rather through several iterations through a series of steps. Design activities can be broadly classified into two important parts:

- Preliminary (or high-level) design and

- Detailed design.

Preliminary and Detailed Design Activities

The meaning and scope of two design activities (i.e. high-level and detailed design) tend to vary considerably from one methodology to another. High-level design means identification of different modules and the control relationships among them and the definition of the interfaces among these modules. The outcome of high-level design is called the program structure or software architecture. Many different types of notations have been used to represent a high-level design. A popular way is to use a tree-like diagram called the structure chart to represent the control hierarchy in a high-level design. However, other notations such as Jackson diagram (1975) or Warnier-Orr (1977, 1981) diagram can also be used. During detailed design, the data structure and the algorithms of the different modules are designed. The outcome of the detailed design stage is usually known as the module-specification document.

Difference between Analysis and Design

The aim of analysis is to understand the problem with a view to eliminate any deficiencies in the requirement specification such as incompleteness, inconsistencies, etc. The model which we are trying to build may be or may not be ready.

The aim of design is to produce a model that will provide a seamless transition to the coding phase, i.e. once the requirements are analyzed and found to be satisfactory, a design model is created which can be easily implemented.

Items Developed During the Software Design Phase

For a design to be easily implemented in a conventional programming language, the following items must be designed during the design phase.

- Different modules required to implement the design solution.

- Control relationship among the identified modules. The relationship is also known as the call relationship or invocation relationship among modules.

- Interface among different modules. The interface among different modules identifies the exact data items exchanged among the modules.

- Data structures of the individual modules.

- Algorithms required to implement each individual module.

Characteristics of a Good Software Design

The definition of "a good software design" can vary depending on the application being designed. For example, the memory size used by a program may be an important issue to characterize a good solution for embedded software development – since embedded applications are often required to be implemented using memory of limited size due to cost, space, or power consumption considerations. For embedded applications, one may sacrifice design comprehensibility to achieve code compactness. For embedded applications, factors like design comprehensibility may take a back seat while judging the goodness of design. Therefore, the criteria used to judge how good a given design solution is can vary widely depending upon the application. Not only is the goodness of design dependent on the targeted application, but also the notion of goodness of a design itself varies widely across software engineers and academicians. However, most researchers and software engineers agree on a few desirable characteristics that every good software design for general application must possess. The characteristics are listed below:

- Correctness: A good design should correctly implement all the functionalities identified in the SRS document.

- Understandability: A good design is easily understandable.

- Efficiency: It should be efficient.

- Maintainability: It should be easily amenable to change.

Possibly the most important goodness criterion is design correctness. A design has to be correct to be acceptable. Given that a design solution is correct, understandability of a design is possibly the most important issue to be considered while judging the goodness of a design. A design that is easy to understand is also easy to develop, maintain and change. Thus, unless a design is easily understandable, it would require tremendous effort to implement and maintain it.

Features of a Design Document

In order to facilitate understandability, the design should have the following features:

- It should use consistent and meaningful names for various design components.

- The design should be modular. The term modularity means that it should use a cleanly decomposed set of modules.

- It should neatly arrange the modules in a hierarchy, e.g. in a tree-like diagram.

Cohesion

Most researchers and engineers agree that a good software design implies clean decomposition of the problem into modules, and the neat arrangement of these modules in a hierarchy. The primary characteristics of neat module decomposition are high cohesion and low coupling. Cohesion is a measure of functional strength of a module. A module having high cohesion and low coupling is said to be functionally independent of other modules. By the term functional independence, we mean that a cohesive module performs a single task or function. A functionally independent module has minimal interaction with other modules.

Classification of Cohesion

The different classes of cohesion that a module may possess are depicted in figure.

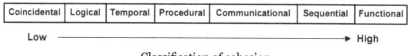

Classification of cohesion

Coincidental cohesion: A module is said to have coincidental cohesion, if it performs a set of tasks that relate to each other very loosely, if at all. In this case, the module contains a random collection of functions. It is likely that the functions have been put in the module out of pure coincidence without any thought or design. For example, in a transaction processing system (TPS), the get-input, print-error, and summarize-members functions are grouped into one module. The grouping does not have any relevance to the structure of the problem.

Logical cohesion: A module is said to be logically cohesive, if all elements of the module perform similar operations, e.g. error handling, data input, data output, etc. An example of logical cohesion is the case where a set of print functions generating different output reports are arranged into a single module.

Temporal cohesion: When a module contains functions that are related by the fact that all the functions must be executed in the same time span, the module is said to exhibit temporal cohesion. The set of functions responsible for initialization, start-up, shut-down of some process, etc. exhibit temporal cohesion.

Procedural cohesion: A module is said to possess procedural cohesion, if the set of functions of the module are all part of a procedure (algorithm) in which certain sequence of steps have to be carried out for achieving an objective, e.g. the algorithm for decoding a message.

Communicational cohesion: A module is said to have communicational cohesion, if all functions of the module refer to or update the same data structure, e.g. the set of functions defined on an array or a stack.

Sequential cohesion: A module is said to possess sequential cohesion, if the elements of a module form the parts of sequence, where the output from one element of the sequence is input to the next. For example, in a TPS, the get-input, validate-input, sort-input functions are grouped into one module.

Functional cohesion: Functional cohesion is said to exist, if different elements of a module cooperate to achieve a single function. For example, a module containing all the functions required to manage employees' pay-roll exhibits functional cohesion. Suppose a module exhibits functional cohesion and we are asked to describe what the module does, then we would be able to describe it using a single sentence.

Coupling

Coupling between two modules is a measure of the degree of interdependence or interaction between the two modules. A module having high cohesion and low coupling is said to be functionally independent of other modules. If two modules interchange large amounts of data, then they are highly interdependent. The degree of coupling between two modules depends on their interface complexity. The interface complexity is basically determined by the number of types of parameters that are interchanged while invoking the functions of the module.

Classification of Coupling

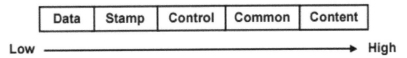

Classification of coupling

Data coupling: Two modules are data coupled, if they communicate through a parameter. An example is an elementary data item passed as a parameter between two modules, e.g. an integer, a float, a character, etc. This data item should be problem related and not used for the control purpose.

Stamp coupling: Two modules are stamp coupled, if they communicate using a composite data item such as a record in PASCAL or a structure in C.

Control coupling: Control coupling exists between two modules, if data from one module is used to direct the order of instructions execution in another. An example of control coupling is a flag set in one module and tested in another module.

Common coupling: Two modules are common coupled, if they share data through some global data items.

Content coupling: Content coupling exists between two modules, if they share code, e.g. a branch from one module into another module.

Functional Independence

A module having high cohesion and low coupling is said to be functionally independent of other modules. By the term functional independence, we mean that a cohesive module performs a single task or function. A functionally independent module has minimal interaction with other modules.

Need for Functional Independence

Functional independence is a key to any good design due to the following reasons:

- Error isolation: Functional independence reduces error propagation. The reason behind this is that if a module is functionally independent, its degree of interaction with the other modules is less. Therefore, any error existing in a module would not directly effect the other modules.

- Scope of reuse: Reuse of a module becomes possible. Because each module does some well-defined and precise function, and the interaction of the module with the other modules is simple and minimal. Therefore, a cohesive module can be easily taken out and reused in a different program.

- Understandability: Complexity of the design is reduced, because different modules can be understood in isolation as modules are more or less independent of each other.

Function-oriented Design

The following are the salient features of a typical function-oriented design approach:

1. A system is viewed as something that performs a set of functions. Starting at this high-level view of the system, each function is successively refined into more detailed functions. For example, consider a function create-new- library-member which essentially creates the record for a new member, assigns a unique membership number to him, and prints a bill towards his membership charge. This function may consist of the following sub- functions:

   - assign-membership-number

   - create-member-record

   - print-bill

Each of these sub-functions may be split into more detailed subfunctions and so on.

2. The system state is centralized and shared among different functions, e.g. data such as member-records is available for reference and updation to several functions such as:

   - create-new-member

   - delete-member

   - update-member-record

Object-oriented Design

In the object-oriented design approach, the system is viewed as collection of objects (i.e. entities). The state is decentralized among the objects and each object manages its own state information. For example, in a Library Automation Software, each library member may be a separate object with its own data and functions to operate on these data. In fact, the functions defined for one object cannot refer or change data of other objects. Objects have their own internal data which define their state. Similar objects constitute a class. In other words, each object is a member of some class. Classes may inherit features from super class. Conceptually, objects communicate by message passing.

Function-oriented Vs. Object-oriented Design Approach

The following are some of the important differences between function-oriented and object-oriented design.

   - Unlike function-oriented design methods, in OOD, the basic abstraction are not real-world functions such as sort, display, track, etc, but real- world entities such as employee, picture, machine, radar system, etc. For example in OOD, an employee pay-roll software is not developed by designing functions such as update-employee-record, get- employee-address, etc. but by designing objects such as employees, departments, etc. Grady Booch sums up this difference as "identify verbs if you are after procedural design and nouns if you are after object-oriented design"

- In OOD, state information is not represented in a centralized shared memory but is distributed among the objects of the system. For example, while developing an employee pay-roll system, the employee data such as the names of the employees, their code numbers, basic salaries, etc. are usually implemented as global data in a traditional programming system; whereas in an object-oriented system these data are distributed among different employee objects of the system. Objects communicate by message passing. Therefore, one object may discover the state information of another object by interrogating it. Of course, somewhere or other the real-world functions must be implemented. In OOD, the functions are usually associated with specific real-world entities (objects); they directly access only part of the system state information.

- Function-oriented techniques such as SA/SD group functions together if, as a group, they constitute a higher-level function. On the other hand, object-oriented techniques group functions together on the basis of the data they operate on.

To illustrate the differences between the object-oriented and the function-oriented design approaches, an example can be considered.

Example: Fire-Alarm System

The owner of a large multi-stored building wants to have a computerized fire alarm system for his building. Smoke detectors and fire alarms would be placed in each room of the building. The fire alarm system would monitor the status of these smoke detectors. Whenever a fire condition is reported by any of the smoke detectors, the fire alarm system should determine the location at which the fire condition is reported by any of the smoke detectors, the fire alarm system should determine the location at which the fire condition has occurred and then sound the alarms only in the neighboring locations. The fire alarm system should also flash an alarm message on the computer console. Fire fighting personnel man the console round the clock. After a fire condition has been successfully handled, the fire alarm system should support resetting the alarms by the fire fighting personnel.

Function-Oriented Approach

```
    /* Global data (system state) accessible by various
    functions */
BOOL

detector_status[MAX_ROOMS];

int detector_locs[MAX_ROOMS];

BOOL alarm_status[MAX_ROOMS];

/* alarm activated when status is set

*/ int alarm_locs[MAX_ROOMS];
```

```
/* room number where alarm is located
*/ int neighbor-alarm[MAX_ROOMS];
/* each detector has at most 10
neighboring
locations
*/
```

The functions which operate on the system state are:

```
        interrogate_detectors();
get_detector_location()
;
determine_neighbor();
ring_alarm();
reset_alarm();
report_fire_location();
```

Object-Oriented Approach:

```
            class detector
            attributes:
                status, location, neighbors
            operations:
                create, sense_status, get_location, find_neighbors
            class alarm
            attributes:
                location, status
            operations:
                create, ring_alarm, get_location, reset_alarm
```

In the object oriented program, an appropriate number of instances of the class detector and alarm should be created. If the function-oriented and the object-oriented programs are examined, it can be seen that in the function-oriented program, the system state is centralized and several functions accessing this central data are defined. In case of the object-oriented program, the state information is distributed among various sensor and alarm objects.

It is not necessary an object-oriented design be implemented by using an object-oriented language only. However, an object-oriented language such as C++ supports the definition of all the basic mechanisms of class, inheritance, objects, methods, etc. and also support all key object-oriented concepts that we have just discussed. Thus, an object-oriented language facilitates the implementation of an OOD. However, an OOD can as well be implemented using a conventional procedural language – though it may require more effort to implement an OOD using a procedural language as compared to the effort required for implementing the same design using an object-oriented language.

Even though object-oriented and function-oriented approaches are remarkably different approaches to software design, yet they do not replace each other but complement each other in some sense. For example, usually one applies the top-down function-oriented techniques to design the internal methods of a class, once the classes are identified. In this case, though outwardly the system appears to have been developed in an object-oriented fashion, but inside each class there may be a small hierarchy of functions designed in a top-down manner.

Responsibility-driven Design

Responsibility-driven design is a design technique in object-oriented programming, which improves encapsulation by using the client–server model. It focuses on the contract by considering the actions that the object is responsible for and the information that the object shares. It was proposed by Rebecca Wirfs-Brock and Brian Wilkerson

Responsibility-driven design is in direct contrast with data-driven design, which promotes defining the behavior of a class along with the data that it holds. Data-driven design is not the same as data-driven programming, which is concerned with using data to determine the control flow, not class design.

In the client–server model they refer to, both the client and the server are classes or instances of classes. At any particular time, either the client or the server represents an object. Both the parties commit to a contract and exchange information by adhering to it. The client can only make the requests specified in the contract and the server must answer these requests. Thus, responsibility-driven design tries to avoid dealing with details, such as the way in which requests are carried out, by instead only specifying the intent of a certain request. The benefit is increased encapsulation, since the specification of the exact way in which a request is carried out is private to the server.

To further the encapsulation of the server, Wirfs-Brock and Wilkerson call for language features that limit outside influence to the behavior of a class. They demand that the visibility of members and functions should be finely grained, such as in Eiffel programming language. Even finer control of the visibility of even classes is available in the Newspeak programming language.

Overview

Responsibility-driven design focuses on the objects as behavioral abstractions which are characterized by their responsibilities. The CRC-card modelling technique is used to generate these behavioral abstractions. The rest of the object structure including data attributes are assigned later, as and when required. This makes the design follow type hierarchy for inheritance which improves encapsulation and makes it easier to identify abstract classes. It can also group the classes together based on their clients which is considered a unique ability.

A good object-oriented design involves an early focus on behaviors to realize the capabilities meeting the stated requirements and a late binding of implementation details to the requirements. This approach especially helps to decentralize control and distribute system behavior which can help manage the complexities of high-functionality large or distributed systems. Similarly, it can help to design and maintain explanation facilities for cognitive models, intelligent agents, and other knowledge-based systems.

Building Blocks

In their book *Object Design: Roles, Responsibilities and Collaborations*, the authors describe the following building blocks that make up responsibility-driven design.

- Application: A software application is referred to as a set of interacting objects.

- Candidates: Candidates or candidate objects are key concepts in the form of objects described on CRC cards. They serve as initial inventions in the process of object design.

- Collaborations: A collaboration is defined as an interaction of objects or roles (or both).

- CRC Cards: CRC stands for Candidates, Responsibilities, Collaborators. They are index cards used in early design for recording candidates. These cards are split up into an unlined and a lined side.

    o Content of lined side: On this side the candidate's name, its responsibilities and its collaborators are recorded.

    o Content of unlined side: On this side the candidate's name, its purpose in the application, stereotype roles and anything worthwhile such as the names of roles in patterns it participates in are recorded.

- Hot Spots: Hot Spots are points in the application where variations occur. They are recorded using Hot Spot Cards.

- Hot Spot Cards: Hot Spot Cards are used for recording variations with just enough detail so you can discriminate important difference. Similar to CRC cards, these are also created from index cards. These cards consist of:

  o   Hot Spot Name

  o   General description of the variation

  o   At least two specific examples where the variation occurs

Objects

Objects are described as things that have machine-like behaviors that can be plugged together to work in concert. These objects play well-defined roles and encapsulate scripted responses and information.

- Object Neighborhoods: Another term for subsystem. It is a logical grouping of collaborators.

- Responsibilities: A responsibility is an obligation to perform a task or know information. These are further categorized according to their usage scenario.

  o   Public Responsibilities: Public responsibilities are the responsibilities an object offers as services to others and the information it provides to others.

  o   Private Responsibilities: Private responsibilities are the actions an object takes in support of public responsibilities.

  o   Subresponsibilities: Sometimes, a large or complicated responsibility is split up into smaller ones called subresponsibilities. They are further categorized based on what they do.

    ▪   Subordinate Responsibilities: These include the major steps in each subresponsibility.

    ▪   Sequencing Responsibilities: These refer to the sequencing of the execution of subordinate responsibilities.

Roles

Object role refers to an exterior view of what general service is offered by the object. It is a set of related responsibilities. It can be implemented as a class or an interface. Interface, however, is the preferred implementation as it increases flexibility by hiding the concrete class which ultimately does the work.

Role Stereotypes: Role stereotypes are simplified roles that come with predefined responsibilities. There are several categories.

- Controller: Object implementing this role makes decisions and closely directs the action of other objects.

- Coordinator: This role reacts to events by delegating tasks to others.

- Information Holder: Information holder knows and provides information.

  o Information Provider: A slight variation of an information holder is the information provider, which takes a more active role in managing and maintaining information. This distinction can be used if a designer needs to get more specific.

- Interfacer: This role transforms information and requests between distinct parts of an application. It is further divided into more specific roles.

  o External Interfacer: External interfacer communicates with other applications rather than its own. It is mainly used for encapsulating non-object-oriented APIs and does not collaborate a lot.

  o Internal Interfacer: Also called intersystem interfacer. It act as a bridge between object neighborhoods.

  o User Interfacer: User interfacer communicates with users by responding to events generated in the UI and then passing them on to more appropriate objects.

- Service Provider: This role performs work and offers computing services.

- Structurer: This role maintains relationships between objects and information about those relationships.

Control Style

An important part in the responsibility-driven design process is the distribution of control responsibilities that results in developing a control style. A control style is concerned about the control flow between subsystems.

- Concept of Control : The responsibilities and collaborations among the classes.

- Control Centers : An important aspect of developing a control style is the invention of so-called control centers. These are places where objects charged with controlling and coordinating reside.

- Control Style Variations : A control style comes in three distinct variations. These are not precise definitions though since a control style can be said to be more centralized or delegated than another.

Centralized Control Style

This control style inflicts a procedural paradigm on the structure of the application and places major-decision making responsibilities in only a few objects or a single object.

Types

- Call-return model : The control of the objects in the application is in hierarchical way. Control starts at root and moves downwards. It is used in a sequential model.

- Manager model : The control of the objects in the application is in with only one object. Generally, it is implemented in concurrent models. It can also be implemented in sequential model using case statement.

Advantages

- Application logic is in one place.

Disadvantages

- Control logic can get overly complex

- Controllers can become dependent on information holders' contents

- Objects can become coupled indirectly through the actions of their controller

- The only interesting work is done in the controller

When to use

When decisions to be made are few, simple, and related to a single task.

Delegated Control Style

A delegated control style lies in between a centralized and dispersed control style. It passes some of the decision making and much of the action to objects surrounding a control center. Each neighboring object has a significant role to play. It can also be called as event driven model, where the control is delegated to the object requesting it to process the event.

Types

- Broadcast model : An event is broadcast to all objects in the application. The object which can handle the event can acquire the control.

- Interrupt-driven model : There will be the interrupt handler to process the interrupt and passes to some object to process it.

Advantages

- It is easy to understand.

- Though there is an external coordinator, Objects can be made smarter to know what they are supposed to do and can be reused in other applications.

- Delegating coordinators tend to know about fewer objects than dominating controllers.

- Dialogs are higher-level.

- It is easy to change as changes typically affect fewer objects.

- It is easier to divide design work among team members.

Disadvantages

- Too much distribution of responsibility can lead to weak objects and weak collaborations

When to use

When one wants to delegate work to objects that are more specialized.

Clustered Control Style

This control style is a variation of the centralized control style wherein control is factored among a group of objects whose actions are coordinated. The main difference between a clustered and delegated control style is that in a clustered control style, the decision making objects are located within a control center whereas in a delegated control style they are mostly outside.

Dispersed Control Style

A dispersed control style does not contain any control centers. The logic is spread across the entire population of objects, keeping each object small and building in as few dependencies among them as possible.

Advantages

- None

Disadvantages

- When you want to find out how something works, you must trace the sequence of requests for services across many objects

- Not very reusable because no single object contributes much

When to use

Never.

Preferred Control Style

After extensive results of experiments conducted, only the senior management has the necessary skills to make use of delegated control style and centralized control style benefits programmers. There is no context mentioned about the mid-level employees.

Conflict with the Law of Demeter

According to Wirfs-Brock and Wilkerson, there is a conflict between the Law of Demeter and responsibility-driven design. The law says that messages can be sent only to the following: message argument, instance variable, new objects, and global variables. Therefore, sending a message to the result of a previous message send isn't allowed. However, "returned values are part of the client/server contract. There need be no correlation between the structure of an object and the object returned by the message."

Function-Oriented Software Design

Structured analysis is used to carry out the top-down decomposition of a set of high-level functions depicted in the problem description and to represent them graphically. During structured analysis, functional decomposition of the system is achieved. That is, each function that the system performs is analyzed and hierarchically decomposed into more detailed functions. Structured analysis technique is based on the following essential underlying principles:

- Top-down decomposition approach.

- Divide and conquer principle. Each function is decomposed independently.

- Graphical representation of the analysis results using Data Flow Diagrams (DFDs).

Data Flow Diagram (DFD)

The DFD (also known as a bubble chart) is a hierarchical graphical model of a system that shows the different processing activities or functions that the system performs and the data interchange among these functions. Each function is considered as a processing station (or process) that consumes some input data and produces some output data. The system is represented in terms of the input data to the system, various processing carried out on these data, and the output data generated by the system. A DFD model uses a very limited number of primitive symbols to represent the functions performed by a system and the data flow among these functions.

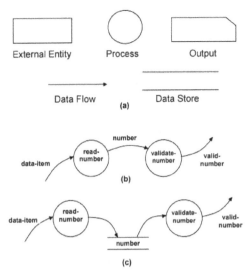

(a) Symbols used for designing DFDs
(b), (c) Synchronous and asynchronous data flow

Here, two examples of data flow that describe input and validation of data are considered. In Figure (b), the two processes are directly connected by a data flow. This means that the 'validate-number' process can start only after the 'read- number' process had supplied data to it. However in Figure (c), the two processes are connected through a data store. Hence, the operations of the two bubbles are independent. The first one is termed 'synchronous' and the second one 'asynchronous'.

Importance of DFDs in a Good Software Design

The main reason why the DFD technique is so popular is probably because of the fact that DFD is a very simple formalism – it is simple to understand and use. Starting with a set of high-level functions that a system performs, a DFD model hierarchically represents various sub-functions. In fact, any hierarchical model is simple to understand. Human mind is such that it can easily understand any hierarchical model of a system – because in a hierarchical model, starting with a very simple and abstract model of a system, different details of the system are slowly introduced through different hierarchies. The data flow diagramming technique also follows a very simple set of intuitive concepts and rules. DFD is an elegant modeling technique that turns out to be useful not only to represent the results of structured analysis of a software problem, but also for several other applications such as showing the flow of documents or items in an organization.

Data Dictionary

A data dictionary lists all data items appearing in the DFD model of a system. The data items listed include all data flows and the contents of all data stores appearing on the DFDs in the DFD model of a system. A data dictionary lists the purpose of all data items and the definition of all composite data items in terms of their component data items. For example, a data dictionary entry may represent that the data grossPay consists of the components regularPay and overtimePay.

$$grossPay = regularPay + overtimePay$$

For the smallest units of data items, the data dictionary lists their name and their type. Composite data items can be defined in terms of primitive data items using the following data definition operators:

+: denotes composition of two data items, e.g. a+b represents data a and b.

[,,]: represents selection, i.e. any one of the data items listed in the brackets can occur. For example, [a,b] represents either a occurs or b occurs.

(): the contents inside the bracket represent optional data which may or may not appear. e.g. a+(b) represents either a occurs or a+b occurs.

{}: represents iterative data definition, e.g. {name}5 represents five name data. {name}* represents zero or more instances of name data.

=:   represents equivalence, e.g. a=b+c means that a represents b and c.

/* */: Anything appearing within /* and */ is considered as a comment.

Example 1: Tic-Tac-Toe Computer Game

Tic-tac-toe is a computer game in which a human player and the computer make alternative moves on a 3´3 square. A move consists of marking previously unmarked square. The player who first places three consecutive marks along a straight line on the square (i.e. along a row, column, or diagonal) wins the game. As soon as either the human player or the computer wins, a message congratulating the winner should be displayed. If neither player manages to get three consecutive marks along a straight line, but all the squares on the board are filled up, then the game is drawn. The computer always tries to win a game.

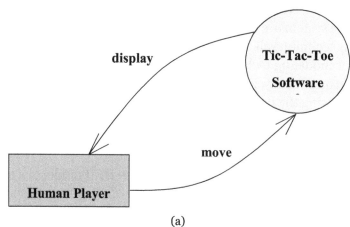

(a)

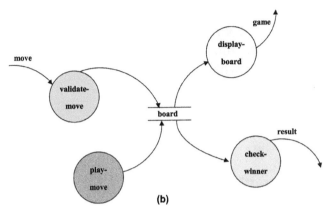

(a), (b) Level 0 and Level 1 DFD for Tic-Tac-Toe game described in Example 1

It may be recalled that the DFD model of a system typically consists of several DFDs: level 0, level 1, etc. However, a single data dictionary should capture all the data appearing in all the DFDs constituting the model. Figure represents the level 0 and level 1 DFDs for the tic-tac- toe game. The data dictionary for the model is given below.

Data dictionary for the DFD model in Example 1

> move: integer /*number between 1 and 9 */
>
> display: game+result
>
> game: board
>
> board: {integer}9
>
> result: ["computer won", "human won" "draw"]

Importance of Data Dictionary

A data dictionary plays a very important role in any software development process because of the following reasons:

- A data dictionary provides a standard terminology for all relevant data for use by the engineers working in a project. A consistent vocabulary for data items is very important, since in large projects different engineers of the project have a tendency to use different terms to refer to the same data, which unnecessary causes confusion.

- The data dictionary provides the analyst with a means to determine the definition of different data structures in terms of their component elements.

Balancing a DFD

The data that flow into or out of a bubble must match the data flow at the next level of

DFD. This is known as balancing a DFD. The concept of balancing a DFD has been illustrated in figure. In the level 1 of the DFD, data items d1 and d3 flow out of the bubble 0.1 and the data item d2 flows into the bubble 0.1. In the next level, bubble 0.1 is decomposed. The decomposition is balanced, as d1 and d3 flow out of the level 2 diagram and d2 flows in.

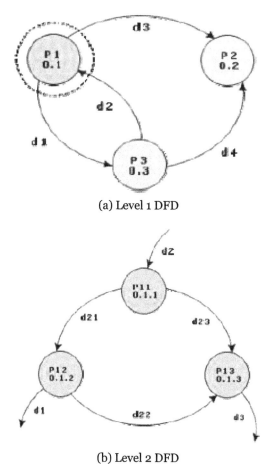

(a) Level 1 DFD

(b) Level 2 DFD

An example showing balanced decomposition

Context Diagram

The context diagram is the most abstract data flow representation of a system. It represents the entire system as a single bubble. This bubble is labeled according to the main function of the system. The various external entities with which the system interacts and the data flow occurring between the system and the external entities are also represented. The data input to the system and the data output from the system are represented as incoming and outgoing arrows. These data flow arrows should be annotated with the corresponding data names. The name 'context diagram' is well justified because it represents the context in which the system is to exist, i.e. the external entities who would interact with the system and the specific data items they would be supplying the system and the data items they would be receiving from the system. The context diagram is also called as the level 0 DFD.

To develop the context diagram of the system, it is required to analyze the SRS document to identify the different types of users who would be using the system and the kinds of data they would be inputting to the system and the data they would be receiving the system. Here, the term "users of the system" also includes the external systems which supply data to or receive data from the system.

The bubble in the context diagram is annotated with the name of the software system being developed (usually a noun). This is in contrast with the bubbles in all other levels which are annotated with verbs. This is expected since the purpose of the context diagram is to capture the context of the system rather than its functionality.

Example 1: RMS Calculating Software.

A software system called RMS calculating software would read three integral numbers from the user in the range of -1000 and +1000 and then determine the root mean square (rms) of the three input numbers and display it. In this example, the context diagram is simple to draw. The system accepts three integers from the user and returns the result to him.

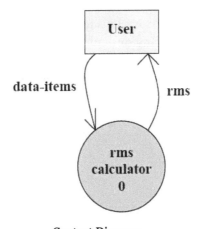

Context Diagram

DFD Model of a System

A DFD model of a system graphically depicts the transformation of the data input to the system to the final result through a hierarchy of levels. A DFD starts with the most abstract definition of the system (lowest level) and at each higher level DFD, more details are successively introduced. To develop a higher-level DFD model, processes are decomposed into their sub-processes and the data flow among these sub-processes is identified.

To develop the data flow model of a system, first the most abstract representation of the problem is to be worked out. The most abstract representation of the problem is also called the context diagram. After, developing the context diagram, the higher-level DFDs have to be developed.

Context Diagram

This has been described earlier.

Level 1 DFD

To develop the level 1 DFD, examine the high-level functional requirements. If there are between 3 to 7 high-level functional requirements, then these can be directly represented as bubbles in the level 1 DFD. We can then examine the input data to these functions and the data output by these functions and represent them appropriately in the diagram.

If a system has more than 7 high-level functional requirements, then some of the related requirements have to be combined and represented in the form of a bubble in the level 1 DFD. Such a bubble can be split in the lower DFD levels. If a system has less than three high-level functional requirements, then some of them need to be split into their sub-functions so that we have roughly about 5 to 7 bubbles on the diagram.

Decomposition

Each bubble in the DFD represents a function performed by the system. The bubbles are decomposed into sub-functions at the successive levels of the DFD. Decomposition of a bubble is also known as factoring or exploding a bubble. Each bubble at any level of DFD is usually decomposed to anything between 3 to 7 bubbles. Too few bubbles at any level make that level superfluous. For example, if a bubble is decomposed to just one bubble or two bubbles, then this decomposition becomes redundant. Also, too many bubbles, i.e. more than 7 bubbles at any level of a DFD makes the DFD model hard to understand. Decomposition of a bubble should be carried on until a level is reached at which the function of the bubble can be described using a simple algorithm.

Numbering of Bubbles

It is necessary to number the different bubbles occurring in the DFD. These numbers help in uniquely identifying any bubble in the DFD by its bubble number. The bubble at the context level is usually assigned the number 0 to indicate that it is the 0 level DFD. Bubbles at level 1 are numbered, 0.1, 0.2, 0.3, etc, etc. When a bubble numbered x is decomposed, its children bubble are numbered x.1, x.2, x.3, etc. In this numbering scheme, by looking at the number of a bubble we can unambiguously determine its level, its ancestors, and its successors.

Example

A supermarket needs to develop the following software to encourage regular customers. For this, the customer needs to supply his/her residence address, telephone number, and the driving license number. Each customer who registers for this scheme is assigned a unique customer number (CN) by the computer. A customer can present his CN to the check out staff when he makes any purchase. In this case, the value of his purchase is credited against his CN. At the end of each year, the supermarket intends to award surprise gifts to 10 customers who make the highest total purchase over the year. Also, it intends to award a 22 caret gold coin to every customer whose purchase exceeded Rs.10,000. The entries against the CN are the reset on the day of every year after the prize winners' lists are generated.

The context diagram for this problem is shown in figure, the level 1 DFD in figure, and the level 2 DFD in figure.

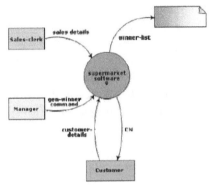

Context diagram for supermarket problem

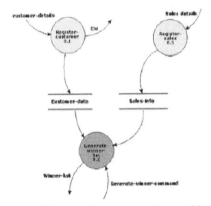

Level 1 diagram for supermarket problem

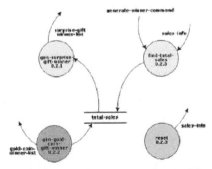

Level 2 diagram for supermarket problem

Data Dictionary for a DFD Model

Every DFD model of a system must be accompanied by a data dictionary. A data dictionary lists all data items appearing in the DFD model of a system. The data items listed include all data flows and the contents of all data stores appearing on the DFDs in the DFD model of a system. We can understand the creation of a data dictionary better by considering an example.

Example: Trading-House Automation System (TAS).

The trading house wants us to develop a computerized system that would automate various book-keeping activities associated with its business. The following are the salient features of the system to be developed:

- The trading house has a set of regular customers. The customers place orders with it for various kinds of commodities. The trading house maintains the names and addresses of its regular customers. Each of these regular customers should be assigned a unique customer identification number (CIN) by the computer. The customers quote their CIN on every order they place.

- Once order is placed, as per current practice, the accounts department of the trading house first checks the credit-worthiness of the customer. The credit-worthiness of the customer is determined by analyzing the history of his payments to different bills sent to him in the past. After automation, this task has to be done by the computer.

- If the customer is not credit-worthy, his orders are not processed any further and an appropriate order rejection message is generated for the customer.

- If a customer is credit-worthy, the items that have been ordered are checked against a list of items that the trading house deals with. The items in the order which the trading house does not deal with, are not processed any further and an appropriate apology message for the customer for these items is generated.

- The items in the customer's order that the trading house deals with are checked for availability in the inventory. If the items are available in the inventory in the desired quantity, then

  o A bill with the forwarding address of the customer is printed.

  o A material issue slip is printed. The customer can produce this material issue slip at the store house and take delivery of the items.

  o Inventory data is adjusted to reflect the sale to the customer.

- If any of the ordered items are not available in the inventory in sufficient quantity to satisfy the order, then these out-of-stock items along with the quantity ordered by the customer and the CIN are stored in a "pending-order" file for the further processing to be carried out when the purchase department issues the "generate indent" command.

- The purchase department should be allowed to periodically issue commands to generate indents. When a command to generate indents is issued, the system should examine the "pending-order" file to determine the orders that are pending and determine the total quantity required for each of the items. It should find out the addresses of the vendors who supply these items by examining a file containing vendor details and then should print out indents to these vendors.

- The system should also answer managerial queries regarding the statistics of different items sold over any given period of time and the corresponding quantity sold and the price realized.

The context diagram for the trading house automation problem is shown in figure, and the level 1 DFD in figure.

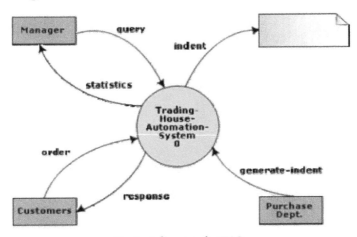

Context diagram for TAS

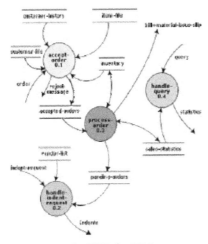

Level 1 DFD for TAS

Data Dictionary for the DFD Model of TAS

response:	[bill + material-issue-slip, reject-message]
query:	period /*query from manager regarding sales statistics */
period	[date + date, month, year, day]
date:	year + month + day
year:	integer
month:	integer
day:	integer
order:	customer-id + {items + quantity}* + order#
accepted-order:	order /* ordered items available in inventory */
reject-message:	order + message /*rejection message*/
pending-orders:	customer-id + {items + quantity}*
customer-address:	name + house# + street# + city + pin name: string
house#:	string
street#:	string
city:	string
pin:	integer
customer-id:	integer
customer-file:	{customer-address}*
bill:	{item + quantity + price}* + total-amount + customer-address + order#
material-issue-slip:	message + item + quantity + customer-address
message:	string
statistics:	{item + quantity + price}*
sales-statistics:	{statistics}* + date
quantity:	integer
order#:	integer /* unique order number generated by the program */

price:	integer
total-amount:	integer
generate-indent:	command
indent:	{indent + quantity}* + vendor-address
indents:	{indent}*
vendor-address:	customer-address
vendor-list:	{vendor-address}*
item-file:	{item}*
item:	string
indent-request:	command

Commonly Made Errors while Constructing a DFD Model

Although DFDs are simple to understand and draw, students and practitioners alike encounter similar types of problems while modelling software problems using DFDs. While learning from experience is powerful thing, it is an expensive pedagogical technique in the business world. It is therefore helpful to understand the different types of mistakes that users usually make while constructing the DFD model of systems.

- Many beginners commit the mistake of drawing more than one bubble in the context diagram. A context diagram should depict the system as a single bubble.

- Many beginners have external entities appearing at all levels of DFDs. All external entities interacting with the system should be represented only in the context diagram. The external entities should not appear at other levels of the DFD.

- It is a common oversight to have either too less or too many bubbles in a DFD. Only 3 to 7 bubbles per diagram should be allowed, i.e. each bubble should be decomposed to between 3 and 7 bubbles.

- Many beginners leave different levels of DFD unbalanced.

- A common mistake committed by many beginners while developing a DFD model is attempting to represent control information in a DFD. It is important to realize that a DFD is the data flow representation of a system, and it does not represent control information. For an example mistake of this kind:

  o Consider the following example. A book can be searched in the library catalog by inputting its name. If the book is available in the library, then the details of the book are displayed. If the book is not listed in the catalog, then an error message is generated. While generating the DFD model for this simple problem, many beginners commit the mistake of drawing an arrow to indicate the error function is invoked after the search book. But, this is a control information and should not be shown on the DFD.

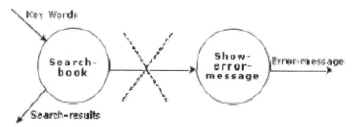

Showing control information on a DFD – incorrect

o   Another error is trying to represent when or in what order different functions (processes) are invoked and not representing the conditions under which different functions are invoked.

o   If a bubble A invokes either the bubble B or the bubble C depending upon some conditions, we need only to represent the data that flows between bubbles A and B or bubbles A and C and not the conditions depending on which the two modules are invoked.

- A data store should be connected only to bubbles through data arrows. A data store cannot be connected to another data store or to an external entity.

- All the functionalities of the system must be captured by the DFD model. No function of the system specified in its SRS document should be overlooked.

- Only those functions of the system specified in the SRS document should be represented, i.e. the designer should not assume functionality of the system not specified by the SRS document and then try to represent them in the DFD.

- Improper or unsatisfactory data dictionary.

- The data and function names must be intuitive. Some students and even practicing engineers use symbolic data names such a, b, c, etc. Such names hinder understanding the DFD model.

Shortcomings of a DFD Model

DFD models suffer from several shortcomings. The important shortcomings of the DFD models are the following:

- DFDs leave ample scope to be imprecise. In the DFD model, the function performed by a bubble is judged from its label. However, a short label may not capture the entire functionality of a bubble. For example, a bubble named find-book-position has only intuitive meaning and does not specify several things, e.g. what happens when some input information are missing or are incorrect. Further, the find-book- position bubble may not convey anything regarding what happens when the required book is missing.

- Control aspects are not defined by a DFD. For instance, the order in which inputs are consumed and outputs are produced by a bubble is not specified. A DFD model does not specify the order in which the different bubbles are executed. Representation of such aspects is very important for modeling real-time systems.

- The method of carrying out decomposition to arrive at the successive levels and the ultimate level to which decomposition is carried out are highly subjective and depend on the choice and judgment of the analyst. Due to this reason, even for the same problem, several alternative DFD representations are possible. Further, many times it is not possible to say which DFD representation is superior or preferable to another one.

- The data flow diagramming technique does not provide any specific guidance as to how exactly to decompose a given function into its sub- functions and we have to use subjective judgment to carry out decomposition.

Structured Design

The aim of structured design is to transform the results of the structured analysis (i.e. a DFD representation) into a structure chart. Structured design provides two strategies to guide transformation of a DFD into a structure chart.

- Transform analysis
- Transaction analysis

Normally, one starts with the level 1 DFD, transforms it into module representation using either the transform or the transaction analysis and then proceeds towards the lower-level DFDs. At each level of transformation, it is important to first determine whether the transform or the transaction analysis is applicable to a particular DFD. These are discussed in the subsequent sub- sections.

Structure Chart

A structure chart represents the software architecture, i.e. the various modules making up the system, the dependency (which module calls which other modules), and the parameters that are passed among the different modules. Hence, the structure chart representation can be easily implemented using some programming language. Since the main focus in a structure chart representation is on the module structure of the software and the interactions among different modules, the procedural aspects (e.g. how a particular functionality is achieved) are not represented.

The basic building blocks which are used to design structure charts are the following:

- Rectangular boxes: Represents a module.

- Module invocation arrows: Control is passed from one module to another module in the direction of the connecting arrow.

- Data flow arrows: Arrows are annotated with data name; named data passes from one module to another module in the direction of the arrow.

- Library modules: Represented by a rectangle with double edges.

- Selection: Represented by a diamond symbol.

- Repetition: Represented by a loop around the control flow arrow.

Structure Chart Vs. Flow Chart

We are all familiar with the flow chart representation of a program. Flow chart is a convenient technique to represent the flow of control in a program. A structure chart differs from a flow chart in three principal ways:

- It is usually difficult to identify the different modules of the software from its flow chart representation.

- Data interchange among different modules is not represented in a flow chart.

- Sequential ordering of tasks inherent in a flow chart is suppressed in a structure chart.

Transform Analysis

Transform analysis identifies the primary functional components (modules) and the high level inputs and outputs for these components. The first step in transform analysis is to divide the DFD into 3 types of parts:

- Input

- Logical processing

- Output

The input portion of the DFD includes processes that transform input data from physical (e.g. character from terminal) to logical forms (e.g. internal tables, lists, etc.). Each input portion is called an afferent branch.

The output portion of a DFD transforms output data from logical to physical form. Each output portion is called an efferent branch. The remaining portion of a DFD is called the central transform.

In the next step of transform analysis, the structure chart is derived by drawing one functional component for the central transform, and the afferent and efferent branches. These are drawn below a root module, which would invoke these modules.

Identifying the highest level input and output transforms requires experience and skill. One possible approach is to trace the inputs until a bubble is found whose output cannot be deduced from its inputs alone. Processes which validate input or add information to them are not central transforms. Processes which sort input or filter data from it are. The first level structure chart is produced by representing each input and output unit as boxes and each central transform as a single box.

In the third step of transform analysis, the structure chart is refined by adding sub-functions required by each of the high-level functional components. Many levels of functional components may be added. This process of breaking functional components into subcomponents is called factoring. Factoring includes adding read and write modules, error-handling modules, initialization and termination process, identifying customer modules, etc. The factoring process is continued until all bubbles in the DFD are represented in the structure chart.

Example: Structure chart for the RMS software

For this example, the context diagram was drawn earlier.

To draw the level 1 DFD, from a cursory analysis of the problem description, we can see that there are four basic functions that the system needs to perform – accept the input numbers from the user, validate the numbers, calculate the root mean square of the input numbers and, then display the result.

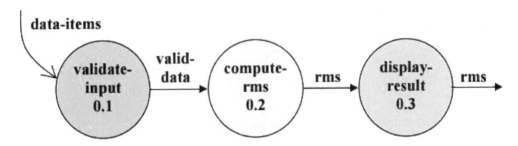

By observing the level 1 DFD, we identify the validate-input as the afferent branch and write-output as the efferent branch. The remaining portion (i.e. compute-rms) forms the central transform. By applying the step 2 and step 3 of transform analysis, we get the structure chart shown in figure.

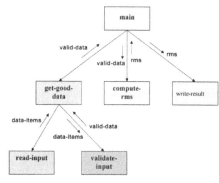

Structure chart

Transaction Analysis

A transaction allows the user to perform some meaningful piece of work. Transaction analysis is useful while designing transaction processing programs. In a transaction-driven system, one of several possible paths through the DFD is traversed depending upon the input data item. This is in contrast to a transform centered system which is characterized by similar processing steps for each data item. Each different way in which input data is handled is a transaction. A simple way to identify a transaction is to check the input data. The number of bubbles on which the input data to the DFD are incident defines the number of transactions. However, some transaction may not require any input data. These transactions can be identified from the experience of solving a large number of examples.

For each identified transaction, trace the input data to the output. All the traversed bubbles belong to the transaction. These bubbles should be mapped to the same module on the structure chart. In the structure chart, draw a root module and below this module draw each identified transaction a module. Every transaction carries a tag, which identifies its type. Transaction analysis uses this tag to divide the system into transaction modules and a transaction-center module.

The structure chart for the supermarket prize scheme software is shown in figure.

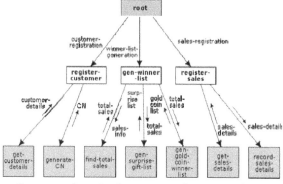

Structure chart for the supermarket prize scheme

References

- Wirfs-Brock, Rebecca; Wilkerson, Brian (1989). "Object-Oriented Design: A Responsibility-Driven Approach". ACM SIGPLAN Notices. 24 (10): 74. doi:10.1145/74878.74885. Retrieved 9 February 2016

- Simison, Graeme. C. & Witt, Graham. C. (2005).Data Modeling Essentials.3rd Edition. Morgan Kauffman Publishers. ISBN 0-12-644551-6

- "The role of context in perceptions of the aesthetics of web pages over time". International Journal of Human–Computer Studies. 2009-01-05. Retrieved 2009-04-02

- Ann Blandford. "Semi-structured qualitative studies". The Encyclopedia of Human-Computer Interaction, 2nd Ed. Interaction Design Foundation. Retrieved 20 April 2014

- Booch, Grady; et al. (2004). Object-Oriented Analysis and Design with Applications (3rd ed.). MA, USA: Addison Wesley. ISBN 0-201-89551-X. Retrieved 30 January 2015

- Wolf, Lauren (23 May 2012). "6 Tips for Designing an Optimal User Interface for Your Digital Event". INXPO. Retrieved 22 May 2013

- Anthony J. H. Simons; Monique Snoeck; Kitty Hung (1998). "Design Patterns as Litmus Paper to Test the Strength of Object-Oriented Methods". doi:10.1007/978-1-4471-0895-5_10

- Whitten, Jeffrey L.; Lonnie D. Bentley, Kevin C. Dittman. (2004). Systems Analysis and Design Methods. 6th edition. ISBN 0-256-19906-X

- Norman, D. A. (2002). "Emotion & Design: Attractive things work better". Interactions Magazine, ix (4). pp. 36–42. Retrieved 20 April 2014

- Freeman, Peter; David Hart (2004). "A Science of design for software-intensive systems". Communications of the ACM. 47 (8): 19–21 [20]. doi:10.1145/1012037.1012054

- Suryanarayana, Girish (November 2014). Refactoring for Software Design Smells. Morgan Kaufmann. p. 258. ISBN 978-0128013977. Retrieved 31 January 2015

- Ralph, P. and Wand, Y. (2009). A proposal for a formal definition of the design concept. In Lyytinen, K., Loucopoulos, P., Mylopoulos, J., and Robinson, W., editors, Design Requirements Workshop (LNBIP 14), pp. 103–136. Springer-Verlag, p. 109 doi:10.1007/978-3-540-92966-6_6

- Karen Holtzblatt and Hugh R. Beyer. "Contextual design". The Encyclopedia of Human-Computer Interaction, 2nd Ed. Interaction Design Foundation. Retrieved 20 April 2014

3

Programming Paradigm: An Overview

Programming paradigm is a method to sort languages on the basis of their features. Various types of programming paradigms include structured programming, procedural programming, declarative programming, imperative programming, object-oriented programming, functional programming etc. The major components of programming paradigm are discussed in this chapter.

Programming Paradigm

Programming paradigms are a way to classify programming languages based on the features of various programming languages. Languages can be classified into multiple paradigm.

Some paradigms are concerned mainly with implications for the execution model of the language, such as allowing side effects, or whether the sequence of operations is defined by the execution model. Other paradigms are concerned mainly with the way that code is organized, such as grouping code into units along with the state that is modified by the code. Yet others are concerned mainly with the style of syntax and grammar.

Common programming paradigms include:

- Imperative which allows side effects,

- Functional which disallows side effects,

- Declarative which does not state the order in which operations execute,

- Object-oriented which groups code together with the state the code modifies,

- Procedural which groups code into functions,

- Logic which has a particular style of execution model coupled to a particular style of syntax and grammar, and

- Symbolic programming which has a particular style of syntax and grammar.

For example, languages that fall into the imperative paradigm have two main features: they state the order in which operations occur, with constructs that explicitly control that order, and they allow side effects, in which state can be modified at one point in time, within one unit of code, and then later read at a different point in time inside a different unit of code. The communication between the units of code is not explicit. Meanwhile, in object-oriented programming, code is organized into objects that contain state that is only modified by the code that is part of the object. Most object-oriented languages are also imperative languages. In contrast, languages that fit the declarative paradigm do not state the order in which to execute operations. Instead, they supply a number of operations that are available in the system, along with the conditions under which each is allowed to execute. The implementation of the language's execution model tracks which operations are free to execute and chooses the order on its own. More at Comparison of multi-paradigm programming languages.

Overview

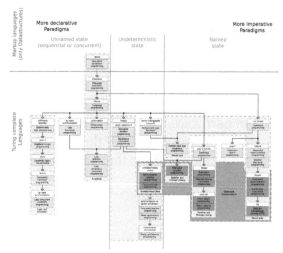

Overview of the Various Programming Paradigms According to
Peter Van Roy

Just as software engineering (as a process) is defined by differing *methodologies*, so the programming languages (as models of computation) are defined by differing *paradigms*. Some languages are designed to support one paradigm (Smalltalk supports object-oriented programming, Haskell supports functional programming), while other programming languages support multiple paradigms (such as Object Pascal, C++, Java, C#, Scala, Visual Basic, Common Lisp, Scheme, Perl, PHP, Python, Ruby, Oz, and F#). For example, programs written in C++, Object Pascal or PHP can be purely procedural, purely object-oriented, or can contain elements of both or other paradigms. Software designers and programmers decide how to use those paradigm elements.

In object-oriented programming, programs are treated as a set of interacting objects. In functional programming, programs are treated as a sequence of stateless function evaluations. When programming computers or systems with many processors, in process-oriented programming, programs are treated as sets of concurrent processes acting on logically shared data structures.

Many programming paradigms are as well known for the techniques they *forbid* as for those they *enable*. For instance, pure functional programming disallows use of side-effects, while structured programming disallows use of the goto statement. Partly for this reason, new paradigms are often regarded as doctrinaire or overly rigid by those accustomed to earlier styles. Yet, avoiding certain techniques can make it easier to understand program behavior, and to prove theorems about program correctness.

Programming paradigms can also be compared with *programming models* which allow invoking an external execution model by using only an API. Programming models can also be classified into paradigms, based on features of the execution model.

For parallel computing, using a programming model instead of a language is common. The reason is that details of the parallel hardware leak into the abstractions used to program the hardware. This causes the programmer to have to map patterns in the algorithm onto patterns in the execution model (which have been inserted due to leakage of hardware into the abstraction). As a consequence, no one parallel programming language maps well to all computation problems. It is thus more convenient to use a base sequential language and insert API calls to parallel execution models, via a programming model. Such parallel programming models can be classified according to abstractions that reflect the hardware, such as shared memory, distributed memory with message passing, notions of *place* visible in the code, and so forth. These can be considered flavors of programming paradigm that apply to only parallel languages and programming models.

History

Different approaches to programming have developed over time, being identified as such either at the time or retrospectively. An early approach consciously identified as such is structured programming, advocated since the mid 1960s. The concept of a "programming paradigm" as such dates at least to 1978, in the Turing Award lecture of Robert W. Floyd, entitled *The Paradigms of Programming*, which cites the notion of paradigm as used by Thomas Kuhn in his *The Structure of Scientific Revolutions* (1962).

Machine Code

The lowest-level programming paradigms are machine code, which directly represents the instructions (the contents of program memory) as a sequence of numbers, and assembly language where the machine instructions are represented by mnemonics and memory addresses can be given symbolic labels. These are sometimes called first- and second-generation languages.

In the 1960s, assembly languages were developed to support library COPY and quite sophisticated conditional macro generation and preprocessing abilities, CALL to (subroutines), external variables and common sections (globals), enabling significant code re-use and isolation from hardware specifics via use of logical operators such as READ/ WRITE/GET/PUT. Assembly was, and still is, used for time critical systems and often in embedded systems as it gives the most direct control of what the machine does.

Procedural Languages

The next advance was the development of procedural languages. These third-generation languages (the first described as high-level languages) use vocabulary related to the problem being solved. For example:

- COmmon Business Oriented Language (COBOL) – uses terms like file, move and copy.

- FORmula TRANslation (FORTRAN) – using mathematical language terminology, it was developed mainly for scientific and engineering problems.

- ALGOrithmic Language (ALGOL) – focused on being an appropriate language to define algorithms, while using mathematical language terminology and targeting scientific and engineering problems just like FORTRAN.

- Programming Language One (PL/I) – a hybrid commercial-scientific general purpose language supporting pointers.

- Beginners All purpose Symbolic Instruction Code (BASIC) – it was developed to enable more people to write programs.

- C – a general-purpose programming language, initially developed by Dennis Ritchie between 1969 and 1973 at AT&T Bell Labs.

All these languages follow the procedural paradigm. That is, they describe, step by step, exactly the procedure that should, according to the particular programmer at least, be followed to solve a specific problem. The efficacy and efficiency of any such solution are both therefore entirely subjective and highly dependent on that programmer's experience, inventiveness, and ability.

Object-oriented Programming

Following the widespread use of procedural languages, object-oriented programming (OOP) languages were created, such as Simula, Smalltalk, C++, C#, Eiffel, PHP, and Java. In these languages, data and methods to manipulate it are kept as one unit called an object. The only way that another object or user can access the data is via the object's *methods*. Thus, the inner workings of an object may be changed without affecting any code that uses the object. There is still some controversy raised by Alexander Stepanov, Richard Stallman and other programmers, concerning the efficacy of the OOP paradigm versus the procedural paradigm. The need for every object to have associative methods leads some skeptics to associate OOP with software bloat; an attempt to resolve this dilemma came through polymorphism.

Because object-oriented programming is considered a paradigm, not a language, it is possible to create even an object-oriented assembler language. High Level Assembly (HLA) is an example of this that fully supports advanced data types and object-oriented assembly language programming – despite its early origins. Thus, differing programming paradigms can be seen rather like *motivational memes* of their advocates, rather than necessarily representing progress from one level to the next. Precise comparisons of the efficacy of competing paradigms are frequently made more difficult because of new and differing terminology applied to similar entities and processes together with numerous implementation distinctions across languages.

Further Paradigms

Literate programming, as a form of imperative programming, structures programs as a human-centered web, as in a hypertext essay: documentation is integral to the program, and the program is structured following the logic of prose exposition, rather than compiler convenience.

Independent of the imperative branch, declarative programming paradigms were developed. In these languages, the computer is told what the problem is, not how to solve the problem – the program is structured as a set of properties to find in the expected result, not as a procedure to follow. Given a database or a set of rules, the computer tries to find a solution matching all the desired properties. An archetype of a declarative language is the fourth generation language SQL, and the family of functional languages and logic programming.

Functional programming is a subset of declarative programming. Programs written using this paradigm use functions, blocks of code intended to behave like mathematical functions. Functional languages discourage changes in the value of variables through assignment, making a great deal of use of recursion instead.

The logic programming paradigm views computation as automated reasoning over a body of knowledge. Facts about the problem domain are expressed as logic formulae, and programs are executed by applying inference rules over them until an answer to the problem is found, or the set of formulae is proved inconsistent.

Symbolic programming is a paradigm that describes programs able to manipulate formulas and program components as data. Programs can thus effectively modify themselves, and appear to "learn", making them suited for applications such as artificial intelligence, expert systems, natural language processing and computer games. Languages that support this paradigm include Lisp and Prolog.

Multi-paradigm

A *multi-paradigm programming language* is a programming language that supports more than one programming paradigm. The design goal of such languages is to allow programmers to use the most suitable programming style and associated language constructs for a given job, considering that no single paradigm solves all problems in the easiest or most efficient way.

One example is C#, which includes imperative and object-oriented paradigms, together with a certain level of support for functional programming with features like delegates (allowing functions to be treated as first-order objects), type inference, anonymous functions and Language Integrated Query. Other examples are F# and Scala, which provide similar functionality to C# but also include full support for functional programming (including currying, pattern matching, algebraic data types, lazy evaluation, tail recursion, immutability, etc.). Perhaps the most extreme example is Oz, which has subsets that adhere to logic (Oz descends from logic programming), functional, object-oriented, dataflow concurrent, and other paradigms. Oz was designed over a ten-year period to combine in a harmonious way concepts that are traditionally associated with different programming paradigms. Lisp, while often taught as a functional language, is known for its malleability and thus its ability to engulf many paradigms.

Imperative Programming

In computer science, imperative programming is a programming paradigm that uses statements that change a program's state. In much the same way that the imperative mood in natural languages expresses commands, an imperative program consists of commands for the computer to perform. Imperative programming focuses on describing *how* a program operates.

The term is often used in contrast to declarative programming, which focuses on *what* the program should accomplish without specifying *how* the program should achieve the result.

Imperative and Procedural Programming

Procedural programming is a type of imperative programming in which the program is built from one or more procedures (also termed subroutines or functions). The terms are often used as synonyms, but the use of procedures has a dramatic effect on how imperative programs appear and how they are constructed. Heavily-procedural programming, in which state changes are localized to procedures or restricted to explicit arguments and returns from procedures, is a form of structured programming. From the 1960s onwards, structured programming and modular programming in general have been promoted as techniques to improve the maintainability and overall quality of imperative programs. The concepts behind object-oriented programming attempt to extend this approach.

Procedural programming could be considered a step towards declarative programming. A programmer can often tell, simply by looking at the names, arguments, and return types of procedures (and related comments), what a particular procedure is supposed to do, without necessarily looking at the details of how it achieves its result. At the same time, a complete program is still imperative since it *fixes* the statements to be executed and their order of execution to a large extent.

Rationale and Foundations of Imperative Programming

The hardware implementation of almost all computers is imperative. Nearly all computer hardware is designed to execute machine code, which is native to the computer, written in the imperative style. From this low-level perspective, the program state is defined by the contents of memory, and the statements are instructions in the native machine language of the computer. Higher-level imperative languages use variables and more complex statements, but still follow the same paradigm. Recipes and process checklists, while not computer programs, are also familiar concepts that are similar in style to imperative programming; each step is an instruction, and the physical world holds the state. Since the basic ideas of imperative programming are both conceptually familiar and directly embodied in the hardware, most computer languages are in the imperative style.

Assignment statements, in imperative paradigm, perform an operation on information located in memory and store the results in memory for later use. High-level imperative languages, in addition, permit the evaluation of complex expressions, which may consist of a combination of arithmetic operations and function evaluations, and the assignment of the resulting value to memory. Looping statements (as in while loops, do while loops, and for loops) allow a sequence of statements to be executed multiple times. Loops can either execute the statements they contain a predefined number of times, or they can execute them repeatedly until some condition changes. Conditional branching statements allow a sequence of statements to be executed only if some condition is met. Otherwise, the statements are skipped and the execution sequence continues from the statement following them. Unconditional branching statements allow an execution sequence to be transferred to another part of a program. These include the jump (called *goto* in many languages), switch, and the subprogram, subroutine, or procedure call (which usually returns to the next statement after the call).

Early in the development of high-level programming languages, the introduction of the block enabled the construction of programs in which a group of statements and declarations could be treated as if they were one statement. This, alongside the introduction of subroutines, enabled complex structures to be expressed by hierarchical decomposition into simpler procedural structures.

Many imperative programming languages (such as Fortran, BASIC, and C) are abstractions of assembly language.

History of Imperative and Object-oriented Languages

The earliest imperative languages were the machine languages of the original computers. In these languages, instructions were very simple, which made hardware implementation easier, but hindered the creation of complex programs. FORTRAN, developed by John Backus at International Business Machines (IBM) starting in 1954, was the first major programming language to remove the obstacles presented by machine code in the creation of complex programs. FORTRAN was a compiled language that allowed named variables, complex expressions, subprograms, and many other features now common in imperative languages. The next two decades saw the development of many other major high-level imperative programming languages. In the late 1950s and 1960s, ALGOL was developed in order to allow mathematical algorithms to be more easily expressed, and even served as the operating system's target language for some computers. MUMPS (1966) carried the imperative paradigm to a logical extreme, by not having any statements at all, relying purely on commands, even to the extent of making the IF and ELSE commands independent of each other, connected only by an intrinsic variable named $TEST. COBOL (1960) and BASIC (1964) were both attempts to make programming syntax look more like English. In the 1970s, Pascal was developed by Niklaus Wirth, and C was created by Dennis Ritchie while he was working at Bell Laboratories. Wirth went on to design Modula-2 and Oberon. For the needs of the United States Department of Defense, Jean Ichbiah and a team at Honeywell began designing Ada in 1978, after a 4-year project to define the requirements for the language. The specification was first published in 1983, with revisions in 1995 and 2005–06.

The 1980s saw a rapid growth in interest in object-oriented programming. These languages were imperative in style, but added features to support objects. The last two decades of the 20th century saw the development of many such languages. Smalltalk-80, originally conceived by Alan Kay in 1969, was released in 1980, by the Xerox Palo Alto Research Center (PARC). Drawing from concepts in another object-oriented language—Simula (which is considered the world's first object-oriented programming language, developed in the 1960s)—Bjarne Stroustrup designed C++, an object-oriented language based on C. Design of C++ began in 1979 and the first implementation was completed in 1983. In the late 1980s and 1990s, the notable imperative languages drawing on object-oriented concepts were Perl, released by Larry Wall in 1987; Python, released by Guido van Rossum in 1990; Visual Basic and Visual C++ (which included Microsoft Foundation Class Library (MFC) 2.0), released by Microsoft in 1991 and 1993 respectively; PHP, released by Rasmus Lerdorf in 1994; Java, released by Sun Microsystems in 1994, and Ruby, released by Yukihiro "Matz" Matsumoto in 1995. Microsoft's .NET Framework (2002) is imperative at its core, as are its main target languages, VB.NET and C# that run on it; however Microsoft's F#, a functional language, also runs on it.

Functional Programming

In computer science, functional programming is a programming paradigm—a style of building the structure and elements of computer programs—that treats computation as the evaluation of mathematical functions and avoids changing-state and mutable data. It is a declarative programming paradigm, which means programming is done with expressions or declarations instead of statements. In functional code, the output value of a function depends only on the arguments that are passed to the function, so calling a function f twice with the same value for an argument x will produce the same result $f(x)$ each time; this is in contrast to procedures depending on local or global state, which may produce different results at different times when called with the same arguments but different program state. Eliminating side effects, i.e. changes in state that do not depend on the function inputs, can make it much easier to understand and predict the behavior of a program, which is one of the key motivations for the development of functional programming.

Functional programming has its origins in lambda calculus, a formal system developed in the 1930s to investigate computability, the Entscheidungsproblem, function definition, function application, and recursion. Many functional programming languages can be viewed as elaborations on the lambda calculus. Another well-known declarative programming paradigm, *logic programming*, is based on relations.

In contrast, imperative programming changes state with commands in the source code, the simplest example being assignment. Imperative programming does have functions—not in the mathematical sense—but in the sense of subroutines. They can have side effects that may change the value of program state. Functions without return values therefore make sense. Because of this, they lack referential transparency, i.e. the same language expression can result in different values at different times depending on the state of the executing program.

Functional programming languages have largely been emphasized in academia rather than in commercial software development. However, prominent programming languages which support functional programming such as Common Lisp, Scheme, Clojure, Wolfram Language (also known as Mathematica), Racket, Erlang, OCaml, Haskell, and F# have been used in industrial and commercial applications by a wide variety of organizations. Functional programming is also supported in some domain-specific programming languages like R (statistics), J, K and Q from Kx Systems (financial analysis), XQuery/XSLT (XML), and Opal. Widespread domain-specific declarative languages like SQL and Lex/Yacc use some elements of functional programming, especially in eschewing mutable values.

Programming in a functional style can also be accomplished in languages that are not specifically designed for functional programming. For example, the imperative Perl programming language has been the subject of a book describing how to apply functional programming concepts. This is also true of the PHP programming language. C++11, Java 8, and C# 3.0 all added constructs to facilitate the functional style. The Julia language also offers functional programming abilities. An interesting case is that of Scala – it is frequently written in a functional style, but the presence of side effects and mutable state place it in a grey area between imperative and functional languages.

History

Lambda calculus provides a theoretical framework for describing functions and their evaluation. Although it is a mathematical abstraction rather than a programming language, it forms the basis of almost all functional programming languages today. An equivalent theoretical formulation, combinatory logic, is commonly perceived as more abstract than lambda calculus and preceded it in invention. Combinatory logic and lambda calculus were both originally developed to achieve a clearer approach to the foundations of mathematics.

An early functional-flavored language was Lisp, developed in the late 1950s for the IBM 700/7000 series scientific computers by John McCarthy while at Massachusetts Institute of Technology (MIT). Lisp first introduced many paradigmatic features of functional programming, though early Lisps were multi-paradigm languages, and incorporated support for numerous programming styles as new paradigms evolved. Later dialects, such as Scheme and Clojure, and offshoots such as Dylan and Julia, sought to simplify and rationalise Lisp around a cleanly functional core, while Common Lisp was designed to preserve and update the paradigmatic features of the numerous older dialects it replaced.

Information Processing Language (IPL) is sometimes cited as the first computer-based functional programming language. It is an assembly-style language for manipulating lists of symbols. It does have a notion of "generator", which amounts to a function accepting a function as an argument, and, since it is an assembly-level language, code can be used as data, so IPL can be regarded as having higher-order functions. However, it relies heavily on mutating list structure and similar imperative features.

Kenneth E. Iverson developed APL in the early 1960s, described in his 1962 book *A Programming Language* (ISBN 9780471430148). APL was the primary influence on John Backus's FP. In the early 1990s, Iverson and Roger Hui created J. In the mid-1990s, Arthur Whitney, who had previously worked with Iverson, created K, which is used commercially in financial industries along with its descendant Q.

John Backus presented FP in his 1977 Turing Award lecture "Can Programming Be Liberated From the von Neumann Style? A Functional Style and its Algebra of Programs". He defines functional programs as being built up in a hierarchical way by means of "combining forms" that allow an "algebra of programs"; in modern language, this means that functional programs follow the principle of compositionality. Backus's paper popularized research into functional programming, though it emphasized function-level programming rather than the lambda-calculus style which has come to be associated with functional programming.

In the 1970s, ML was created by Robin Milner at the University of Edinburgh, and David Turner initially developed the language SASL at the University of St Andrews and later the language Miranda at the University of Kent. Also in Edinburgh in the 1970s, Burstall and Darlington developed the functional language NPL. NPL was based on Kleene Recursion Equations and was first introduced in their work on program transformation. Burstall, MacQueen and Sannella then incorporated the polymorphic type checking from ML to produce the language Hope. ML eventually developed into several dialects, the most common of which are now OCaml and Standard ML. Meanwhile, the development of Scheme, a simple lexically scoped and (impurely) functional dialect of Lisp, as described in the influential Lambda Papers and the classic 1985 textbook *Structure and Interpretation of Computer Programs*, brought awareness of the power of functional programming to the wider programming-languages community.

In the 1980s, Per Martin-Löf developed intuitionistic type theory (also called *constructive* type theory), which associated functional programs with constructive proofs of arbitrarily complex mathematical propositions expressed as dependent types. This led to powerful new approaches to interactive theorem proving and has influenced the development of many subsequent functional programming languages.

The Haskell language began with a consensus in 1987 to form an open standard for functional programming research; implementation releases have been ongoing since 1990.

Concepts

A number of concepts and paradigms are specific to functional programming, and generally foreign to imperative programming (including object-oriented programming). However, programming languages are often hybrids of several programming paradigms, so programmers using "mostly imperative" languages may have utilized some of these concepts.

First-class and Higher-order Functions

Higher-order functions are functions that can either take other functions as arguments or return them as results. In calculus, an example of a higher-order function is the differential operator d / dx, which returns the derivative of a function f.

Higher-order functions are closely related to first-class functions in that higher-order functions and first-class functions both allow functions as arguments and results of other functions. The distinction between the two is subtle: "higher-order" describes a mathematical concept of functions that operate on other functions, while "first-class" is a computer science term that describes programming language entities that have no restriction on their use (thus first-class functions can appear anywhere in the program that other first-class entities like numbers can, including as arguments to other functions and as their return values).

Higher-order functions enable partial application or currying, a technique in which a function is applied to its arguments one at a time, with each application returning a new function that accepts the next argument. This allows one to succinctly express, for example, the successor function as the addition operator partially applied to the natural number one.

Pure Functions

Pure functions (or expressions) have no side effects (memory or I/O). This means that pure functions have several useful properties, many of which can be used to optimize the code:

- If the result of a pure expression is not used, it can be removed without affecting other expressions.

- If a pure function is called with arguments that cause no side-effects, the result is constant with respect to that argument list (sometimes called referential transparency), i.e. if the pure function is again called with the same arguments, the same result will be returned (this can enable caching optimizations such as memoization).

- If there is no data dependency between two pure expressions, then their order can be reversed, or they can be performed in parallel and they cannot interfere with one another (in other terms, the evaluation of any pure expression is thread-safe).

- If the entire language does not allow side-effects, then any evaluation strategy can be used; this gives the compiler freedom to reorder or combine the evaluation of expressions in a program (for example, using deforestation).

While most compilers for imperative programming languages detect pure functions and perform common-subexpression elimination for pure function calls, they cannot always do this for pre-compiled libraries, which generally do not expose this information, thus preventing optimizations that involve those external functions. Some compilers, such as gcc, add extra keywords for a programmer to explicitly mark external functions as pure, to enable such optimizations. Fortran 95 also allows functions to be designated "pure".

Recursion

Iteration (looping) in functional languages is usually accomplished via recursion. Recursive functions invoke themselves, allowing an operation to be performed over and over until the base case is reached. Though some recursion requires maintaining a stack, tail recursion can be recognized and optimized by a compiler into the same code used to implement iteration in imperative languages. The Scheme language standard requires implementations to recognize and optimize tail recursion. Tail recursion optimization can be implemented by transforming the program into continuation passing style during compiling, among other approaches.

Common patterns of recursion can be factored out using higher order functions, with catamorphisms and anamorphisms (or "folds" and "unfolds") being the most obvious examples. Such higher order functions play a role analogous to built-in control structures such as loops in imperative languages.

Most general purpose functional programming languages allow unrestricted recursion and are Turing complete, which makes the halting problem undecidable, can cause unsoundness of equational reasoning, and generally requires the introduction of inconsistency into the logic expressed by the language's type system. Some special purpose languages such as Coq allow only well-founded recursion and are strongly normalizing (nonterminating computations can be expressed only with infinite streams of values called codata). As a consequence, these languages fail to be Turing complete and expressing certain functions in them is impossible, but they can still express a wide class of interesting computations while avoiding the problems introduced by unrestricted recursion. Functional programming limited to well-founded recursion with a few other constraints is called total functional programming.

Strict Versus Non-strict Evaluation

Functional languages can be categorized by whether they use *strict (eager)* or *non-strict (lazy)* evaluation, concepts that refer to how function arguments are processed when an expression is being evaluated. The technical difference is in the denotational semantics of expressions containing failing or divergent computations. Under strict evaluation, the evaluation of any term containing a failing subterm will itself fail. For example, the expression:

```
print length([2+1, 3*2, 1/0, 5-4])
```

will fail under strict evaluation because of the division by zero in the third element of the list. Under lazy evaluation, the length function will return the value 4 (i.e., the number of items in the list), since evaluating it will not attempt to evaluate the terms making up the list. In brief, strict evaluation always fully evaluates function arguments before invoking the function. Lazy evaluation does not evaluate function arguments unless their values are required to evaluate the function call itself.

The usual implementation strategy for lazy evaluation in functional languages is graph reduction. Lazy evaluation is used by default in several pure functional languages, including Miranda, Clean, and Haskell.

Hughes 1984 argues for lazy evaluation as a mechanism for improving program modularity through separation of concerns, by easing independent implementation of producers and consumers of data streams. Launchbury 1993 describes some difficulties that lazy evaluation introduces, particularly in analyzing a program's storage requirements, and proposes an operational semantics to aid in such analysis. Harper 2009 proposes including both strict and lazy evaluation in the same language, using the language's type system to distinguish them.

Type Systems

Especially since the development of Hindley–Milner type inference in the 1970s, functional programming languages have tended to use typed lambda calculus, rejecting all invalid programs at compilation time and risking false positive errors, as opposed to the untyped lambda calculus, that accepts all valid programs at compilation time and risks false negative errors, used in Lisp and its variants (such as Scheme), although they reject all invalid programs at runtime, when the information is enough to not reject valid programs. The use of algebraic datatypes makes manipulation of complex data structures convenient; the presence of strong compile-time type checking makes programs more reliable in absence of other reliability techniques like test-driven development, while type inference frees the programmer from the need to manually declare types to the compiler in most cases.

Some research-oriented functional languages such as Coq, Agda, Cayenne, and Epigram are based on intuitionistic type theory, which allows types to depend on terms. Such types are called dependent types. These type systems do not have decidable type inference and are difficult to understand and program with. But dependent types can express arbitrary propositions in predicate logic. Through the Curry–Howard isomorphism, then, well-typed programs in these languages become a means of writing formal mathematical proofs from which a compiler can generate certified code. While these languages are mainly of interest in academic research (including in formalized mathematics), they have begun to be used in engineering as well. Compcert is a compiler for a subset of the C programming language that is written in Coq and formally verified.

A limited form of dependent types called generalized algebraic data types (GADT's) can be implemented in a way that provides some of the benefits of dependently typed programming while avoiding most of its inconvenience. GADT's are available in the Glasgow Haskell Compiler, in OCaml (since version 4.00) and in Scala (as "case classes"), and have been proposed as additions to other languages including Java and C#.

Referential Transparency

Functional programs do not have assignment statements, that is, the value of a variable in a functional program never changes once defined. This eliminates any chances of side effects because any variable can be replaced with its actual value at any point of execution. So, functional programs are referentially transparent.

Consider C assignment statement `x = x * 10,` this changes the value assigned to the variable `x`. Let us say that the initial value of `x` was 1, then two consecutive evaluations of the variable x will yield `10` and `100` respectively. Clearly, replacing `x = x * 10` with either `10` or `100` gives a program with different meaning, and so the expression *is not* referentially transparent. In fact, assignment statements are never referentially transparent.

Now, consider another function such as int plusone`(int x)  {return x+1;}` *is* transparent, as it will not implicitly change the input x and thus has no such side effects. Functional programs exclusively use this type of function and are therefore referentially transparent.

Functional Programming in Non-functional Languages

It is possible to use a functional style of programming in languages that are not traditionally considered functional languages. For example, both D and Fortran 95 explicitly support pure functions.

JavaScript, Lua and Python had first class functions from their inception. Amrit Prem added support to Python for "lambda", "map", "reduce", and "filter" in 1994, as well as closures in Python 2.2, though Python 3 relegated "reduce" to the functools standard library module. First-class functions have been introduced into other mainstream languages such as PHP 5.3, Visual Basic 9, C# 3.0, and C++11.

In Java, anonymous classes can sometimes be used to simulate closures; however, anonymous classes are not always proper replacements to closures because they have more limited capabilities. Java 8 supports lambda expressions as a replacement for some anonymous classes. However, the presence of checked exceptions in Java can make functional programming inconvenient, because it can be necessary to catch checked exceptions and then rethrow them—a problem that does not occur in other JVM languages that do not have checked exceptions, such as Scala.

In C#, anonymous classes are not necessary, because closures and lambdas are fully supported. Libraries and language extensions for immutable data structures are being developed to aid programming in the functional style in C#.

Many object-oriented design patterns are expressible in functional programming terms: for example, the strategy pattern simply dictates use of a higher-order function, and the visitor pattern roughly corresponds to a catamorphism, or fold.

Similarly, the idea of immutable data from functional programming is often included in imperative programming languages, for example the tuple in Python, which is an immutable array.

Data Structures

Purely functional data structures are often represented in a different way than their imperative counterparts. For example, array with constant-time access and update is a basic component of most imperative languages and many imperative data-structure, such as hash table and binary heap, are based on arrays. Arrays can be replaced by map or random access list, which admits purely functional implementation, but the access and update time is logarithmic. Therefore, purely functional data structures can be used in languages which are non-functional, but they may not be the most efficient tool available, especially if persistency is not required.

Comparison to Imperative Programming

Functional programming is very different from imperative programming. The most significant differences stem from the fact that functional programming avoids side effects, which are used in imperative programming to implement state and I/O. Pure functional programming completely prevents side-effects and provides referential transparency.

Higher-order functions are rarely used in older imperative programming. A traditional imperative program might use a loop to traverse and modify a list. A functional program, on the other hand, would probably use a higher-order "map" function that takes a function and a list, generating and returning a new list by applying the function to each list item.

Simulating State

There are tasks (for example, maintaining a bank account balance) that often seem most naturally implemented with state. Pure functional programming performs these tasks, and I/O tasks such as accepting user input and printing to the screen, in a different way.

The pure functional programming language Haskell implements them using monads, derived from category theory. Monads offer a way to abstract certain types of computational patterns, including (but not limited to) modeling of computations with mutable state (and other side effects such as I/O) in an imperative manner without losing purity. While existing monads may be easy to apply in a program, given appropriate templates and examples, many students find them difficult to understand conceptually, e.g., when asked to define new monads (which is sometimes needed for certain types of libraries).

Another way in which functional languages can simulate state is by passing around a data structure that represents the current state as a parameter to function calls. On each function call, a copy of this data structure is created with whatever differences are the result of the function. This is referred to as 'state-passing style'.

Impure functional languages usually include a more direct method of managing mutable state. Clojure, for example, uses managed references that can be updated by applying pure functions to the current state. This kind of approach enables mutability while still promoting the use of pure functions as the preferred way to express computations.

Alternative methods such as Hoare logic and uniqueness have been developed to track side effects in programs. Some modern research languages use effect systems to make the presence of side effects explicit.

Efficiency Issues

Functional programming languages are typically less efficient in their use of CPU and memory than imperative languages such as C and Pascal. This is related to the fact that some mutable data structures like arrays have a very straightforward implementation using present hardware (which is a highly evolved Turing machine). Flat arrays may be accessed very efficiently with deeply pipelined CPUs, prefetched efficiently through caches (with no complex pointer chasing), or handled with SIMD instructions. It is also not easy to create their equally efficient general-purpose immutable counterparts. For purely functional languages, the worst-case slowdown is logarithmic in the number of memory cells used, because mutable memory can be represented by a purely functional data structure with logarithmic access time (such as a balanced tree). However, such slowdowns are not universal. For programs that perform intensive numerical computations, functional languages such as OCaml and Clean are only slightly slower than C. For programs that handle large matrices and multidimensional databases, array functional languages (such as J and K) were designed with speed optimizations.

Immutability of data can in many cases lead to execution efficiency by allowing the compiler to make assumptions that are unsafe in an imperative language, thus increasing opportunities for inline expansion.

Lazy evaluation may also speed up the program, even asymptotically, whereas it may slow it down at most by a constant factor (however, it may introduce memory leaks if used improperly). Launchbury 1993 discusses theoretical issues related to memory leaks from lazy evaluation, and O'Sullivan *et al.* 2008 give some practical advice for analyzing and fixing them. However, the most general implementations of lazy evaluation making extensive use of dereferenced code and data perform poorly on modern processors with deep pipelines and multi-level caches (where a cache miss may cost hundreds of cycles).

Coding Styles

Imperative programs have the environment and a sequence of steps manipulating the environment. Functional programs have an expression that is successively substituted until it reaches normal form. An example illustrates this with different solutions to the same programming goal (calculating Fibonacci numbers).

Python

Printing first 10 Fibonacci numbers, iterative

```python
def fibonacci(n, first=0, second=1):
  while n != 0:
    print(first, end="\n") # side-effect
    n, first, second = n - 1, second, first + second # assignment
fibonacci(10)
```

Printing first 10 Fibonacci numbers, functional expression style

```python
fibonacci = (lambda n, first=0, second=1:
  "" if n == 0 else
  str(first) + "\n" + fibonacci(n - 1, second, first + second))
print(fibonacci(10), end="")
```

Printing a list with first 10 Fibonacci numbers, with generators

```python
def fibonacci(n, first=0, second=1):
  while n != 0:
    yield first
    n, first, second = n - 1, second, first + second # assignment
print(list(fibonacci(10)))
```

Printing a list with first 10 Fibonacci numbers, functional expression style

```python
fibonacci = (lambda n, first=0, second=1:
  [] if n == 0 else
  [first] + fibonacci(n - 1, second, first + second))
print(fibonacci(10))
```

Haskell

Printing first 10 Fibonacci numbers, functional expression style

```haskell
fibonacci_aux = \n first second->
  if n == 0 then "" else
  show first ++ "\n" ++ Fibonacci_aux (n - 1) second (first + second)
```

```
fibonacci = \n-> fibonacci_aux n 0 1

main = putStr (fibonacci 10)
```

Printing a list with first 10 Fibonacci numbers, functional expression style

```
fibonacci_aux = \n first second->

  if n == 0 then [] else

  [first] ++ fibonacci_aux (n - 1) second (first + second)

fibonacci = \n-> fibonacci_aux n 0 1

main = putStrLn (show (fibonacci 10))
```

Printing the 11th Fibonacci number, functional expression style

```
fibonacci = \n-> if n == 0 then 0

         else if n == 1 then 1

            else fibonacci(n - 1) + fibonacci(n - 2)

main = putStrLn (show (fibonacci 10))
```

Printing the 11th Fibonacci number, functional expression style, tail recursive

```
fibonacci_aux = \n first second->

  if n == 0 then first else

  fibonacci_aux (n - 1) second (first + second)

fibonacci = \n-> Fibonacci_aux n 0 1

main = putStrLn (show (fibonacci 10))
```

Printing the 11th Fibonacci number, functional expression style with recursive lists

```
fibonacci_aux = \first second-> first : fibonacci_aux second (first + sec-
ond)

select = \n zs-> if n==0 then head zs

         else select (n - 1) (tail zs)

fibonacci = \n-> select n (fibonacci_aux 0 1)

main = putStrLn (show (fibonacci 10))
```

Printing the 11th Fibonacci number, functional expression style with primitives for recursive lists

```
fibonacci_aux = \first second-> first : fibonacci_aux second (first + sec-
```

```
ond)

fibonacci = \n-> (fibonacci_aux 0 1) !! n

main = putStrLn (show (fibonacci 10))
```

Printing the 11th Fibonacci number, functional expression style with primitives for recursive lists, more concisely

```
fibonacci_aux = 0:1:zipWith (+) fibonacci_aux (tail fibonacci_aux)

fibonacci = \n-> fibonacci_aux !! n

main = putStrLn (show (fibonacci 10))
```

Printing the 11th Fibonacci number, functional declaration style, tail recursive

```
fibonacci_aux 0 first _ = first

fibonacci_aux n first second = fibonacci_aux (n - 1) second (first + second)

fibonacci n = fibonacci_aux n 0 1

main = putStrLn (show (fibonacci 10))
```

Printing the 11th Fibonacci number, functional declaration style, using lazy infinite lists and primitives

```
fibs = 1 : 1 : zipWith (+) fibs (tail fibs)

-- an infinite list of the fibonacci numbers

-- fibs is defined in terms of fibs

fibonacci = (fibs !!)

main = putStrLn $ show $ fibonacci 11
```

Perl 6

As influenced by Haskell and others, Perl 6 has several functional and declarative approaches to problems. For example, you can declaratively build up a well-typed recursive version (the type constraints are optional) through signature pattern matching:

```
# define constraints that are common to all candidates

proto fib ( UInt:D \n --> UInt:D ) {*}

multi fib ( 0 --> 0 ) { }

multi fib ( 1 --> 1 ) { }

multi fib ( \n ) {
```

```
  fib(n - 1) + fib(n - 2)

}

for ^10 -> $n { say fib($n) }
```

An alternative to this is to construct a lazy iterative sequence, which appears as an almost direct illustration of the sequence:

```
my @fib = 0, 1, *+* ... *; # Each additional entry is the sum of the
previous two

                           # and this sequence extends lazily indefinitely

say @fib[^10];             # Display the first 10 entries
```

Erlang

Erlang is a functional, concurrent, general-purpose programming language. A Fibonacci algorithm implemented in Erlang (Note: This is only for demonstrating the Erlang syntax. Use other algorithms for fast performance):

```
-module(fib).   % This is the file 'fib.erl', the module and the filename
must match

-export([fib/1]). % This exports the function 'fib' of arity 1

fib(1) -> 1; % If 1, then return 1, otherwise (note the semicolon ;
meaning 'else')

fib(2) -> 1; % If 2, then return 1, otherwise

fib(N) -> fib(N - 2) + fib(N - 1).
```

Elixir

Elixir is a functional, concurrent, general-purpose programming language that runs on the Erlang virtual machine (BEAM).

The Fibonacci function can be written in Elixir as follows:

```
defmodule Fibonacci do

  def fib(0), do: 0

  def fib(1), do: 1

  def fib(n), do: fib(n-1) + fib(n-2)

end
```

Lisp

The Fibonacci function can be written in Common Lisp as follows:

```
(defun fib (n &optional (a 0) (b 1))
 (if (= n 0)
   a
   (fib (- n 1) b (+ a b))))
```

The program can then be called as

```
(fib 10)
```

Clojure

The Fibonacci function can be written in Clojure as follows:

```
(defn fib
 [n]
 (loop [a 0 b 1 i n]
  (if (zero? i)
   a
    (recur b (+ a b) (dec i)))))
```

The program can then be called as

```
(fib 7)
```

D

D has support for functional programming:

```
import std.stdio;
import std.range;
void main()
{
  /* 'f' is a range representing the first 10 Fibonacci numbers */
  auto f = recurrence!((seq, i) => seq + seq)(0, 1)
          .take(10);
```

```
  writeln(f);

}
```

R

R is an environment for statistical computing and graphics. It is also a functional programming language.

The Fibonacci function can be written in R as a recursive function as follows:

```
fib <- function(n) {

  if (n <= 2) 1

  else fib(n - 1) + fib(n - 2)

}
```

Or it can be written as a singly recursive function:

```
fib <- function(n,a=1,b=1) {

  if (n == 1) a

  else fib(n-1,b,a+b)

}
```

Or it can be written as an iterative function:

```
fib <- function(n) {

  if (n == 1) 1

  else if (n == 2) 1

  else {

  fibval<-c(1,1)

  for (i in 3:n) fibval<-c(0,fibval)+fibval

  fibval

  }

}
```

The function can then be called as

```
fib(10)
```

SequenceL

SequenceL is a functional, concurrent, general-purpose programming language. The Fibonacci function can be written in SequenceL as follows:

```
fib(n) := n when n < 2 else
    fib(n - 1) + fib(n - 2);
```

The function can then be called as

```
fib(10)
```

To reduce the memory consumed by the call stack when computing a large Fibonacci term, a tail-recursive version can be used. A tail-recursive function is implemented by the SequenceL compiler as a memory-efficient looping structure:

```
fib(n) := fib_Helper(0, 1, n);

fib_Helper(prev, next, n) :=
    prev when n < 1 else
    next when n = 1 else
    fib_Helper(next, next + prev, n - 1);
```

Tcl

The Fibonacci function can be written in Tcl as a recursive function as follows:

```
proc fibo {x} {
  expr {$x<2? $x: [fibo [incr x -1]] + [fibo [incr x -1]]}
}
```

Use in Industry

Functional programming has long been popular in academia, but with few industrial applications. However, recently several prominent functional programming languages have been used in commercial or industrial systems. For example, the Erlang programming language, which was developed by the Swedish company Ericsson in the late 1980s, was originally used to implement fault-tolerant telecommunications systems. It has since become popular for building a range of applications at companies such as T-Mobile, Nortel, Facebook, Électricité de France and WhatsApp. The Scheme dialect of Lisp was used as the basis for several applications on early Apple Macintosh computers, and has more recently been applied to problems such as training simulation software and telescope control. OCaml, which was introduced in the mid-1990s, has seen commercial use in areas such as financial analysis, driver verification, industrial robot programming, and static analysis of embedded software. Haskell, although initially intended as a research language, has also been applied by a range of companies, in areas such as aerospace systems, hardware design, and web programming.

Other functional programming languages that have seen use in industry include Scala, F#, (both being functional-OO hybrids with support for both purely functional and imperative programming) Wolfram Language, Lisp, Standard ML and Clojure.

In Education

Functional programming is being used as a method to teach problem solving, algebra and geometric concepts. It has also been used as a tool to teach classical mechanics in Structure and Interpretation of Classical Mechanics.

Declarative Programming

In computer science, declarative programming is a programming paradigm—a style of building the structure and elements of computer programs—that expresses the logic of a computation without describing its control flow.

Many languages that apply this style attempt to minimize or eliminate side effects by describing *what* the program must accomplish in terms of the problem domain, rather than describe *how* to accomplish it as a sequence of the programming language primitives (the *how* being left up to the language's implementation). This is in contrast with imperative programming, which implements algorithms in explicit steps.

Declarative programming often considers programs as theories of a formal logic, and computations as deductions in that logic space. Declarative programming may greatly simplify writing parallel programs.

Common declarative languages include those of database query languages (e.g., SQL, XQuery), regular expressions, logic programming, functional programming, and configuration management systems.

Definition

Declarative programming is often defined as any style of programming that is not imperative. A number of other common definitions exist that attempt to give the term a definition other than simply contrasting it with imperative programming. For example:

- A program that describes *what* computation should be performed and not *how* to compute it

- Any programming language that lacks side effects (or more specifically, is referentially transparent)

- A language with a clear correspondence to mathematical logic.

These definitions overlap substantially.

Declarative programming contrasts with imperative and procedural programming. Declarative programming is a non-imperative style of programming in which programs describe their desired results without explicitly listing commands or steps that must be performed. Functional and logical programming languages are characterized by a declarative programming style. In logical programming languages, programs consist of logical statements, and the program executes by searching for proofs of the statements.

In a pure functional language, such as Haskell, all functions are without side effects, and state changes are only represented as functions that transform the state, which is explicitly represented as a first class object in the program. Although pure functional languages are non-imperative, they often provide a facility for describing the effect of a function as a series of steps. Other functional languages, such as Lisp, OCaml and Erlang, support a mixture of procedural and functional programming.

Some logical programming languages, such as Prolog, and database query languages, such as SQL, while declarative in principle, also support a procedural style of programming.

Subparadigms

Declarative programming is an umbrella term that includes a number of better-known programming paradigms.

Constraint Programming

Constraint programming states relations between variables in the form of constraints that specify the properties of the target solution. The set of constraints is solved by giving a value to each variable so that the solution is consistent with the maximum number of constraints. Constraint programming often complements other paradigms: functional, logical, or even imperative programming.

Domain-specific Languages

Well-known examples of declarative domain-specific languages (DSLs) include the yacc parser generator input language, the Make build specification language, Puppet's configuration management language, regular expressions, and a subset of SQL (SELECT queries, for example). DSLs have the advantage of being useful while not necessarily needing to be Turing-complete, which makes it easier for a language to be purely declarative.

Many markup languages such as HTML, MXML, XAML, XSLT or other user-interface markup languages are often declarative. HTML, for example, only describes what should appear on a webpage - it specifies neither control flow rendering a page nor its possible interactions with a user.

As of 2013 some software systems combine traditional user-interface markup languages (such as HTML) with declarative markup that defines what (but not how) the back-end server systems should do to support the declared interface. Such systems, typically using a domain-specific XML namespace, may include abstractions of SQL database syntax or parameterised calls to web services using representational state transfer (REST) and SOAP.

Hybrid Languages

Makefiles, for example, specify dependencies in a declarative fashion, but include an imperative list of actions to take as well. Similarly, yacc specifies a context free grammar declaratively, but includes code snippets from a host language, which is usually imperative (such as C).

Logic Programming

Logic programming languages such as Prolog state and query relations. The specifics of *how* these queries are answered is up to the implementation and its theorem prover, but typically take the form of some sort of unification. Like functional programming, many logic programming languages permit side effects, and as a result are not strictly declarative.

Modeling

Models, or mathematical representations, of physical systems may be implemented in computer code that is declarative. The code contains a number of equations, not imperative assignments, that describe ("declare") the behavioral relationships. When a model is expressed in this formalism, a computer is able to perform algebraic manipulations to best formulate the solution algorithm. The mathematical causality is typically imposed at the boundaries of the physical system, while the behavioral description of the system itself is declarative or acausal. Declarative modeling languages and environments include Analytica, Modelica and Simile.

Object-oriented Programming

Object-oriented programming (OOP) is a programming paradigm based on the concept of "objects", which may contain data, in the form of fields, often known as *attributes;* and code, in the form of procedures, often known as *methods*. A feature of objects is that an object's procedures can access and often modify the data fields of the object with which they are associated (objects have a notion of "this" or "self"). In OOP, computer programs are designed by making them out of objects that interact with one another. There is significant diversity of OOP languages, but the most popular ones are class-based, meaning that objects are instances of classes, which typically also determine their type.

Many of the most widely used programming languages (such as C++, Delphi, Java, Python etc.) are multi-paradigm programming languages that support object-oriented programming to a greater or lesser degree, typically in combination with imperative, procedural programming. Significant object-oriented languages include Java, C++, C#, Python, PHP, Ruby, Perl, Object Pascal, Objective-C, Dart, Swift, Scala, Common Lisp, and Smalltalk.

Features

Object-oriented Programming uses objects, but not all of the associated techniques and structures are supported directly in languages that claim to support OOP. The features listed below are, however, common among languages considered strongly class- and object-oriented (or multi-paradigm with OOP support), with notable exceptions mentioned.

Shared with Non-OOP Predecessor Languages

Object-oriented programming languages typically share low-level features with high-level procedural programming languages (which were invented first). The fundamental tools that can be used to construct a program include:

- Variables that can store information formatted in a small number of built-in data types like integers and alphanumeric characters. This may include data structures like strings, lists, and hash tables that are either built-in or result from combining variables using memory pointers

- Procedures – also known as functions, methods, routines, or subroutines – that take input, generate output, and manipulate data. Modern languages include structured programming constructs like loops and conditionals.

Modular programming support provides the ability to group procedures into files and modules for organizational purposes. Modules are namespaced so code in one module will not be accidentally confused with the same procedure or variable name in another file or module.

Objects and Classes

Languages that support object-oriented programming typically use inheritance for code reuse and extensibility in the form of either classes or prototypes. Those that use classes support two main concepts:

- Classes – the definitions for the data format and available procedures for a given type or class of object; may also contain data and procedures (known as class methods) themselves, i.e. classes contains the data members and member functions

- Objects – instances of classes

Objects sometimes correspond to things found in the real world. For example, a graphics program may have objects such as "circle", "square", "menu". An online shopping system might have objects such as "shopping cart", "customer", and "product". Sometimes objects represent more abstract entities, like an object that represents an open file, or an object that provides the service of translating measurements from U.S. customary to metric.

Each object is said to be an instance of a particular class (for example, an object with its name field set to "Mary" might be an instance of class Employee). Procedures in object-oriented programming are known as methods; variables are also known as fields, members, attributes, or properties. This leads to the following terms:

- Class variables – belong to the *class as a whole*; there is only one copy of each one

- Instance variables or attributes – data that belongs to individual *objects*; every object has its own copy of each one

- Member variables – refers to both the class and instance variables that are defined by a particular class

- Class methods – belong to the *class as a whole* and have access only to class variables and inputs from the procedure call

- Instance methods – belong to *individual objects*, and have access to instance variables for the specific object they are called on, inputs, and class variables

Objects are accessed somewhat like variables with complex internal structure, and in many languages are effectively pointers, serving as actual references to a single instance of said object in memory within a heap or stack. They provide a layer of abstraction which can be used to separate internal from external code. External code can use an object by calling a specific instance method with a certain set of input parameters, read an instance variable, or write to an instance variable. Objects are created by calling a special type of method in the class known as a constructor. A program may create many instances of the same class as it runs, which operate independently. This is an easy way for the same procedures to be used on different sets of data.

Object-oriented programming that uses classes is sometimes called class-based programming, while prototype-based programming does not typically use classes. As a result, a significantly different yet analogous terminology is used to define the concepts of *object* and *instance*.

In some languages classes and objects can be composed using other concepts like traits and mixins.

Dynamic Dispatch/message Passing

It is the responsibility of the object, not any external code, to select the procedural code to execute in response to a method call, typically by looking up the method at run time in a table associated with the object. This feature is known as dynamic dispatch, and distinguishes an object from an abstract data type (or module), which has a fixed (static) implementation of the operations for all instances. If there are multiple methods that might be run for a given name, it is known as multiple dispatch.

A method call is also known as *message passing*. It is conceptualized as a message (the name of the method and its input parameters) being passed to the object for dispatch.

Encapsulation

Encapsulation is an Object Oriented Programming concept that binds together the data and functions that manipulate the data, and that keeps both safe from outside interference and misuse. Data encapsulation led to the important OOP concept of data hiding.

If a class does not allow calling code to access internal object data and permits access through methods only, this is a strong form of abstraction or information hiding known as encapsulation. Some languages (Java, for example) let classes enforce access restrictions explicitly, for example denoting internal data with the private keyword and designating methods intended for use by code outside the class with the public keyword. Methods may also be designed public, private, or intermediate levels such as protected (which allows access from the same class and its subclasses, but not objects of a different class). In other languages (like Python) this is enforced only by convention (for example, private methods may have names that start with an underscore). Encapsulation prevents external code from being concerned with the internal workings of an object. This facilitates code refactoring, for example allowing the author of the class to change how objects of that class represent their data internally without changing any external code (as long as "public" method calls work the same way). It also encourages programmers to put all the code that is concerned with a certain set of data in the same class, which organizes it for easy comprehension by other programmers. Encapsulation is a technique that encourages decoupling.

Composition, Inheritance, and Delegation

Objects can contain other objects in their instance variables; this is known as object composition. For example, an object in the Employee class might contain (point to) an object in the Address class, in addition to its own instance variables like "first_name" and "position". Object composition is used to represent "has-a" relationships: every employee has an address, so every Employee object has a place to store an Address object.

Languages that support classes almost always support inheritance. This allows classes to be arranged in a hierarchy that represents "is-a-type-of" relationships. For example, class Employee might inherit from class Person. All the data and methods available to the parent class also appear in the child class with the same names. For example, class Person might define variables "first_name" and "last_name" with method "make_full_name()". These will also be available in class Employee, which might add the variables "position" and "salary". This technique allows easy re-use of the same procedures and data definitions, in addition to potentially mirroring real-world relationships in an intuitive way. Rather than utilizing database tables and programming subroutines, the developer utilizes objects the user may be more familiar with: objects from their application domain.

Subclasses can override the methods defined by superclasses. Multiple inheritance is allowed in some languages, though this can make resolving overrides complicated. Some languages have special support for mixins, though in any language with multiple inheritance, a mixin is simply a class that does not represent an is-a-type-of relationship. Mixins are typically used to add the same methods to multiple classes. For example, class UnicodeConversionMixin might provide a method unicode_to_ascii() when included in class FileReader and class WebPageScraper, which don't share a common parent.

Abstract classes cannot be instantiated into objects; they exist only for the purpose of inheritance into other "concrete" classes which can be instantiated. In Java, the final keyword can be used to prevent a class from being subclassed.

The doctrine of composition over inheritance advocates implementing has-a relationships using composition instead of inheritance. For example, instead of inheriting from class Person, class Employee could give each Employee object an internal Person object, which it then has the opportunity to hide from external code even if class Person has many public attributes or methods. Some languages, like Go do not support inheritance at all.

The "open/closed principle" advocates that classes and functions "should be open for extension, but closed for modification".

Delegation is another language feature that can be used as an alternative to inheritance.

Polymorphism

Subtyping, a form of polymorphism, is when calling code can be agnostic as to whether an object belongs to a parent class or one of its descendants. For example, a function might call "make_full_name()" on an object, which will work whether the object is of class Person or class Employee. This is another type of abstraction which simplifies code external to the class hierarchy and enables strong separation of concerns.

Open Recursion

In languages that support open recursion, object methods can call other methods on the same object (including themselves), typically using a special variable or keyword called this or self. This variable is *late-bound*; it allows a method defined in one class to invoke another method that is defined later, in some subclass thereof.

History

Terminology invoking "objects" and "oriented" in the modern sense of object-oriented programming made its first appearance at MIT in the late 1950s and early 1960s. In the environment of the artificial intelligence group, as early as 1960, "object" could refer to identified items (LISP atoms) with properties (attributes); Alan Kay was later to cite a detailed understanding of LISP internals as a strong influence on his thinking in 1966. Another early MIT example was Sketchpad created by Ivan Sutherland in 1960–61; in the glossary of the 1963 technical report based on his dissertation about Sketchpad, Sutherland defined notions of "object" and "instance" (with the class concept covered by "master" or "definition"), albeit specialized to graphical interaction. Also, an MIT ALGOL version, AED-0, established a direct link between data structures ("plexes", in that dialect) and procedures, prefiguring what were later termed "messages", "methods", and "member functions".

The formal programming concept of objects was introduced in the mid-1960s with Simula 67, a major revision of Simula I, a programming language designed for discrete event simulation, created by Ole-Johan Dahl and Kristen Nygaard of the Norwegian Computing Center in Oslo.

Simula 67 was influenced by SIMSCRIPT and C.A.R. "Tony" Hoare's proposed "record classes". Simula introduced the notion of classes and instances or objects (as well as subclasses, virtual procedures, coroutines, and discrete event simulation) as part of an explicit programming paradigm. The language also used automatic garbage collection that had been invented earlier for the functional programming language Lisp. Simula was used for physical modeling, such as models to study and improve the movement of ships and their content through cargo ports. The ideas of Simula 67 influenced many later languages, including Smalltalk, derivatives of LISP (CLOS), Object Pascal, and C++.

The Smalltalk language, which was developed at Xerox PARC (by Alan Kay and others) in the 1970s, introduced the term *object-oriented programming* to represent the pervasive use of objects and messages as the basis for computation. Smalltalk creators were influenced by the ideas introduced in Simula 67, but Smalltalk was designed to be a fully dynamic system in which classes could be created and modified dynamically rather than statically as in Simula 67. Smalltalk and with it OOP were introduced to a wider audience by the August 1981 issue of *Byte Magazine*.

In the 1970s, Kay's Smalltalk work had influenced the Lisp community to incorporate object-based techniques that were introduced to developers via the Lisp machine. Experimentation with various extensions to Lisp (such as LOOPS and Flavors introducing multiple inheritance and mixins) eventually led to the Common Lisp Object System, which integrates functional programming and object-oriented programming and allows extension via a Meta-object protocol. In the 1980s, there were a few attempts to design processor architectures that included hardware support for objects in memory but these were not successful. Examples include the Intel iAPX 432 and the Linn Smart Rekursiv.

In 1985, Bertrand Meyer produced the first design of the Eiffel language. Focused on software quality, Eiffel is among the purely object-oriented languages, but differs in the sense that the language itself is not only a programming language, but a notation supporting the entire software lifecycle. Meyer described the Eiffel software development method, based on a small number of key ideas from software engineering and computer science, in Object-Oriented Software Construction. Essential to the quality focus of Eiffel is Meyer's reliability mechanism, Design by Contract, which is an integral part of both the method and language.

Object-oriented programming developed as the dominant programming methodology in the early and mid 1990s when programming languages supporting the techniques became widely available. These included Visual FoxPro 3.0, C++, and Delphi. Its dominance was further enhanced by the rising popularity of graphical user interfaces, which rely heavily upon object-oriented programming techniques. An example of a closely related dynamic GUI library and OOP language can be found in the Cocoa frameworks on Mac OS X, written in Objective-C, an object-oriented, dynamic messaging extension to C based on Smalltalk. OOP toolkits also enhanced the popularity of event-driven programming (although this concept is not limited to OOP).

At ETH Zürich, Niklaus Wirth and his colleagues had also been investigating such topics as data abstraction and modular programming (although this had been in common use in the 1960s or earlier). Modula-2 (1978) included both, and their succeeding design, Oberon, included a distinctive approach to object orientation, classes, and such.

Object-oriented features have been added to many previously existing languages, including Ada, BASIC, Fortran, Pascal, and COBOL. Adding these features to languages that were not initially designed for them often led to problems with compatibility and maintainability of code.

More recently, a number of languages have emerged that are primarily object-oriented, but that are also compatible with procedural methodology. Two such languages are Python and Ruby. Probably the most commercially important recent object-oriented languages are Java, developed by Sun Microsystems, as well as C# and Visual Basic. NET (VB.NET), both designed for Microsoft's .NET platform. Each of these two frameworks shows, in its own way, the benefit of using OOP by creating an abstraction from implementation. VB.NET and C# support cross-language inheritance, allowing classes defined in one language to subclass classes defined in the other language.

OOP Languages

Simula (1967) is generally accepted as being the first language with the primary features of an object-oriented language. It was created for making simulation programs, in which what came to be called objects were the most important information representation. Smalltalk (1972 to 1980) is another early example, and the one with which much of the theory of OOP was developed. Concerning the degree of object orientation, the following distinctions can be made:

- Languages called "pure" OO languages, because everything in them is treated consistently as an object, from primitives such as characters and punctuation, all the way up to whole classes, prototypes, blocks, modules, etc. They were designed specifically to facilitate, even enforce, OO methods. Examples: Python, Ruby, Scala, Smalltalk, Eiffel, Emerald, JADE, Self.

- Languages designed mainly for OO programming, but with some procedural elements. Examples: Java, C++, C#, Delphi/Object Pascal, VB.NET.

- Languages that are historically procedural languages, but have been extended with some OO features. Examples: PHP, Perl, Visual Basic (derived from BASIC), MATLAB, COBOL 2002, Fortran 2003, ABAP, Ada 95, Pascal.

- Languages with most of the features of objects (classes, methods, inheritance), but in a distinctly original form. Examples: Oberon (Oberon-1 or Oberon-2).

- Languages with abstract data type support which may be used to resemble OO programming, but without all features of object-orientation. This includes object-*based* and prototype-based languages. Examples: JavaScript, Lua, Modula-2, CLU.

- Chameleon languages that support multiple paradigms, including OO. Tcl stands out among these for TclOO, a hybrid object system that supports both prototype-based programming and class-based OO.

OOP in Dynamic Languages

In recent years, object-oriented programming has become especially popular in dynamic programming languages. Python, PowerShell, Ruby and Groovy are dynamic languages built on OOP principles, while Perl and PHP have been adding object-oriented features since Perl 5 and PHP 4, and ColdFusion since version 6.

The Document Object Model of HTML, XHTML, and XML documents on the Internet has bindings to the popular JavaScript/ECMAScript language. JavaScript is perhaps the best known prototype-based programming language, which employs cloning from prototypes rather than inheriting from a class (contrast to class-based programming). Another scripting language that takes this approach is Lua.

OOP in a Network Protocol

The messages that flow between computers to request services in a client-server environment can be designed as the linearizations of objects defined by class objects known to both the client and the server. For example, a simple linearized object would consist of a length field, a code point identifying the class, and a data value. A more complex example would be a command consisting of the length and code point of the command and values consisting of linearized objects representing the command's parameters. Each such command must be directed by the server to an object whose class (or superclass) recognizes the command and is able to provide the requested service. Clients and servers are best modeled as complex object-oriented structures. Distributed Data Management Architecture (DDM) took this approach and used class objects to define objects at four levels of a formal hierarchy:

- Fields defining the data values that form messages, such as their length, code-point and data values.

- Objects and collections of objects similar to what would be found in a Smalltalk program for messages and parameters.

- Managers similar to AS/400 objects, such as a directory to files and files consisting of metadata and records. Managers conceptually provide memory and processing resources for their contained objects.

- A client or server consisting of all the managers necessary to implement a full processing environment, supporting such aspects as directory services, security and concurrency control.

The initial version of DDM defined distributed file services. It was later extended to be the foundation of Distributed Relational Database Architecture (DRDA).

Design Patterns

Challenges of object-oriented design are addressed by several methodologies. Most common is known as the design patterns codified by Gamma *et al.*. More broadly, the term "design patterns" can be used to refer to any general, repeatable solution to a commonly occurring problem in software design. Some of these commonly occurring problems have implications and solutions particular to object-oriented development.

Inheritance and Behavioral Subtyping

It is intuitive to assume that inheritance creates a semantic "is a" relationship, and thus to infer that objects instantiated from subclasses can always be *safely* used instead of those instantiated from the superclass. This intuition is unfortunately false in most OOP languages, in particular in all those that allow mutable objects. Subtype polymorphism as enforced by the type checker in OOP languages (with mutable objects) cannot guarantee behavioral subtyping in any context. Behavioral subtyping is undecidable in general, so it cannot be implemented by a program (compiler). Class or object hierarchies must be carefully designed, considering possible incorrect uses that cannot be detected syntactically. This issue is known as the Liskov substitution principle.

Gang of Four Design Patterns

Design Patterns: Elements of Reusable Object-Oriented Software is an influential book published in 1995 by Erich Gamma, Richard Helm, Ralph Johnson, and John Vlissides, often referred to humorously as the "Gang of Four". Along with exploring the capabilities and pitfalls of object-oriented programming, it describes 23 common programming problems and patterns for solving them. As of April 2007, the book was in its 36th printing.

The book describes the following patterns:

- *Creational patterns* (5): Factory method pattern, Abstract factory pattern, Singleton pattern, Builder pattern, Prototype pattern

- *Structural patterns* (7): Adapter pattern, Bridge pattern, Composite pattern, Decorator pattern, Facade pattern, Flyweight pattern, Proxy pattern

- *Behavioral patterns* (11): Chain-of-responsibility pattern, Command pattern, Interpreter pattern, Iterator pattern, Mediator pattern, Memento pattern, Observer pattern, State pattern, Strategy pattern, Template method pattern, Visitor pattern

Object-orientation and Databases

Both object-oriented programming and relational database management systems (RDBMSs) are extremely common in software today. Since relational databases don't store objects directly (though some RDBMSs have object-oriented features to approximate this), there is a general need to bridge the two worlds. The problem of bridging object-oriented programming accesses and data patterns with relational databases is known as object-relational impedance mismatch. There are a number of approaches to cope with this problem, but no general solution without downsides. One of the most common approaches is object-relational mapping, as found in IDE languages such as Visual FoxPro and libraries such as Java Data Objects and Ruby on Rails' ActiveRecord.

There are also object databases that can be used to replace RDBMSs, but these have not been as technically and commercially successful as RDBMSs.

Real-world Modeling and Relationships

OOP can be used to associate real-world objects and processes with digital counterparts. However, not everyone agrees that OOP facilitates direct real-world mapping or that real-world mapping is even a worthy goal; Bertrand Meyer argues in *Object-Oriented Software Construction* that a program is not a model of the world but a model of some part of the world; "Reality is a cousin twice removed". At the same time, some principal limitations of OOP have been noted. For example, the circle-ellipse problem is difficult to handle using OOP's concept of inheritance.

However, Niklaus Wirth (who popularized the adage now known as Wirth's law: "Software is getting slower more rapidly than hardware becomes faster") said of OOP in his paper, "Good Ideas through the Looking Glass", "This paradigm closely reflects the structure of systems 'in the real world', and it is therefore well suited to model complex systems with complex behaviours" (contrast KISS principle).

Steve Yegge and others noted that natural languages lack the OOP approach of strictly prioritizing *things* (objects/nouns) before *actions* (methods/verbs). This problem may cause OOP to suffer more convoluted solutions than procedural programming.

OOP and Control Flow

OOP was developed to increase the reusability and maintainability of source code. Transparent representation of the control flow had no priority and was meant to be handled by a compiler. With the increasing relevance of parallel hardware and multi-threaded coding, developing transparent control flow becomes more important, something hard to achieve with OOP.

Responsibility- Vs. Data-driven Design

Responsibility-driven design defines classes in terms of a contract, that is, a class should be defined around a responsibility and the information that it shares. This is contrasted by Wirfs-Brock and Wilkerson with data-driven design, where classes are defined around the data-structures that must be held. The authors hold that responsibility-driven design is preferable.

SOLID and GRASP Guidelines

SOLID is a mnemonic invented by Michael Feathers that stands for and advocates five programming practices:

- Single responsibility principle
- Open/closed principle
- Liskov substitution principle
- Interface segregation principle
- Dependency inversion principle

GRASP (General Responsibility Assignment Software Patterns) is another set of guidelines advocated by Craig Larman.

Criticism

The OOP paradigm has been criticised for a number of reasons, including not meeting its stated goals of reusability and modularity, and for overemphasizing one aspect of software design and modeling (data/objects) at the expense of other important aspects (computation/algorithms).

Luca Cardelli has claimed that OOP code is "intrinsically less efficient" than procedural code, that OOP can take longer to compile, and that OOP languages have "extremely poor modularity properties with respect to class extension and modification", and tend to be extremely complex. The latter point is reiterated by Joe Armstrong, the principal inventor of Erlang, who is quoted as saying:

> The problem with object-oriented languages is they've got all this implicit environment that they carry around with them. You wanted a banana but what you got was a gorilla holding the banana and the entire jungle.

A study by Potok et al. has shown no significant difference in productivity between OOP and procedural approaches.

Christopher J. Date stated that critical comparison of OOP to other technologies, relational in particular, is difficult because of lack of an agreed-upon and rigorous definition of OOP; however, Date and Darwen have proposed a theoretical foundation on OOP that uses OOP as a kind of customizable type system to support RDBMS.

In an article Lawrence Krubner claimed that compared to other languages (LISP dialects, functional languages, etc.) OOP languages have no unique strengths, and inflict a heavy burden of unneeded complexity.

Alexander Stepanov compares object orientation unfavourably to generic programming:

I find OOP technically unsound. It attempts to decompose the world in terms of interfaces that vary on a single type. To deal with the real problems you need multisorted algebras — families of interfaces that span multiple types. I find OOP philosophically unsound. It claims that everything is an object. Even if it is true it is not very interesting — saying that everything is an object is saying nothing at all.

Paul Graham has suggested that OOP's popularity within large companies is due to "large (and frequently changing) groups of mediocre programmers". According to Graham, the discipline imposed by OOP prevents any one programmer from "doing too much damage".

Steve Yegge noted that, as opposed to functional programming:

Object Oriented Programming puts the Nouns first and foremost. Why would you go to such lengths to put one part of speech on a pedestal? Why should one kind of concept take precedence over another? It's not as if OOP has suddenly made verbs less important in the way we actually think. It's a strangely skewed perspective.

Rich Hickey, creator of Clojure, described object systems as overly simplistic models of the real world. He emphasized the inability of OOP to model time properly, which is getting increasingly problematic as software systems become more concurrent.

Eric S. Raymond, a Unix programmer and open-source software advocate, has been critical of claims that present object-oriented programming as the "One True Solution", and has written that object-oriented programming languages tend to encourage thickly layered programs that destroy transparency. Raymond compares this unfavourably to the approach taken with Unix and the C programming language.

Rob Pike, a programmer involved in the creation of UTF-8 and Go, has called object-oriented programming "the Roman numerals of computing" and has said that OOP languages frequently shift the focus from data structures and algorithms to types. Furthermore, he cites an instance of a Java professor whose "idiomatic" solution to a problem was to create six new classes, rather than to simply use a lookup table.

Formal Semantics

Objects are the run-time entities in an object-oriented system. They may represent a person, a place, a bank account, a table of data, or any item that the program has to handle.

There have been several attempts at formalizing the concepts used in object-oriented programming. The following concepts and constructs have been used as interpretations of OOP concepts:

- Co algebraic data types

- Abstract data types (which have existential types) allow the definition of modules but these do not support dynamic dispatch

- Recursive types

- Encapsulated state

- Inheritance

- Records are basis for understanding objects if function literals can be stored in fields (like in functional programming languages), but the actual calculi need be considerably more complex to incorporate essential features of OOP. Several extensions of System F<: that deal with mutable objects have been studied; these allow both subtype polymorphism and parametric polymorphism (generics)

Attempts to find a consensus definition or theory behind objects have not proven very successful (however, Abadi & Cardelli, *A Theory of Objects* for formal definitions of many OOP concepts and constructs), and often diverge widely. For example, some definitions focus on mental activities, and some on program structuring. One of the simpler definitions is that OOP is the act of using "map" data structures or arrays that can contain functions and pointers to other maps, all with some syntactic and scoping sugar on top. Inheritance can be performed by cloning the maps (sometimes called "prototyping").

Procedural Programming

Procedural programming is a programming paradigm, derived from structured programming, based upon the concept of the *procedure call*. Procedures, also known as routines, subroutines, or functions, simply contain a series of computational steps to be carried out. Any given procedure might be called at any point during a program's execution, including by other procedures or itself. The first major procedural programming languages first appeared circa 1960, including Fortran, ALGOL, COBOL and BASIC. Pascal and C were published closer to the 1970s, while Ada was released in 1980. Go is an example of a more modern procedural language, first published in 2009.

Computer processors provide hardware support for procedural programming through a stack register and instructions for calling procedures and returning from them. Hardware support for other types of programming is possible, but no attempt was commercially successful (for example Lisp machines or Java processors).

Procedures and Modularity

Modularity is generally desirable, especially in large, complicated programs. Inputs are usually specified syntactically in the form of *arguments* and the outputs delivered as *return values*.

Scoping is another technique that helps keep procedures modular. It prevents the procedure from accessing the variables of other procedures (and vice versa), including previous instances of itself, without explicit authorization.

Less modular procedures, often used in small or quickly written programs, tend to interact with a large number of variables in the execution environment, which other procedures might also modify.

Because of the ability to specify a simple interface, to be self-contained, and to be reused, procedures are a convenient vehicle for making pieces of code written by different people or different groups, including through programming libraries.

Comparison with Other Programming Paradigms

Imperative Programming

Procedural programming languages are also imperative languages, because they make explicit references to the state of the execution environment. This could be anything from *variables* (which may correspond to processor registers) to something like the position of the "turtle" in the Logo programming language.

Often, the terms "procedural programming" and "imperative programming" are used synonymously. However, procedural programming relies heavily on blocks and scope, whereas imperative programming as a whole may or may not have such features. As such, procedural languages generally use reserved words that act on blocks, such as if, while, and for, to implement control flow, whereas non-structured imperative languages use goto statements and branch tables for the same purpose.

Object-oriented Programming

The focus of procedural programming is to break down a programming task into a collection of variables, data structures, and subroutines, whereas in object-oriented programming it is to break down a programming task into objects that expose behavior (methods) and data (members or attributes) using interfaces. The most important distinction is that while procedural programming uses procedures to operate on data structures, object-oriented programming bundles the two together, so an "object", which is an instance of a class, operates on its "own" data structure.

Nomenclature varies between the two, although they have similar semantics:

Procedural	Object-oriented
procedure	method
record	object
module	class
procedure call	message

Functional Programming

The principles of modularity and code reuse in practical functional languages are fundamentally the same as in procedural languages, since they both stem from structured programming. So for example:

- Procedures correspond to functions. Both allow the reuse of the same code in various parts of the programs, and at various points of its execution.

- By the same token, procedure calls correspond to function application.

- Functions and their invocations are modularly separated from each other in the same manner, by the use of function arguments, return values and variable scopes.

The main difference between the styles is that functional programming languages remove or at least deemphasize the imperative elements of procedural programming. The feature set of functional languages is therefore designed to support writing programs as much as possible in terms of pure functions:

- Whereas procedural languages model execution of the program as a sequence of imperative commands that may implicitly alter shared state, functional programming languages model execution as the evaluation of complex expressions that only depend on each other in terms of arguments and return values. For this reason, functional programs can have a free order of code execution, and the languages may offer little control over the order in which various parts of the program are executed. (For example, the arguments to a procedure invocation in Scheme are executed in an arbitrary order.)

- Functional programming languages support (and heavily use) first-class functions, anonymous functions and closures, although these concepts are being included in newer procedural languages.

- Functional programming languages tend to rely on tail call optimization and higher-order functions instead of imperative looping constructs.

Many functional languages, however, are in fact impurely functional and offer imperative/procedural constructs that allow the programmer to write programs in procedural style, or in a combination of both styles. It is common for input/output code in functional languages to be written in a procedural style.

There do exist a few esoteric functional languages (like Unlambda) that eschew structured programming precepts for the sake of being difficult to program in (and therefore challenging). These languages are the exception to the common ground between procedural and functional languages.

Logic Programming

In logic programming, a program is a set of premises, and computation is performed by attempting to prove candidate theorems. From this point of view, logic programs are declarative, focusing on what the problem is, rather than on how to solve it.

However, the backward reasoning technique, implemented by SLD resolution, used to solve problems in logic programming languages such as Prolog, treats programs as goal-reduction procedures. Thus clauses of the form:

```
H :- B , ..., B .
     1        n
```

have a dual interpretation, both as procedures

```
to show/solve H, show/solve B  and ... and B
                              1              n
```

and as logical implications:

```
B  and ... and B  implies H.
 1              n
```

Experienced logic programmers use the procedural interpretation to write programs that are effective and efficient, and they use the declarative interpretation to help ensure that programs are correct.

Structured Programming

Structured programming is a programming paradigm aimed at improving the clarity, quality, and development time of a computer program by making extensive use of subroutines, block structures, for and while loops—in contrast to using simple tests and jumps such as the *go to* statement which could lead to "spaghetti code" causing difficulty to both follow and maintain.

It emerged in the late 1950s with the appearance of the ALGOL 58 and ALGOL 60 programming languages, with the latter including support for block structures. Contributing factors to its popularity and widespread acceptance, at first in academia and later among practitioners, include the discovery of what is now known as the structured program theorem in 1966, and the publication of the influential "Go To Statement Considered Harmful" open letter in 1968 by Dutch computer scientist Edsger W. Dijkstra, who coined the term "structured programming".

Structured programming is most frequently used with deviations that allow for clearer programs in some particular cases, such as when exception handling has to be performed.

Elements

Control Structures

Following the structured program theorem, all programs are seen as composed of control structures:

- "Sequence"; ordered statements or subroutines executed in sequence.

- "Selection"; one or a number of statements is executed depending on the state of the program. This is usually expressed with keywords such as if..then..else..endif.

- "Iteration"; a statement or block is executed until the program reaches a certain state, or operations have been applied to every element of a collection. This is usually expressed with keywords such as while, repeat, for or do..until. Often it is recommended that each loop should only have one entry point (and in the original structural programming, also only one exit point, and a few languages enforce this).

- "Recursion"; a statement is executed by repeatedly calling itself until termination conditions are met. While similar in practice to iterative loops, recursive loops may be more computationally efficient, and are implemented differently as a cascading stack.

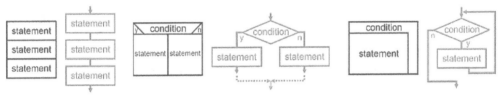

Graphical representations of the three basic patterns using NS diagrams (blue) and flow charts (green).

Subroutines

Subroutines; callable units such as procedures, functions, methods, or subprograms are used to allow a sequence to be referred to by a single statement.

Blocks

Blocks are used to enable groups of statements to be treated as if they were one statement. *Block-structured* languages have a syntax for enclosing structures in some formal way, such as an if-statement bracketed by if..fi as in ALGOL 68, or a code section bracketed by BEGIN..END, as in PL/I, whitespace indentation as in Python - or the curly braces {...} of C and many later languages.

Structured Programming Languages

It is possible to do structured programming in any programming language, though it is preferable to use something like a procedural programming language. Some of the languages initially used for structured programming include: ALGOL, Pascal, PL/I and Ada – but most new procedural programming languages since that time have included features to encourage structured programming, and sometimes deliberately left out features – notably GOTO – in an effort to make unstructured programming more difficult. *Structured programming* (sometimes known as modular programming) enforces a logical structure on the program being written to make it more efficient and easier to understand and modify.

History

Theoretical Foundation

The structured program theorem provides the theoretical basis of structured programming. It states that three ways of combining programs—sequencing, selection, and iteration—are sufficient to express any computable function. This observation did not originate with the structured programming movement; these structures are sufficient to describe the instruction cycle of a central processing unit, as well as the operation of a Turing machine. Therefore, a processor is always executing a "structured program" in this sense, even if the instructions it reads from memory are not part of a structured program. However, authors usually credit the result to a 1966 paper by Böhm and Jacopini, possibly because Dijkstra cited this paper himself. The structured program theorem does not address how to write and analyze a usefully structured program. These issues were addressed during the late 1960s and early 1970s, with major contributions by Dijkstra, Robert W. Floyd, Tony Hoare, Ole-Johan Dahl, and David Gries.

Debate

P. J. Plauger, an early adopter of structured programming, described his reaction to the structured program theorem:

> Us converts waved this interesting bit of news under the noses of the unreconstructed assembly-language programmers who kept trotting forth twisty bits of logic and saying, 'I betcha can't structure this.' Neither the proof by Böhm and Jacopini nor our repeated successes at writing structured code brought them around one day sooner than they were ready to convince themselves.

Donald Knuth accepted the principle that programs must be written with provability in mind, but he disagreed (and still disagrees) with abolishing the GOTO statement. In his 1974 paper, "Structured Programming with Goto Statements", he gave examples where he believed that a direct jump leads to clearer and more efficient code without sacrificing provability. Knuth proposed a looser structural constraint: It should be possible to draw a program's flow chart with all forward branches on the left, all backward branches on the right, and no branches crossing each other. Many of those knowledgeable in compilers and graph theory have advocated allowing only reducible flow graphs

Structured programming theorists gained a major ally in the 1970s after IBM researcher Harlan Mills applied his interpretation of structured programming theory to the development of an indexing system for the *New York Times* research file. The project was a great engineering success, and managers at other companies cited it in support of adopting structured programming, although Dijkstra criticized the ways that Mills's interpretation differed from the published work.

As late as 1987 it was still possible to raise the question of structured programming in a computer science journal. Frank Rubin did so in that year with an open letter titled ""GOTO considered harmful" considered harmful". Numerous objections followed, including a response from Dijkstra that sharply criticized both Rubin and the concessions other writers made when responding to him.

Outcome

By the end of the 20th century nearly all computer scientists were convinced that it is useful to learn and apply the concepts of structured programming. High-level programming languages that originally lacked programming structures, such as FORTRAN, COBOL, and BASIC, now have them.

Common Deviations

While goto has now largely been replaced by the structured constructs of selection (if/then/else) and repetition (while and for), few languages are purely structured. The most common deviation, found in many languages, is the use of a return statement for early exit from a subroutine. This results in multiple exit points, instead of the single exit point required by structured programming. There are other constructions to handle cases that are awkward in purely structured programming.

Early Exit

The most common deviation from structured programming is early exit from a function or loop. At the level of functions, this is a `return` statement. At the level of loops, this is a break statement (terminate the loop) or `continue` statement (terminate the current iteration, proceed with next iteration). In structured programming, these can be replicated by adding additional branches or tests, but for returns from nested code this can add significant complexity. C is an early and prominent example of these constructs. Some newer languages also have "labeled breaks", which allow breaking out of more than just the innermost loop. Exceptions also allow early exit, but have further consequences, and thus are treated below.

Multiple exits can arise for a variety of reasons, most often either that the subroutine has no more work to do (if returning a value, it has completed the calculation), or has encountered "exceptional" circumstances that prevent it from continuing, hence needing exception handling.

The most common problem in early exit is that cleanup or final statements are not executed – for example, allocated memory is not deallocated, or open files are not closed, causing memory leaks or resource leaks. These must be done at each return site, which is brittle and can easily result in bugs. For instance, in later development, a return statement could be overlooked by a developer, and an action which should be performed at the end of a subroutine (e.g., a trace statement) might not be performed in all cases. Languages without a return statement, such as standard Pascal don't have this problem.

Most modern languages provide language-level support to prevent such leaks. Most commonly this is done via unwind protection, which ensures that certain code is guaranteed to be run when execution exits a block; this is a structured alternative to having a cleanup block and a `goto`. This is most often known as `try...finally`, and considered a part of exception handling. Various techniques exist to encapsulate resource management. An alternative approach, found primarily in C++, is Resource Acquisition Is Initialization, which uses normal stack unwinding (variable deallocation) at function exit to call destructors on local variables to deallocate resources.

Kent Beck, Martin Fowler and co-authors have argued in their refactoring books that nested conditionals may be harder to understand than a certain type of flatter structure using multiple exits predicated by guard clauses. Their 2009 book flatly states that "one exit point is really not a useful rule. Clarity is the key principle: If the method is clearer with one exit point, use one exit point; otherwise don't". They offer a cookbook solution for transforming a function consisting only of nested conditionals into a sequence of guarded return (or throw) statements, followed by a single unguarded block, which is intended to contain the code for the common case, while the guarded statements are supposed to deal with the less common ones (or with errors). Herb Sutter and Andrei Alexandrescu also argue in their 2004 C++ tips book that the single-exit point is an obsolete requirement.

In his 2004 textbook, David Watt writes that "single-entry multi-exit control flows are often desirable". Using Tennent's framework notion of sequencer, Watt uniformly describes the control flow constructs found in contemporary programming languages and attempts to explain why certain types of sequencers are preferable to others in the context of multi-exit control flows. Watt writes that unrestricted gotos (jump sequencers) are bad because the destination of the jump is not self-explanatory to the reader of a program until the reader finds and examines the actual label or address that is the target of the jump. In contrast, Watt argues that the conceptual intent of a return sequencer is clear from its own context, without having to examine its destination. Watt writes that a class of sequencers known as *escape sequencers*, defined as a "sequencer that terminates execution of a textually enclosing command or procedure", encompasses both breaks from loops (including multi-level breaks) and return statements. Watt also notes that while jump sequencers (gotos) have been somewhat restricted in languages like C, where the target must be an inside the local block or an encompassing outer block, that restriction alone is not sufficient to make the intent of gotos in C self-describing and so they can still produce "spaghetti code". Watt also examines how exception sequencers differ from escape and jump sequencers.

In contrast to the above, Bertrand Meyer wrote in his 2009 textbook that instructions like break and continue "are just the old goto in sheep's clothing" and strongly advised against their use.

Exception Handling

Based on the coding error from the Ariane 501 disaster, software developer Jim Bonang argues that any exceptions thrown from a function violate the single-exit paradigm, and proposes that all inter-procedural exceptions should be forbidden. In C++ syntax, this is done by declaring all function signatures as throw() Bonang proposes that all single-exit conforming C++ should be written along the lines of:

```cpp
bool myCheck1() throw()

{

 bool success = false;

 try {

   // do something that may throw exceptions

   if(myCheck2() == false) {

     throw SomeInternalException();

   }

   // other code similar to the above

   success = true;

 }

 catch(...) { // all exceptions caught and logged

 }

 return success;

}
```

Peter Ritchie also notes that, in principle, even a single throw right before the return in a function constitutes a violation of the single-exit principle, but argues that Dijkstra's rules were written in a time before exception handling became a paradigm in programming languages, so he proposes to allow any number of throw points in addition to a single return point. He notes that solutions which wrap exceptions for the sake of creating a single-exit have higher nesting depth and thus are more difficult to comprehend, and even accuses those who propose to apply such solutions to programming languages which support exceptions of engaging in cargo cult thinking.

David Watt also analyzes exception handling in the framework of sequencers Watt notes that an abnormal situation (generally exemplified with arithmetic overflows or input/output failures like file not found) is a kind of error that "is detected in some low-level program unit, but [for which] a handler is more naturally located in a high-level program unit". For example, a program might contain several calls to read files, but the action to perform when a file is not found depends on the meaning (purpose) of the file in question to the program and thus a handling routine for this abnormal situation cannot be located in low-level system code. Watts further notes that introducing status flags testing in the caller, as single-exit structured programming or even (multi-exit) return sequencers would entail, results in a situation where "the application code tends to get cluttered by tests of status flags" and that "the programmer might forgetfully or lazily omit to test a status flag. In fact, abnormal situations represented by status flags are by default ignored!" He notes that in contrast to status flags testing, exceptions have the opposite default behavior, causing the program to terminate unless the programmer explicitly deals with the exception in some way, possibly by adding code to willfully ignore it. Based on these arguments, Watt concludes that jump sequencers or escape sequencers (discussed in the previous section) aren't as suitable as a dedicated exception sequencer with the semantics discussed above.

The textbook by Louden and Lambert emphasizes that exception handling differs from structured programming constructs like `while` loops because the transfer of control "is set up at a different point in the program than that where the actual transfer takes place. At the point where the transfer actually occurs, there may be no syntactic indication that control will in fact be transferred." Computer science professor Arvind Kumar Bansal also notes that in languages which implement exception handling, even control structures like `for`, which have the single-exit property in absence of exceptions, no longer have it in presence of exceptions, because an exception can prematurely cause an early exit in any part of the control structure; for instance if `init()` throws an exception in `for (init(); check(); increm())`, then the usual exit point after check() is not reached. Citing multiple prior studies by others (1999-2004) and their own results, Westley Weimer and George Necula wrote that a significant problem with exceptions is that they "create hidden control-flow paths that are difficult for programmers to reason about".

The necessity to limit code to single-exit points appears in some contemporary programming environments focused on parallel computing, such as OpenMP. The various parallel constructs from OpenMP, like `parallel do`, do not allow early exits from inside to the outside of the parallel construct; this restriction includes all manner of exits, from break to C++ exceptions, but all of these are permitted inside the parallel construct if the jump target is also inside it.

Multiple Entry

More rarely, subprograms allow multiple *entry*. This is most commonly only *re*-entry into a coroutine (or generator/semicoroutine), where a subprogram yields control (and possibly a value), but can then be resumed where it left off. There are a number of common uses of such programming, notably for streams (particularly input/output), state machines, and concurrency. From a code execution point of view, yielding from a coroutine is closer to structured programming than returning from a subroutine, as the subprogram has not actually terminated, and will continue when called again – it is not an early exit. However, coroutines mean that multiple subprograms have execution state – rather than a single call stack of subroutines – and thus introduce a different form of complexity.

It is very rare for subprograms to allow entry to an arbitrary position in the subprogram, as in this case the program state (such as variable values) is uninitialized or ambiguous, and this is very similar to a goto.

State Machines

Some programs, particularly parsers and communications protocols, have a number of states that follow each other in a way that is not easily reduced to the basic structures, and some programmers implement the state-changes with a jump to the new state. This type of state-switching is often used in the Linux kernel.

However, it is possible to structure these systems by making each state-change a separate subprogram and using a variable to indicate the active state. Alternatively, these can be implemented via coroutines, which dispense with the trampoline.

Important Features of a Structured Program

A structured program uses three types of program constructs i.e. selection, sequence and iteration. Structured programs avoid unstructured control flows by restricting the use of GOTO statements. A structured program consists of a well partitioned set of modules. Structured programming uses single entry, single-exit program constructs such as if-then-else, do-while, etc. Thus, the structured programming principle emphasizes designing neat control structures for programs.

Important Advantages of Structured Programming

Structured programs are easier to read and understand. Structured programs are easier to maintain. They require less effort and time for development. They are amenable to easier debugging and usually fewer errors are made in the course of writing such programs.

Evolution of Software Design Techniques Over the Last 50 Years

During the 1950s, most programs were being written in assembly language. These programs were limited to about a few hundreds of lines of assembly code, i.e. were very small in size. Every programmer developed programs in his own individual style - based on his intuition. This type of programming was called Exploratory Programming.

The next significant development which occurred during early 1960s in the area computer programming was the high-level language programming. Use of high-level language programming reduced development efforts and development time significantly. Languages like FORTRAN, ALGOL, and COBOL were introduced at that time.

As the size and complexity of programs kept on increasing, the exploratory programming style proved to be insufficient. Programmers found it increasingly difficult not only to write cost-effective and correct programs, but also to understand and maintain programs written by others. To cope with this problem, experienced programmers advised other programmers to pay particular attention to the design of the program's control flow structure (in late 1960s). In the late 1960s, it was found that the "GOTO" statement was the main culprit which makes control structure of a program complicated and messy. At that time most of the programmers used assembly languages extensively. They considered use of "GOTO" statements in high-level languages were very natural because of their familiarity with JUMP statements which are very frequently used in assembly language programming. So they did not really accept that they can write programs without using GOTO statements, and considered the frequent use of GOTO statements inevitable. At this time, Dijkstra [1968] published his (now famous) article "GOTO Statements Considered Harmful". Expectedly, many programmers were enraged to read this article. They published several counter articles highlighting the advantages and inevitably of GOTO statements. But, soon it was conclusively proved that only three programming constructs – sequence, selection, and iteration – were sufficient to express any programming logic. This formed the basis of the structured programming methodology.

After structured programming, the next important development was data structure-oriented design. Programmers argued that for writing a good program, it is important to pay more attention to the design of data structure, of the program rather than to the design of its control structure. Data structure- oriented design techniques actually help to derive program structure from the data structure of the program. Example of a very popular data structure-oriented design technique is Jackson's Structured Programming (JSP) methodology, developed by Michael Jackson in the1970s.

Next significant development in the late 1970s was the development of data flow-oriented design technique. Experienced programmers stated that to have a good program structure, one has to study how the data flows from input to the output of the program. Every program reads data and then processes that data to produce some output. Once the data flow structure is identified, then from there one can derive the program structure.

Object-oriented design (1980s) is the latest and very widely used technique. It has an intuitively appealing design approach in which natural objects (such as employees, pay-roll register, etc.) occurring in a problem are first identified. Relationships among objects (such as composition, reference and inheritance) are determined. Each object essentially acts as a data hiding entity.

Exploratory Style Vs. Modern Style of Software Development

An important difference is that the exploratory software development style is based on error correction while the software engineering principles are primarily based on error prevention. Inherent in the software engineering principles is the realization that it is much more cost-effective to prevent errors from occurring than to correct them as and when they are detected. Even when errors occur, software engineering principles emphasize detection of errors as close to the point where the errors are committed as possible. In the exploratory style, errors are detected only during the final product testing. In contrast, the modern practice of software development is to develop the software through several well-defined stages such as requirements specification, design, coding, testing, etc., and attempts are made to detect and fix as many errors as possible in the same phase in which they occur.

In the exploratory style, coding was considered synonymous with software development. For instance, exploratory programming style believed in developing a working system as quickly as possible and then successively modifying it until it performed satisfactorily.

In the modern software development style, coding is regarded as only a small part of the overall software development activities. There are several development activities such as design and testing which typically require much more effort than coding.

A lot of attention is being paid to requirements specification. Significant effort is now being devoted to develop a clear specification of the problem before any development activity is started.

Now there is a distinct design phase where standard design techniques are employed.

Periodic reviews are being carried out during all stages of the development process. The main objective of carrying out reviews is phase containment of errors, i.e. detect and correct errors as soon as possible. Defects are usually not detected as soon as they occur, rather they are noticed much later in the life cycle. Once a defect is detected, we have to go back to the phase where it was introduced and rework those phases - possibly change the design or change the code and so on.

Today, software testing has become very systematic and standard testing techniques are available. Testing activity has also become all encompassing in the sense that test cases are being developed right from the requirements specification stage.

There is better visibility of design and code. By visibility we mean production of good quality, consistent and standard documents during every phase. In the past, very little attention was paid to producing good quality and consistent documents. In the exploratory style, the design and test activities, even if carried out (in whatever way), were not documented satisfactorily. Today, consciously good quality documents are being developed during product development. This has made fault diagnosis and maintenance smoother.

Now, projects are first thoroughly planned. Project planning normally includes preparation of various types of estimates, resource scheduling, and development of project tracking plans. Several techniques and tools for tasks such as configuration management, cost estimation, scheduling, etc. are used for effective software project management.

Several metrics are being used to help in software project management and software quality assurance.

Subroutine

In computer programming, a subroutine is a sequence of program instructions that perform a specific task, packaged as a unit. This unit can then be used in programs wherever that particular task should be performed.

Subprograms may be defined within programs, or separately in libraries that can be used by multiple programs. In different programming languages, a subroutine may be called a procedure, a function, a routine, a method, or a subprogram. The generic term callable unit is sometimes used.

The name *subprogram* suggests a subroutine behaves in much the same way as a computer program that is used as one step in a larger program or another subprogram. A subroutine is often coded so that it can be started (called) several times and from several places during one execution of the program, including from other subroutines, and then branch back (*return*) to the next instruction after the *call*, once the subroutine's task is done. Maurice Wilkes, David Wheeler, and Stanley Gill are credited with the invention of this concept, which they termed a *closed subroutine*, contrasted with an *open subroutine* or macro.

Subroutines are a powerful programming tool, and the syntax of many programming languages includes support for writing and using them. Judicious use of subroutines (for example, through the structured programming approach) will often substantially reduce the cost of developing and maintaining a large program, while increasing its quality and reliability. Subroutines, often collected into libraries, are an important mechanism for sharing and trading software. The discipline of object-oriented programming is based on objects and methods (which are subroutines attached to these objects or object classes).

In the compiling method called threaded code, the executable program is basically a sequence of subroutine calls.

Main Concepts

The content of a subroutine is its body, which is the piece of program code that is executed when the subroutine is called or invoked.

A subroutine may be written so that it expects to obtain one or more data values from the calling program (its parameters or formal parameters). The calling program provides actual values for these parameters, called arguments. Different programming languages may use different conventions for passing arguments:

Convention	Description	Common use
Call by value	Argument is evaluated and copy of value is passed to subroutine	Default in most Algol-like languages after Algol 60, such as Pascal, Delphi, Simula, CPL, PL/M, Modula, Oberon, Ada, and many others. C, C++, Java (References to objects and arrays are also passed by value)
Call by reference	Reference to argument, typically its address is passed	Selectable in most Algol-like languages after Algol 60, such as Algol 68, Pascal, Delphi, Simula, CPL, PL/M, Modula, Oberon, Ada, and many others. C++, Fortran, PL/I
Call by result	Parameter value is copied back to argument on return from the subroutine	Ada OUT parameters
Call by value-result	Parameter value is copied back on entry to the subroutine and again on return	Algol
Call by name	Like a macro – replace the parameters with the unevaluated argument expressions	Algol, Scala
Call by constant value	Like call by value except that the parameter is treated as a constant	PL/I NONASSIGNABLE parameters, Ada IN parameters

The subroutine may return a computed value to its caller (its return value), or provide various result values or output parameters. Indeed, a common use of subroutines is to implement mathematical functions, in which the purpose of the subroutine is purely to compute one or more results whose values are entirely determined by the parameters passed to the subroutine. (Examples might include computing the logarithm of a number or the determinant of a matrix.)

A subroutine call may also have side effects such as modifying data structures in a computer memory, reading from or writing to a peripheral device, creating a file, halting the program or the machine, or even delaying the program's execution for a specified time. A subprogram with side effects may return different results each time it is called, even if it is called with the same arguments. An example is a random number function, available in many languages, that returns a different pseudo-random number each time it is called. The widespread use of subroutines with side effects is a characteristic of imperative programming languages.

A subroutine can be coded so that it may call itself recursively, at one or more places, to perform its task. This method allows direct implementation of functions defined by mathematical induction and recursive divide and conquer algorithms.

A subroutine whose purpose is to compute one boolean-valued function (that is, to answer a yes/no question) is sometimes called a predicate. In logic programming languages, often all subroutines are called predicates, since they primarily determine success or failure. For example, any type of function is a subroutine but not main().

Language Support

High-level programming languages usually include specific constructs to:

- Delimit the part of the program (body) that makes up the subroutine

- Assign an identifier (name) to the subroutine

- Specify the names and data types of its parameters and return values

- Provide a private naming scope for its temporary variables

- Identify variables outside the subroutine that are accessible within it

- Call the subroutine

- Provide values to its parameters

- Specify the return values from within its body

- Return to the calling program

- Dispose of the values returned by a call

- Handle any exceptional conditions encountered during the call

- Package subroutines into a module, library, object, class, etc.

Some programming languages, such as Pascal, Fortran, Ada and many dialects of BASIC, distinguish between functions or function subprograms, which provide an explicit return value to the calling program, and subroutines or procedures, which do not. In those languages, function calls are normally embedded in expressions (e.g., a sqrt function may be called as `y = z + sqrt(x)`). Procedure calls either behave syntactically as statements (e.g., a `print` procedure may be called as `if x > 0 then print(x)` or are explicitly invoked by a statement such as `CALL` or `GOSUB` (e.g. `call print(x)`). Other languages, such as C and Lisp, do not distinguish between functions and subroutines.

In strictly functional programming languages such as Haskell, subprograms can have no side effects, which means that various internal states of the program will not change. Functions will always return the same result if repeatedly called with the same arguments. Such languages typically only support functions, since subroutines that do not return a value have no use unless they can cause a side effect.

In programming languages such as C, C++, and C#, subroutines may also simply be called functions, mathematical functions or functional programming, which are different concepts.

A language's compiler will usually translate procedure calls and returns into machine instructions according to a well-defined calling convention, so that subroutines can be compiled separately from the programs that call them. The instruction sequences corresponding to call and return statements are called the procedure's prologue and epilogue.

Advantages

The advantages of breaking a program into subroutines include:

- Decomposing a complex programming task into simpler steps: this is one of the two main tools of structured programming, along with data structures

- Reducing duplicate code within a program

- Enabling reuse of code across multiple programs

- Dividing a large programming task among various programmers, or various stages of a project

- Hiding implementation details from users of the subroutine

- Improving traceability (i.e. most languages offer ways to obtain the call trace which includes the names of the involved subroutines and perhaps even more information such as file names and line numbers); by not decomposing the code into subroutines, debugging would be impaired severely

Disadvantages

Invoking a subroutine (versus using in-line code) imposes some computational overhead in the call mechanism.

A subroutine typically requires standard housekeeping code – both at entry to, and exit from, the function (function prologue and epilogue – usually saving general purpose registers and return address as a minimum).

History

The idea of a subroutine was worked out after computing machines had already existed for some time. The arithmetic and conditional jump instructions were planned ahead of time and have changed relatively little; but the special instructions used for procedure calls have changed greatly over the years. The earliest computers and microprocessors, such as the Small-Scale Experimental Machine and the RCA 1802, did not have a single subroutine call instruction. Subroutines could be implemented, but they required programmers to use the call sequence—a series of instructions—at each call site. Some very early computers and microprocessors, such as the IBM 1620, the Intel 8008, and the PIC microcontrollers, have a single-instruction subroutine call that uses dedicated hardware stack to store return addresses—such hardware supports only a few levels of subroutine nesting, but can support recursive subroutines. Machines before the mid 1960s—such as the UNIVAC I, the PDP-1, and the IBM 1130—typically use a calling convention which saved the instruction counter in the first memory location of the called subroutine. This allows arbitrarily deep levels of subroutine nesting, but does not support recursive subroutines. The PDP-11 (1970) is one of the first computers with a stack-pushing subroutine call instruction; this feature supports both arbitrarily deep subroutine nesting and also supports recursive subroutines.

Language Support

In the very early assemblers, subroutine support was limited. Subroutines were not explicitly separated from each other or from the main program, and indeed the source code of a subroutine could be interspersed with that of other subprograms. Some assemblers would offer predefined macros to generate the call and return sequences. By the 1960s, assemblers usually had much more sophisticated support for both inline and separately assembled subroutines that could be linked together.

Subroutine Libraries

Even with this cumbersome approach, subroutines proved very useful. For one thing they allowed use of the same code in many different programs. Moreover, memory was a very scarce resource on early computers, and subroutines allowed significant savings in the size of programs.

Many early computers loaded the program instructions into memory from a punched paper tape. Each subroutine could then be provided by a separate piece of tape, loaded or spliced before or after the main program (or "mainline"); and the same subroutine tape could then be used by many different programs. A similar approach applied in computers which used punched cards for their main input. The name *subroutine library* originally meant a library, in the literal sense, which kept indexed collections of tapes or card-decks for collective use.

Return by Indirect Jump

To remove the need for self-modifying code, computer designers eventually provided an *indirect jump* instruction, whose operand, instead of being the return address itself, was the location of a variable or processor register containing the return address.

On those computers, instead of modifying the subroutine's return jump, the calling program would store the return address in a variable so that when the subroutine completed, it would execute an indirect jump that would direct execution to the location given by the predefined variable.

Jump to Subroutine

Another advance was the *jump to subroutine* instruction, which combined the saving of the return address with the calling jump, thereby minimizing overhead significantly.

In the IBM System/360, for example, the branch instructions BAL or BALR, designed for procedure calling, would save the return address in a processor register specified in the instruction. To return, the subroutine had only to execute an indirect branch instruction (BR) through that register. If the subroutine needed that register for some other purpose (such as calling another subroutine), it would save the register's contents to a private memory location or a register stack.

In systems such as the HP 2100, the JSB instruction would perform a similar task, except that the return address was stored in the memory location that was the target of the branch. Execution of the procedure would actually begin at the next memory location. In the HP 2100 assembly language, one would write, for example

```
    ...

    JSB MYSUB   (Calls subroutine MYSUB.)

BB  ...         (Will return here after MYSUB is done.)
```

to call a subroutine called MYSUB from the main program. The subroutine would be coded as

```
MYSUB NOP       (Storage for MYSUB's return address.)

AA  ...         (Start of MYSUB's body.)

    ...

    JMP MYSUB,I (Returns to the calling program.)
```

The JSB instruction placed the address of the NEXT instruction (namely, BB) into the location specified as its operand (namely, MYSUB), and then branched to the NEXT location after that (namely, AA = MYSUB + 1). The subroutine could then return to the main program by executing the indirect jump JMP MYSUB,I which branched to the location stored at location MYSUB.

Compilers for Fortran and other languages could easily make use of these instructions when available. This approach supported multiple levels of calls; however, since the return address, parameters, and return values of a subroutine were assigned fixed memory locations, it did not allow for recursive calls.

Incidentally, a similar method was used by Lotus 1-2-3, in the early 1980s, to discover the recalculation dependencies in a spreadsheet. Namely, a location was reserved in each cell to store the *return* address. Since circular references are not allowed for natural recalculation order, this allows a tree walk without reserving space for a stack in memory, which was very limited on small computers such as the IBM PC.

Call Stack

Most modern implementations use a call stack, a special case of the stack data structure, to implement subroutine calls and returns. Each procedure call creates a new entry, called a *stack frame*, at the top of the stack; when the procedure returns, its stack frame is deleted from the stack, and its space may be used for other procedure calls. Each stack frame contains the *private data* of the corresponding call, which typically includes the procedure's parameters and internal variables, and the return address.

The call sequence can be implemented by a sequence of ordinary instructions (an approach still used in reduced instruction set computing (RISC) and very long instruction word (VLIW) architectures), but many traditional machines designed since the late 1960s have included special instructions for that purpose.

The call stack is usually implemented as a contiguous area of memory. It is an arbitrary design choice whether the bottom of the stack is the lowest or highest address within this area, so that the stack may grow forwards or backwards in memory; however, many architectures chose the latter.

Some designs, notably some Forth implementations, used two separate stacks, one mainly for control information (like return addresses and loop counters) and the other for data. The former was, or worked like, a call stack and was only indirectly accessible to the programmer through other language constructs while the latter was more directly accessible.

When stack-based procedure calls were first introduced, an important motivation was to save precious memory. With this scheme, the compiler does not have to reserve separate space in memory for the private data (parameters, return address, and local variables) of each procedure. At any moment, the stack contains only the private data of the calls that are currently *active* (namely, which have been called but haven't returned yet). Because of the ways in which programs were usually assembled from libraries, it was (and still is) not uncommon to find programs that include thousands of subroutines, of which only a handful are active at any given moment. For such programs, the call stack mechanism could save significant amounts of memory. Indeed, the call stack mechanism can be viewed as the earliest and simplest method for automatic memory management.

However, another advantage of the call stack method is that it allows recursive subroutine calls, since each nested call to the same procedure gets a separate instance of its private data.

Delayed Stacking

One disadvantage of the call stack mechanism is the increased cost of a procedure call and its matching return. The extra cost includes incrementing and decrementing the stack pointer (and, in some architectures, checking for stack overflow), and accessing the local variables and parameters by frame-relative addresses, instead of absolute addresses. The cost may be realized in increased execution time, or increased processor complexity, or both.

This overhead is most obvious and objectionable in *leaf procedures* or *leaf functions*, which return without making any procedure calls themselves. To reduce that overhead, many modern compilers try to delay the use of a call stack until it is really needed. For example, the call of a procedure P may store the return address and parameters of the called procedure in certain processor registers, and transfer control to the procedure's body by a simple jump. If procedure P returns without making any other call, the call stack is not used at all. If P needs to call another procedure Q, it will then use the call stack to save the contents of any registers (such as the return address) that will be needed after Q returns.

C and C++ Examples

In the C and C++ programming languages, subprograms are termed *functions* (or *member functions* when associated with a class). These languages use the special keyword void to indicate that a function takes no parameters (especially in C) or does not return any value. Note that C/C++ functions can have side-effects, including modifying any variables whose addresses are passed as parameters (i.e., *passed by reference*). Examples:

```
void function1(void) { /* some code */ }
```

The function does not return a value and has to be called as a stand-alone function, e.g.,

```
function1();
```

```
int function2(void)

{

   return 5;

}
```

This function returns a result (the number 5), and the call can be part of an expression, e.g., x + `function2()`

```
char function3(int number)

{

   char selection[] = {'S','M','T','W','T','F','S'};

   return selection[number];

}
```

This function converts a number between 0 and 6 into the initial letter of the corresponding day of the week, namely 0 to 'S', 1 to 'M', ..., 6 to 'S'. The result of calling it might be assigned to a variable, e.g., num_day = `function3(number);`.

```
void function4(int *pointer_to_var)
{
   (*pointer_to_var)++;
}
```

This function does not return a value but modifies the variable whose address is passed as the parameter; it would be called with "`function4(&variable_to_increment);`".

Visual Basic 6 Examples

In the Visual Basic 6 language, subprograms are termed *functions* or *subs* (or *methods* when associated with a class). Visual Basic 6 uses various terms called *types* to define what is being passed as a parameter. By default, an unspecified variable is registered as a variant type and can be passed as *ByRef* (default) or *ByVal*. Also, when a function or sub is declared, it is given a public, private, or friend designation, which determines whether it can be accessed outside the module or project that it was declared in.

- By value [ByVal] – a way of passing the value of an argument to a procedure instead of passing the address. This allows the procedure to access a copy of the variable. As a result, the variable's actual value can't be changed by the procedure to which it is passed.

- By reference [ByRef] – a way of passing the address of an argument to a procedure instead of passing the value. This allows the procedure to access the actual variable. As a result, the variable's actual value can be changed by the procedure to which it is passed. Unless otherwise specified, arguments are passed by reference.

- Public (optional) – indicates that the function procedure is accessible to all other procedures in all modules. If used in a module that contains an Option Private, the procedure is not available outside the project.

- Private (optional) – indicates that the function procedure is accessible only to other procedures in the module where it is declared.

- Friend (optional) – used only in a class module. Indicates that the Function procedure is visible throughout the project, but not visible to a controller of an instance of an object.

```
Private Function Function1()

   ' Some Code Here

End Function
```

The function does not return a value and has to be called as a stand-alone function, e.g., `Function1`

```
Private Function Function2() as Integer

   Function2 = 5

End Function
```

This function returns a result (the number 5), and the call can be part of an expression, e.g., `x + Function2()`

```
Private Function Function3(ByVal intValue as Integer) as String

   Dim strArray(6) as String

   strArray = Array("M", "T", "W", "T", "F", "S", "S")

   Function3 = strArray(intValue)

End Function
```

This function converts a number between 0 and 6 into the initial letter of the corresponding day of the week, namely 0 to 'M', 1 to 'T', ..., 6 to 'S'. The result of calling it might be assigned to a variable, e.g., `num_day = Function3(number)`.

```
Private Function Function4(ByRef intValue as Integer)

   intValue = intValue + 1

End Function
```

This function does not return a value but modifies the variable whose address is passed as the parameter; it would be called with "`Function4(variable_to_increment)`".

PL/I Example

In PL/I a called procedure may be passed a *descriptor* providing information about the argument, such as string lengths and array bounds. This allows the procedure to be more general and eliminates the need for the programmer to pass such information. By default PL/I passes arguments by reference. A (trivial) subroutine to change the sign of each element of a two-dimensional array might look like:

```
change_sign: procedure(array);

  declare array(*,*) float;

  array = -array;

  end change_sign;
```

This could be called with various arrays as follows:

```
/* first array bounds from -5 to +10 and 3 to 9 */

declare array1 (-5:10, 3:9)float;

/* second array bounds from 1 to 16 and 1 to 16 */

declare array2 (16,16) float;

call change_sign(array1);

call change_sign(array2);
```

Local Variables, Recursion and Reentrancy

A subprogram may find it useful to make use of a certain amount of *scratch* space; that is, memory used during the execution of that subprogram to hold intermediate results. Variables stored in this scratch space are termed *local variables*, and the scratch space is termed an *activation record*. An activation record typically has a return address that tells it where to pass control back to when the subprogram finishes.

A subprogram may have any number and nature of call sites. If recursion is supported, a subprogram may even call itself, causing its execution to suspend while another *nested* execution of the same subprogram occurs. Recursion is a useful means to simplify some complex algorithms, and breaking down complex problems. Recursive languages generally provide a new copy of local variables on each call. If the programmer desires the value of local variables to stay the same between calls, they can be declared *static* in some languages, or global values or common areas can be used. Here is an example of recursive subroutine in C/C++ to find Fibonacci numbers:

```
int fib(int n)

{

        if(n<=1) return n;

        return fib(n-1)+fib(n-2);

}
```

Early languages like Fortran did not initially support recursion because variables were statically allocated, as well as the location for the return address. Most computers before the late 1960s such as the PDP-8 did not have support for hardware stack registers.

Modern languages after ALGOL such as PL/1 and C almost invariably use a stack, usually supported by most modern computer instruction sets to provide a fresh activation record for every execution of a subprogram. That way, the nested execution is free to modify its local variables without concern for the effect on other suspended executions in progress. As nested calls accumulate, a call stack structure is formed, consisting of one activation record for each suspended subprogram. In fact, this stack structure is virtually ubiquitous, and so activation records are commonly termed *stack frames*.

Some languages such as Pascal and Ada also support nested subroutines, which are subroutines callable only within the scope of an outer (parent) subroutine. Inner subroutines have access to the local variables of the outer subroutine that called them. This is accomplished by storing extra context information within the activation record, also termed a *display*.

If a subprogram can function properly even when called while another execution is already in progress, that subprogram is said to be *reentrant*. A recursive subprogram must be reentrant. Reentrant subprograms are also useful in multi-threaded situations, since multiple threads can call the same subprogram without fear of interfering with each other. In the IBM CICS transaction processing system, *quasi-reentrant* was a slightly less restrictive, but similar, requirement for application programs that were shared by many threads.

In a multi-threaded environment, there is generally more than one stack. An environment that fully supports coroutines or lazy evaluation may use data structures other than stacks to store their activation records.

Overloading

In strongly typed languages, it is sometimes desirable to have a number of functions with the same name, but operating on different types of data, or with different parameter profiles. For example, a square root function might be defined to operate on reals, complex values or matrices. The algorithm to be used in each case is different, and the return result may be different. By writing three separate functions with the same name, the programmer has the convenience of not having to remember different names for each type of data. Further if a subtype can be defined for the reals, to separate positive and negative reals, two functions can be written for the reals, one to return a real when the parameter is positive, and another to return a complex value when the parameter is negative.

In object-oriented programming, when a series of functions with the same name can accept different parameter profiles or parameters of different types, each of the functions is said to be overloaded.

Here is an example of subroutine overloading in C++:

```cpp
#include <iostream>
double area(double h, double w) {

  return h * w;

}

double area(double r) {

  return r * r * 3.14;

}

int main() {

  double rectangle_area = area(3, 4);

  double circle_area = area(5);

  std::cout << "Area of a rectangle is " << rectangle_area << std::endl;

  std::cout << "Area of a circle is " << circle_area << std::endl;

  return 0;

}
```

In this code there are two functions of same name but they have different parameters.

As another example, a subroutine might construct an object that will accept directions, and trace its path to these points on screen. There are a plethora of parameters that could be passed in to the constructor (colour of the trace, starting x and y co-ordinates, trace speed). If the programmer wanted the constructor to be able to accept only the color parameter, then he could call another constructor that accepts only color, which in turn calls the constructor with all the parameters passing in a set of *default values* for all the other parameters (X and Y would generally be centered on screen or placed at the origin, and the speed would be set to another value of the coder's choosing).

Closures

A *closure* is a subprogram together with the values of some of its variables captured from the environment in which it was created. Closures were a notable feature of the Lisp programming language, introduced by John McCarthy. Depending on the implementation, closures can serve as a mechanism for side-effects.

Conventions

A wide number of conventions for the coding of subroutines have been developed. Pertaining to their naming, many developers have adopted the approach that the name of a subroutine should be a verb when it does a certain task, an adjective when it makes some inquiry, and a noun when it is used to substitute variables.

Some programmers suggest that a subroutine should perform only one task, and if a subroutine does perform more than one task, it should be split up into more subroutines. They argue that subroutines are key components in code maintenance, and their roles in the program must remain distinct.

Proponents of modular programming (modularizing code) advocate that each subroutine should have minimal dependency on other pieces of code. For example, the use of global variables is generally deemed unwise by advocates for this perspective, because it adds tight coupling between the subroutine and these global variables. If such coupling is not necessary, their advice is to refactor subroutines to accept passed parameters instead. However, increasing the number of parameters passed to subroutines can affect code readability.

Return Codes

Besides its *main* or *normal* effect, a subroutine may need to inform the calling program about *exceptional* conditions that may have occurred during its execution. In some languages and programming standards, this is often done through a *return code*, an integer value placed by the subroutine in some standard location, which encodes the normal and exceptional conditions.

In the IBM System/360, where a return code was expected from the subroutine, the return value was often designed to be a multiple of 4—so that it could be used as a direct branch table index into a branch table often located immediately after the call instruction to avoid extra conditional tests, further improving efficiency. In the System/360 assembly language, one would write, for example:

```
BAL 14,SUBRTN01  go to subroutine, storing return address in R14

   B  TABLE(15)     use returned value in reg 15 to index the branch
table,
```

```
*                          branching to the appropriate branch instr.
TABLE    B   OK            return code =00   GOOD              }
         B   BAD           return code =04   Invalid input      } Branch table
         B   ERROR         return code =08   Unexpected condition }
```

Optimization of Subroutine Calls

There is a significant runtime overhead in a calling a subroutine, including passing the arguments, branching to the subprogram, and branching back to the caller. The overhead often includes saving and restoring certain processor registers, allocating and reclaiming call frame storage, etc.. In some languages, each subroutine call also implies automatic testing of the subroutine's return code, or the handling of exceptions that it may raise. In object-oriented languages, a significant source of overhead is the intensively used dynamic dispatch for method calls.

There are some seemingly obvious optimizations of procedure calls that cannot be applied if the procedures may have side effects. For example, in the expression (f(x)-1)/(f(x)+1), the function f must be called twice, because the two calls may return different results. Moreover, the value of x must be fetched again before the second call, since the first call may have changed it. Determining whether a subprogram may have a side effect is very difficult (indeed, undecidable). So, while those optimizations are safe in purely functional programming languages, compilers of typical imperative programming usually have to assume the worst.

Inlining

A method used to eliminate this overhead is *inline expansion* or *inlining* of the subprogram's body at each call site (versus branching to the subroutine and back). Not only does this avoid the call overhead, but it also allows the compiler to optimize the procedure's *body* more effectively by taking into account the context and arguments at that call. The inserted body can be optimized by the compiler. Inlining however, will usually increase the code size, unless the program contains only one call to the subroutine, or the subroutine body is less code than the call overhead.

Block (Programming)

In computer programming, a block or code block is a lexical structure of source code which is grouped together. Blocks consist of one or more declarations and statements. A programming language that permits the creation of blocks, including blocks nested within other blocks, is called a block-structured programming language. Blocks are fundamental to structured programming, where control structures are formed from blocks.

The function of blocks in programming is to enable groups of statements to be treated as if they were one statement, and to narrow the lexical scope of variables, procedures and functions declared in a block so that they do not conflict with variables having the same name used elsewhere in a program for different purposes. In a block-structured programming language, the names of variables and other objects such as procedures which are declared in outer blocks are visible inside other inner blocks, unless they are shadowed by an object of the same name.

History

Ideas of block structure were developed in the 1950s during the development of the first autocodes, and were formalized in the Algol 58 and Algol 60 reports. Algol 58 introduced the notion of the "compound statement", which was related solely to control flow. The subsequent *Revised Report* which described the syntax and semantics of Algol 60 introduced the notion of a block and block scope, with a block consisting of " A sequence of declarations followed by a sequence of statements and enclosed between begin and end..." in which "every declaration appears in a block in this way and is valid only for that block."

Syntax

Blocks use different syntax in different languages. Two broad families are:

- The ALGOL family in which blocks are delimited by the keywords "begin" and "end"

- The C family in which blocks are delimited by curly braces - "{" and "}"

Some other techniques used are as follows :

- Parentheses - "(" and ")", as in batch language and ALGOL 68.

- Indentation, as in Python

- S-expressions with a syntactic keyword such as lambda or let (as in the Lisp family)

- In 1968 (with ALGOL 68), then in Edsger W. Dijkstra's 1974 Guarded Command Language the conditional and iterative code block are alternatively terminated with the block reserved word *reversed*: e.g. if ~ then ~ elif ~ else ~ fi, case ~ in ~ out ~ esac and for ~ while ~ do ~ od

Limitations

Some languages which support blocks with variable declarations do not fully support all declarations; for instance many C-derived languages do not permit a function definition within a block (nested functions). And unlike its ancestor Algol, Pascal does not support the use of blocks with their own declarations inside the begin and end of an existing block, only compound statements enabling sequences of statements to be grouped together in if, while, repeat and other control statements.

Basic Semantics

The semantic meaning of a block is twofold. Firstly, it provides the programmer with a way for creating arbitrarily large and complex structures that can be treated as units. Secondly, it enables the programmer to limit the scope of variables and sometimes other objects that have been declared.

In primitive languages such as early Fortran and BASIC, there were a few built-in statement types, and little or no means of extending them in a structured manner. For instance, until 1978 standard Fortran had no "block if" statement, so to write a standard-complying code to implement simple decisions the programmer had to resort to gotos:

```
C     LANGUAGE: ANSI STANDARD FORTRAN 66

C     INITIALIZE VALUES TO BE CALCULATED

      PAYSTX = .FALSE.

      PAYSST = .FALSE.

      TAX = 0.0

      SUPTAX = 0.0

C     SKIP TAX DEDUCTION IF EMPLOYEE EARNS LESS THAN TAX THRESHOLD

      IF (WAGES .LE. TAXTHR) GOTO 100

      PAYSTX = .TRUE.

      TAX = (WAGES - TAXTHR) * BASCRT

C     SKIP SUPERTAX DEDUCTION IF EMPLOYEE EARNS LESS THAN SUPERTAX
      THRESHOLD

      IF (WAGES .LE. SUPTHR) GOTO 100

      PAYSST = .TRUE.

      SUPTAX = (WAGES - SUPTHR) * SUPRAT

  100 TAXED = WAGES - TAX - SUPTAX
```

Even in this very brief Fortran fragment, written to the Fortran 66 standard, it is not easy to see the structure of the program, because that structure is not reflected in the language. Without careful study it is not easy to see the circumstances in which a given statement is executed.

Blocks allow the programmer to treat a group of statements as a unit, and the default values which had to appear in initialization in this style of programming can, with a block structure, be placed closer to the decision:

```pascal
{ Language: Jensen and Wirth Pascal }
 if wages > tax_threshold then
   begin
   paystax := true;
   tax := (wages - tax_threshold) * tax_rate
   { The block structure makes it easier to see how the code could
    be refactored for clarity, and also makes it easier to do,
   because the structure of the inner conditional can easily be moved
   out of the outer conditional altogether and the effects of doing
   so are easily predicted. }
   if wages > supertax_threshold then
     begin
     pays_supertax := true;
     supertax := (wages - supertax_threshold) * supertax_rate
     end
   else begin
     pays_supertax := false;
     supertax := 0
     end
   end
 else begin
   paystax := false; pays_supertax := false;
   tax := 0; supertax := 0
   end;
 taxed := wages - tax - supertax;
```

Use of blocks in the above fragment of Pascal enables the programmer to be clearer about what he or she intends, and to combine the resulting blocks into a nested hierarchy of conditional statements. The structure of the code reflects the programmer's thinking more closely, making it easier to understand and modify.

From looking at the above code the programmer can easily see that he or she can make the source code even clearer by taking the inner if statement out of the outer one altogether, placing the two blocks one after the other to be executed consecutively. Semantically there is little difference in this case, and the use of block structure, supported by indenting for readability, makes it easy for the programmer to refactor the code.

In primitive languages, variables had broad scope. For instance, an integer variable called IEMPNO might be used in one part of a Fortran subroutine to denote an employee social security number (ssn), but during maintenance work on the same subroutine, a programmer might accidentally use the same variable, IEMPNO, for a different purpose, and this could result in a bug that was difficult to trace. Block structure makes it easier for programmers to control scope to a minute level.

```
;; Language: R5RS Standard Scheme

(let ((empno (ssn-of employee-name)))

 (while (is-manager empno)

  (let ((employees (length (underlings-of empno))))

    (printf "~a has ~a employees working under him:~%" employee-name
employees)

    (for-each

    (lambda (empno)

    ;; Within this lambda expression the variable empno refers to the
ssn

    ;; of an underling. The variable empno in the outer expression,

    ;; referring to the manager's ssn, is shadowed.

    (printf "Name: ~a, role: ~a~%"

        (name-of empno)

        (role-of empno)))

    (underlings-of empno)))))
```

In the above Scheme fragment, empno is used to identify both the manager and his or her underlings each by their respective ssn, but because the underling ssn is declared within an inner block it does not interact with the variable of the same name that contains the manager's ssn. In practice, considerations of clarity would probably lead the programmer to choose distinct variable names, but he or she has the choice and it is more difficult to introduce a bug inadvertently.

Hoisting

In a few circumstances, code in a block is evaluated as if the code were actually at the top of the block or outside the block. This is often colloquially known as *hoisting*, and includes:

- Loop-invariant code motion, a compiler optimization where code in the loop that is invariant is evaluated before the loop;

- Variable hoisting, scope rule in JavaScript, where variables have function scope, and behave as if they were declared (but not defined) at the top of a function.

Structured Program Theorem

The structured program theorem, also called Böhm-Jacopini theorem, is a result in programming language theory. It states that a class of control flow graphs (historically called charts in this context) can compute any computable function if it combines subprograms in only three specific ways (control structures). These are

1. Executing one subprogram, and then another subprogram (sequence)

2. Executing one of two subprograms according to the value of a boolean expression (selection)

3. Executing a subprogram until a boolean expression is true (iteration)

The structured chart subject to these constraints may however use additional variables in the form of bits (stored in an extra integer variable in the original proof) in order to keep track of information that the original program represents by the program location. The construction was based on Böhm's programming language P''.

Origin and Variants

The theorem is typically credited to a 1966 paper by Corrado Böhm and Giuseppe Jacopini. David Harel wrote in 1980 that the Böhm–Jacopini paper enjoyed "universal popularity", particularly with proponents of structured programming. Harel also noted that "due to its rather technical style [the 1966 Böhm–Jacopini paper] is apparently more often cited than read in detail" and, after reviewing a large number of papers published up to 1980, Harel argued that the contents of the Böhm–Jacopini proof was usually misrepresented as a folk theorem that essentially contains a simpler result, a result which itself can be traced to the inception of modern computing theory in the papers of von Neumann and Kleene.

Harel also writes that the more generic name was proposed by H.D. Mills as "The Structure Theorem" in the early 1970s.

Single-while-loop, Folk Version of the Theorem

This version of the theorem replaces all the original program's control flow with a single global while loop that simulates a program counter going over all possible labels (flowchart boxes) in the original non-structured program. Harel traced the origin of this folk theorem to two papers marking the beginning of computing. One is the 1946 description of the von Neumann architecture, which explains how a program counter operates in terms of a while loop. Harel notes that the single loop used by the folk version of the structured programming theorem basically just provides operational semantics for the execution of a flowchart on a von Neumann computer. Another, even older source that Harel traced the folk version of the theorem is Stephen Kleene's normal form theorem from 1936.

Donald Knuth criticized this form of the proof, which results in pseudocode like the one below, by pointing out that the structure of the original program is completely lost in this transformation. Similarly, Bruce Ian Mills wrote about this approach that "The spirit of block structure is a style, not a language. By simulating a Von Neumann machine, we can produce the behavior of any spaghetti code within the confines of a block-structured language. This does not prevent it from being spaghetti."

```
p := 1;

while p > 0 do begin

 if p = 1 then begin

  perform step 1 from the flowchart;

  p := resulting successor step number of step 1 from the flowchart (0
if no successor);

 end;

 if p = 2 then begin

  perform step 2 from the flowchart;

  p := resulting successor step of step 2 from the flowchart (0 if no
successor);

 end;

 ...
```

```
if p = n then begin

 perform step n from the flowchart;

 p := resulting successor step of step n from the flowchart (0 if no
successor);

 end;

end.
```

Böhm and Jacopini's Proof

The proof in Böhm and Jacopini's paper proceeds by induction on the structure of the flow chart. Because it employed pattern matching in graphs, the proof of Böhm and Jacopini's was not really practical as a program transformation algorithm, and thus opened the door for additional research in this direction.

Implications and Refinements

The Böhm-Jacopini proof did not settle the question of whether to adopt structured programming for software development, partly because the construction was more likely to obscure a program than to improve it. On the contrary, it signalled the beginning of the debate. Edsger Dijkstra's famous letter, "Go To Statement Considered Harmful," followed in 1968.

Some academics took a purist approach to the Böhm-Jacopini result and argued that even instructions like `break` and `return` from the middle of loops are bad practice as they are not needed in the Böhm-Jacopini proof, and thus they advocated that all loops should have a single exit point. This purist approach is embodied in the Pascal programming language (designed in 1968–1969), which up to the mid-1990s was the preferred tool for teaching introductory programming classes in academia.

Edward Yourdon notes that in the 1970s there was even philosophical opposition to transforming unstructured programs into structured ones by automated means, based on the argument that one needed to think in structured programming fashion from the get go. The pragmatic counterpoint was that such transformations benefited a large body of existing programs. Among the first proposals for an automated transformation was a 1971 paper by Edward Ashcroft and Zohar Manna.

The direct application of the Böhm-Jacopini theorem may result in additional local variables being introduced in the structured chart, and may also result in some code duplication. The latter issue is called the loop and a half problem in this context. Pascal is affected by both of these problems and according to empirical studies cited by Eric S. Roberts, student programmers had difficulty formulating correct solutions in Pascal for several simple problems, including writing a function for searching an element in an array. A 1980 study by Henry Shapiro cited by Roberts found that using only the

Pascal-provided control structures, the correct solution was given by only 20% of the subjects, while no subject wrote incorrect code for this problem if allowed to write a return from the middle of a loop.

In 1973, S. Rao Kosaraju proved that it's possible to avoid adding additional variables in structured programming, as long as arbitrary-depth, multi-level breaks from loops are allowed. Furthermore, Kosaraju proved that a strict hierarchy of programs exists, nowadays called the *Kosaraju hierarchy*, in that for every integer n, there exists a program containing a multi-level break of depth n that cannot be rewritten as program with multi-level breaks of depth less than n (without introducing additional variables). Kosaraju cites the multi-level break construct to the BLISS programming language. The multi-level breaks, in the form a leave *label* keyword were actually introduced in the BLISS-11 version of that language; the original BLISS only had single-level breaks. The BLISS family of languages didn't provide an unrestricted goto. The Java programming language would later follow this approach as well.

A simpler result from Kosaraju's paper is that a program is reducible to a structured program (without adding variables) if and only if it does not contain a loop with two distinct exits. Reducibility was defined by Kosaraju, loosely speaking, as computing the same function and using the same "primitive actions" and predicates as the original program, but possibly using different control flow structures. (This is a narrower notion of reducibility than what Böhm-Jacopini used.) Inspired by this result, in section VI of his highly-cited paper that introduced the notion of cyclomatic complexity, Thomas J. McCabe described an analogue of Kuratowski's theorem for the control flow graphs (CFG) of non-structured programs, which is to say, the minimal subgraphs that make the CFG of a program non-structured. These subgraphs have a very good description in natural language. They are:

1. Branching out of a loop (other than from the loop cycle test)

2. Branching into a loop

3. Branching into a decision (i.e. into an if "branch")

4. Branching out of a decision

McCabe actually found that these four graphs are not independent when appearing as subgraphs, meaning that a necessary and sufficient condition for a program to be non-structured is for its CFG to have as subgraph one of any subset of three of these four graphs. He also found that if a non-structured program contains one of these four sub-graphs, it must contain another distinct one from the set of four. This latter result helps explain how the control flow of non-structured program becomes entangled in what is popularly called "spaghetti code". McCabe also devised a numerical measure that, given an arbitrary program, quantifies how far off it is from the ideal of being a structured program; McCabe called his measure essential complexity.

McCabe's characterization of the forbidden graphs for structured programming can be considered incomplete, at least if the Dijkstra's D structures are considered the building blocks.

Up to 1990 there were quite a few proposed methods for eliminating gotos from existing program, while preserving most of their structure. The various approaches to this problem also proposed several notions of equivalence, which are stricter than simply Turing equivalence, in order to avoid output like the folk theorem discussed above. The strictness of the chosen notion of equivalence dictates the minimal set of control flow structures needed. The 1988 JACM paper by Lyle Ramshaw surveys the field up to that point, as well proposing its own method. Ramshaw's algorithm was used for example in some Java decompilers because the Java virtual machine code has branch instructions with targets expressed as offsets, but the high-level Java language only has multi-level break and continue statements. Ammarguellat (1992) proposed a transformation method that goes back to enforcing single-exit.

Application to Cobol

In the 1980s IBM researcher Harlan Mills oversaw the development of the COBOL Structuring Facility, which applied a structuring algorithm to COBOL code. Mills's transformation involved the following steps for each procedure.

1. Identify the basic blocks in the procedure.

2. Assign a unique label to each block's entry path, and label each block's exit paths with the labels of the entry paths they connect to. Use 0 for return from the procedure and 1 for the procedure's entry path.

3. Break the procedure into its basic blocks.

4. For each block that is the destination of only one exit path, reconnect that block to that exit path.

5. Declare a new variable in the procedure (called L for reference).

6. On each remaining unconnected exit path, add a statement that sets L to the label value on that path.

7. Combine the resulting programs into a selection statement that executes the program with the entry path label indicated by L

8. Construct a loop that executes this selection statement as long as L is not 0.

9. Construct a sequence that initializes L to 1 and executes the loop.

Note that this construction can be improved by converting some cases of the selection statement into subprocedures.

References

- "DAMP 2009: Workshop on Declarative Aspects of Multicore Programming". Cse.unsw.edu.au. 2009-01-20. Retrieved 2013-08-15

- R.M. Burstall and J. Darlington. A transformation system for developing recursive programs. Journal of the Association for Computing Machinery 24(1):44–67 (1977)

- Ross, Doug. "The first software engineering language". LCS/AI Lab Timeline:. MIT Computer Science and Artificial Intelligence Laboratory. Retrieved 13 May 2010

- Chambers, John M. (1998). Programming with Data: A Guide to the S Language. Springer Verlag. pp. 67–70. ISBN 978-0-387-98503-9

- Michael A. Covington (2010-08-23). "CSCI/ARTI 4540/6540: First Lecture on Symbolic Programming and LISP" (PDF). University of Georgia. Retrieved 2013-11-20

- Turner, D.A. (2004-07-28). "Total Functional Programming". Journal of Universal Computer Science. 10 (7): 751–768. doi:10.3217/jucs-010-07-0751

- Dahl, Ole Johan (2004). "The Birth of Object Orientation: the Simula Languages" (PDF). doi:10.1007/978-3-540-39993-3_3. Retrieved 9 June 2016

- Larry C. Paulson (28 June 1996). ML for the Working Programmer. Cambridge University Press. ISBN 978-0-521-56543-1. Retrieved 10 February 2013

- Peter Van Roy (2009-05-12). "Programming Paradigms for Dummies: What Every Programmer Should Know" (PDF). info.ucl.ac.be. Retrieved 2014-01-27

- Kindler, E.; Krivy, I. (2011). "Object-Oriented Simulation of systems with sophisticated control". International Journal of General Systems: 313–343

- Odersky, Martin; Spoon, Lex; Venners, Bill (December 13, 2010). Programming in Scala: A Comprehensive Step-by-step Guide (2nd ed.). Artima Inc. pp. 883/852. ISBN 978-0-9815316-4-9

- "The useR! 2006 conference schedule includes papers on the commercial use of R". R-project. org. 2006-06-08. Retrieved 2011-06-20

- Williams, M. H. (1983). "Flowchart Schemata and the Problem of Nomenclature". The Computer Journal. 26 (3): 270–276. doi:10.1093/comjnl/26.3.270

- Lewis, John; Loftus, William (2008). Java Software Solutions Foundations of Programming Design 6th ed. Pearson Education Inc. ISBN 0-321-53205-8

- Armstrong, Joe (June 2007). A history of Erlang. Third ACM SIGPLAN Conference on History of Programming Languages. San Diego, California. Retrieved 2009-08-29

- Ramshaw, L. (1988). "Eliminating go to's while preserving program structure". Journal of the ACM. 35 (4): 893–920. doi:10.1145/48014.48021

- John C. Mitchell, Concepts in programming languages, Cambridge University Press, 2003, ISBN 0-521-78098-5, p.278

- Dimitre Novatchev. "The Functional Programming Language XSLT — A proof through examples". TopXML. Retrieved May 27, 2006

4

User Interface and Design

User interface is the area where interactions between humans and machines take place. Ease of use, ease of access and error prevention are some of the essential features of user interface design. User interface design helps create a design that keeps these aspects in focus while maximizing user-friendliness. The chapter closely examines the key concepts of user interface and its design to provide an extensive understanding of the subject.

User Interface

Example of a tangible user interface

The user interface (UI), in the industrial design field of human–computer interaction, is the space where interactions between humans and machines occur. The goal of this interaction is to allow effective operation and control of the machine from the human end, whilst the machine simultaneously feeds back information that aids the operators' decision-making process. Examples of this broad concept of user interfaces include the interactive aspects of computer operating systems, hand tools, heavy machinery operator controls, and process controls. The design considerations applicable when creating user interfaces are related to or involve such disciplines as ergonomics and psychology.

Generally, the goal of user interface design is to produce a user interface which makes it easy (self-explanatory), efficient, and enjoyable (user-friendly) to operate a machine in the way which produces the desired result. This generally means that the operator needs to provide minimal input to achieve the desired output, and also that the machine minimizes undesired outputs to the human.

With the increased use of personal computers and the relative decline in societal awareness of heavy machinery, the term user interface is generally assumed to mean the graphical user interface, while industrial control panel and machinery control design discussions more commonly refer to human-machine interfaces.

Other terms for user interface are man–machine interface (MMI) and when the machine in question is a computer human–computer interface.

Overview

A graphical user interface following the desktop metaphor.

The user interface or *human–machine interface* is the part of the machine that handles the human–machine interaction. Membrane switches, rubber keypads and touchscreens are examples of the physical part of the Human Machine Interface which we can see and touch.

In complex systems, the human–machine interface is typically computerized. The term *human–computer interface* refers to this kind of system. In the context of computing the term typically extends as well to the software dedicated to control the physical elements used for human-computer interaction.

The engineering of the human–machine interfaces is enhanced by considering ergonomics (human factors). The corresponding disciplines are human factors engineering (HFE) and usability engineering (UE), which is part of systems engineering.

Tools used for incorporating human factors in the interface design are developed based on knowledge of computer science, such as computer graphics, operating systems, programming languages. Nowadays, we use the expression graphical user interface for human–machine interface on computers, as nearly all of them are now using graphics.

Terminology

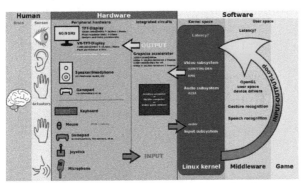

A human–machine interface usually involves peripheral hardware for the INPUT and for the OUTPUT. Often, there is an additional component implemented in software, like e.g. a graphical user interface.

There is a difference between a user interface and an operator interface or a human–machine interface (HMI).

- The term "user interface" is often used in the context of (personal) computer systems and electronic devices.

    o Where a network of equipment or computers are interlinked through an MES (Manufacturing Execution System)-or Host to display information.

    o A human-machine interface (HMI) is typically local to one machine or piece of equipment, and is the interface method between the human and the equipment/machine. An operator interface is the interface method by which multiple equipment that are linked by a host control system is accessed or controlled.

    o The system may expose several user interfaces to serve different kinds of users. For example, a computerized library database might provide two user interfaces, one for library patrons (limited set of functions, optimized for ease of use) and the other for library personnel (wide set of functions, optimized for efficiency).

- The user interface of a mechanical system, a vehicle or an industrial installation is sometimes referred to as the human–machine interface (HMI). HMI is a modification of the original term MMI (man-machine interface). In practice, the abbreviation MMI is still frequently used although some may claim that MMI stands for something different now. Another abbreviation is HCI, but is more commonly used for human–computer interaction. Other terms used are operator interface console (OIC) and operator interface terminal (OIT). However it is abbreviated, the terms refer to the 'layer' that separates a human that is operating a machine from the machine itself. Without a clean and usable interface, humans would not be able to interact with information systems.

In science fiction, HMI is sometimes used to refer to what is better described as direct neural interface. However, this latter usage is seeing increasing application in the real-life use of (medical) prostheses—the artificial extension that replaces a missing body part (e.g., cochlear implants).

In some circumstances, computers might observe the user and react according to their actions without specific commands. A means of tracking parts of the body is required, and sensors noting the position of the head, direction of gaze and so on have been used experimentally. This is particularly relevant to immersive interfaces.

History

The history of user interfaces can be divided into the following phases according to the dominant type of user interface:

1945–1968: Batch Interface

IBM 029

In the batch era, computing power was extremely scarce and expensive. User interfaces were rudimentary. Users had to accommodate computers rather than the other way around; user interfaces were considered overhead, and software was designed to keep the processor at maximum utilization with as little overhead as possible.

The input side of the user interfaces for batch machines were mainly punched cards or equivalent media like paper tape. The output side added line printers to these media. With the limited exception of the system operator's console, human beings did not interact with batch machines in real time at all.

Submitting a job to a batch machine involved, first, preparing a deck of punched cards describing a program and a dataset. Punching the program cards wasn't done on the computer itself, but on keypunches, specialized typewriter-like machines that were notoriously balky, unforgiving, and prone to mechanical failure. The software interface was similarly unforgiving, with very strict syntaxes meant to be parsed by the smallest possible compilers and interpreters.

Holes are punched in the card according to a prearranged code transferring the facts from the census questionnaire into statistics

Once the cards were punched, one would drop them in a job queue and wait. Eventually. operators would feed the deck to the computer, perhaps mounting magnetic tapes to supply another dataset or helper software. The job would generate a printout, containing final results or (all too often) an abort notice with an attached error log. Successful runs might also write a result on magnetic tape or generate some data cards to be used in later computation.

The turnaround time for a single job often spanned entire days. If one were very lucky, it might be hours; real-time response was unheard of. But there were worse fates than the card queue; some computers actually required an even more tedious and error-prone process of toggling in programs in binary code using console switches. The very earliest machines actually had to be partly rewired to incorporate program logic into themselves, using devices known as plugboards.

Early batch systems gave the currently running job the entire computer; program decks and tapes had to include what we would now think of as operating system code to talk to I/O devices and do whatever other housekeeping was needed. Midway through the batch period, after 1957, various groups began to experiment with so-called "load-and-go" systems. These used a monitor program which was always resident on the computer. Programs could call the monitor for services. Another function of the monitor was to do better error checking on submitted jobs, catching errors earlier and more intelligently and generating more useful feedback to the users. Thus, monitors represented a first step towards both operating systems and explicitly designed user interfaces.

1969–present: Command-line user Interface

Command-line interfaces (CLIs) evolved from batch monitors connected to the system console. Their interaction model was a series of request-response transactions, with requests expressed as textual commands in a specialized vocabulary. Latency was far lower than for batch systems, dropping from days or hours to seconds. Accordingly, command-line systems allowed the user to change his or her mind about later stages of the transaction in response to real-time or near-real-time feedback on earlier results.

Software could be exploratory and interactive in ways not possible before. But these interfaces still placed a relatively heavy mnemonic load on the user, requiring a serious investment of effort and learning time to master.

Teletype Model 33 ASR

The earliest command-line systems combined teleprinters with computers, adapting a mature technology that had proven effective for mediating the transfer of information over wires between human beings. Teleprinters had originally been invented as devices for automatic telegraph transmission and reception; they had a history going back to 1902 and had already become well-established in newsrooms and elsewhere by 1920. In reusing them, economy was certainly a consideration, but psychology and the Rule of Least Surprise mattered as well; teleprinters provided a point of interface with the system that was familiar to many engineers and users.

DEC VT100 terminal

The widespread adoption of video-display terminals (VDTs) in the mid-1970s ushered in the second phase of command-line systems. These cut latency further, because characters could be thrown on the phosphor dots of a screen more quickly than a printer head or carriage can move. They helped quell conservative resistance to interactive programming by cutting ink and paper consumables out of the cost picture, and were to the first TV generation of the late 1950s and 60s even more iconic and comfortable than teleprinters had been to the computer pioneers of the 1940s.

Just as importantly, the existence of an accessible screen — a two-dimensional display of text that could be rapidly and reversibly modified — made it economical for software designers to deploy interfaces that could be described as visual rather than textual. The pioneering applications of this kind were computer games and text editors; close descendants of some of the earliest specimens, such as rogue(6), and vi(1), are still a live part of Unix tradition.

1985: SAA user Interface or Text-Based user Interface

In 1985, with the beginning of Microsoft Windows and other graphical user interfaces, IBM created what is called the Systems Application Architecture (SAA) standard which include the Common User Access (CUA) derivative. CUA successfully created what we know and use today in Windows, and most of the more recent DOS or Windows Console Applications will use that standard as well.

This defined that a pulldown menu system should be at the top of the screen, status bar at the bottom, shortcut keys should stay the same for all common functionality (F2 to Open for example would work in all applications that followed the SAA standard). This greatly helped the speed at which users could learn an application so it caught on quick and became an industry standard.

1968–present: Graphical user Interface

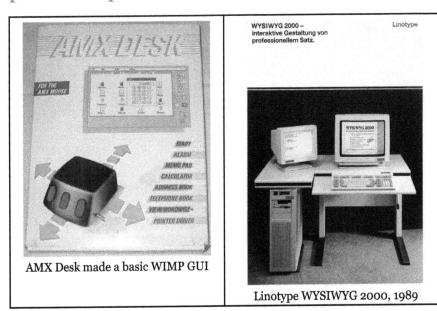

AMX Desk made a basic WIMP GUI

Linotype WYSIWYG 2000, 1989

- 1968 – Douglas Engelbart demonstrated NLS, a system which uses a mouse, pointers, hypertext, and multiple windows.

- 1970 – Researchers at Xerox Palo Alto Research Center (many from SRI) develop WIMP paradigm (Windows, Icons, Menus, Pointers)

- 1973 – Xerox Alto: commercial failure due to expense, poor user interface, and lack of programs

- 1979 – Steve Jobs and other Apple engineers visit Xerox. Pirates of Silicon Valley dramatizes the events, but Apple had already been working on the GUI before the visit

- 1981 – Xerox Star: focus on WYSIWYG. Commercial failure (25K sold) due to cost ($16K each), performance (minutes to save a file, couple of hours to recover from crash), and poor marketing

- 1984 – Apple Macintosh popularizes the GUI. Super Bowl commercial shown once, most expensive ever made at that time

- 1984 – MIT's X Window System: hardware-independent platform and networking protocol for developing GUIs on UNIX-like systems

- 1985 – Windows 1.0 – provided GUI interface to MS-DOS. No overlapping windows (tiled instead).

- 1985 – Microsoft and IBM start work on OS/2 meant to eventually replace MS-DOS and Windows

- 1986 – Apple threatens to sue Digital Research because their GUI desktop looked too much like Apple's Mac.

- 1987 – Windows 2.0 – Overlapping and resizable windows, keyboard and mouse enhancements

- 1987 – Macintosh II: first full-color Mac

- 1988 – OS/2 1.10 Standard Edition (SE) has GUI written by Microsoft, looks a lot like Windows 2

Interface Design

Primary methods used in the interface design include prototyping and simulation.

Typical human–machine interface design consists of the following stages: interaction specification, interface software specification and prototyping:

- Common practices for interaction specification include user-centered design, persona, activity-oriented design, scenario-based design, resiliency design.

- Common practices for interface software specification include use cases, constrain enforcement by interaction protocols (intended to avoid use errors).

- Common practices for prototyping are based on interactive design based on libraries of interface elements (controls, decoration, etc.).

Quality

All great interfaces share eight qualities or characteristics:

1. Clarity: The interface avoids ambiguity by making everything clear through language, flow, hierarchy and metaphors for visual elements.

2. Concision: It's easy to make the interface clear by over-clarifying and labeling everything, but this leads to interface bloat, where there is just too much stuff on the screen at the same time. If too many things are on the screen, finding what you're looking for is difficult, and so the interface becomes tedious to use. The real challenge in making a great interface is to make it concise and clear at the same time.

3. Familiarity: Even if someone uses an interface for the first time, certain elements can still be familiar. Real-life metaphors can be used to communicate meaning.

4. Responsiveness: A good interface should not feel sluggish. This means that the interface should provide good feedback to the user about what's happening and whether the user's input is being successfully processed.

5. Consistency: Keeping your interface consistent across your application is important because it allows users to recognize usage patterns.

6. Aesthetics: While you don't need to make an interface attractive for it to do its job, making something look good will make the time your users spend using your application more enjoyable; and happier users can only be a good thing.

7. Efficiency: Time is money, and a great interface should make the user more productive through shortcuts and good design.

8. Forgiveness: A good interface should not punish users for their mistakes but should instead provide the means to remedy them.

Principle of Least Astonishment

The principle of least astonishment (POLA) is a general principle in the design of all kinds of interfaces. It is based on the idea that human beings can only pay full attention to one thing at one time, leading to the conclusion that novelty should be minimized.

Habit Formation

If an interface is used persistently, the user will unavoidably develop habits for using the interface. The designer's role can thus be characterized as ensuring the user forms good habits. If the designer is experienced with other interfaces, they will similarly develop habits, and often make unconscious assumptions regarding how the user will interact with the interface.

Types

HP Series 100 HP-150 Touchscreen

- Direct manipulation interface is the name of a general class of user interfaces that allow users to manipulate objects presented to them, using actions that correspond at least loosely to the physical world.

- Graphical user interfaces (GUI) accept input via devices such as a computer keyboard and mouse and provide articulated graphical output on the computer monitor. There are at least two different principles widely used in GUI design: Object-oriented user interfaces (OOUIs) and application oriented interfaces.

- Web-based user interfaces or web user interfaces (WUI) that accept input and provide output by generating web pages which are transmitted via the Internet and viewed by the user using a web browser program. Newer implementations utilize PHP, Java, JavaScript, AJAX, Apache Flex, .NET Framework, or similar technologies to provide real-time control in a separate program, eliminating the need to refresh a traditional HTML based web browser. Administrative web interfaces for web-servers, servers and networked computers are often called control panels.

- Touchscreens are displays that accept input by touch of fingers or a stylus. Used in a growing amount of mobile devices and many types of point of sale, industrial processes and machines, self-service machines etc.

- Command line interfaces, where the user provides the input by typing a command string with the computer keyboard and the system provides output by printing text on the computer monitor. Used by programmers and system administrators, in engineering and scientific environments, and by technically advanced personal computer users.

- Touch user interface are graphical user interfaces using a touchpad or touch-screen display as a combined input and output device. They supplement or replace other forms of output with haptic feedback methods. Used in computerized simulators etc.

- Hardware interfaces are the physical, spatial interfaces found on products in the real world from toasters, to car dashboards, to airplane cockpits. They are generally a mixture of knobs, buttons, sliders, switches, and touchscreens.

- Attentive user interfaces manage the user attention deciding when to interrupt the user, the kind of warnings, and the level of detail of the messages presented to the user.

- Batch interfaces are non-interactive user interfaces, where the user specifies all the details of the *batch job* in advance to batch processing, and receives the output when all the processing is done. The computer does not prompt for further input after the processing has started.

- Conversational interfaces enable users to command the computer with plain text English (e.g., via text messages, or chatbots) or voice commands, instead of graphic elements. These interfaces often emulate human-to-human conversations.

- Conversational interface agents attempt to personify the computer interface in the form of an animated person, robot, or other character (such as Microsoft's Clippy the paperclip), and present interactions in a conversational form.

- Crossing-based interfaces are graphical user interfaces in which the primary task consists in crossing boundaries instead of pointing.

- Gesture interfaces are graphical user interfaces which accept input in a form of hand gestures, or mouse gestures sketched with a computer mouse or a stylus.

- Holographic user interfaces provide input to electronic or electro-mechanical devices by passing a finger through reproduced holographic images of what would otherwise be tactile controls of those devices, floating freely in the air, detected by a wave source and without tactile interaction.

- Intelligent user interfaces are human-machine interfaces that aim to improve the efficiency, effectiveness, and naturalness of human-machine interaction by representing, reasoning, and acting on models of the user, domain, task, discourse, and media (e.g., graphics, natural language, gesture).

- Motion tracking interfaces monitor the user's body motions and translate them into commands, currently being developed by Apple.

- Multi-screen interfaces, employ multiple displays to provide a more flexible interaction. This is often employed in computer game interaction in both the commercial arcades and more recently the handheld markets.

- Non-command user interfaces, which observe the user to infer his / her needs and intentions, without requiring that he / she formulate explicit commands.

- Object-oriented user interfaces (OOUI) are based on object-oriented programming metaphors, allowing users to manipulate simulated objects and their properties.

- Reflexive user interfaces where the users control and redefine the entire system via the user interface alone, for instance to change its command verbs. Typically this is only possible with very rich graphic user interfaces.

- Search interface is how the search box of a site is displayed, as well as the visual representation of the search results.

- Tangible user interfaces, which place a greater emphasis on touch and physical environment or its element.

- Task-focused interfaces are user interfaces which address the information overload problem of the desktop metaphor by making tasks, not files, the primary unit of interaction.

- Text-based user interfaces are user interfaces which output a text. TUIs can either contain a command-line interface or a text-based WIMP environment.

- Voice user interfaces, which accept input and provide output by generating voice prompts. The user input is made by pressing keys or buttons, or responding verbally to the interface.

- Natural-language interfaces – Used for search engines and on webpages. User types in a question and waits for a response.

- Zero-input interfaces get inputs from a set of sensors instead of querying the user with input dialogs.

- Zooming user interfaces are graphical user interfaces in which information objects are represented at different levels of scale and detail, and where the user can change the scale of the viewed area in order.

Types of user interfaces

User interfaces can be classified into the following three categories:

- Command language based interfaces

- Menu-based interfaces

- Direct manipulation interfaces

Command Language-based Interface

A command language-based interface – as the name itself suggests, is based on design-ing a command language which the user can use to issue the commands. The user is expected to frame the appropriate commands in the language and type them in appro-priately whenever required. A simple command language-based interface might sim-ply assign unique names to the different commands. However, a more sophisticated command language-based interface may allow users to compose complex commands by using a set of primitive commands. Such a facility to compose commands dramat-ically reduces the number of command names one would have to remember. Thus, a command language-based interface can be made concise requiring minimal typing by the user. Command language-based interfaces allow fast interaction with the computer and simplify the input of complex commands.

Menu-based Interface

An important advantage of a menu-based interface over a command language-based interface is that a menu-based interface does not require the users to remember the exact syntax of the commands. A menu-based interface is based on recognition of the command names, rather than recollection. Further, in a menu-based interface the typ-ing effort is minimal as most interactions are carried out through menu selections us-ing a pointing device. This factor is an important consideration for the occasional user who cannot type fast.

However, experienced users find a menu-based user interface to be slower than a com-mand language-based interface because an experienced user can type fast and can get speed advantage by composing different primitive commands to express complex com-mands. Composing commands in a menu-based interface is not possible. This is be-cause of the fact that actions involving logical connectives (and, or, etc.) are awkward to specify in a menu-based system. Also, if the number of choices is large, it is difficult to select from the menu. In fact, a major challenge in the design of a menu-based interface is to structure large number of menu choices into manageable forms.

Direct Manipulation Interfaces

Direct manipulation interfaces present the interface to the user in the form of visual models (i.e. icons or objects). For this reason, direct manipulation interfaces are some-times called as iconic interface. In this type of interface, the user issues commands by performing actions on the visual representations of the objects, e.g. pull an icon rep-resenting a file into an icon representing a trash box, for deleting the file. Important advantages of iconic interfaces include the fact that the icons can be recognized by the users very easily, and that icons are language-independent. However, direct manipula-tion interfaces can be considered slow for experienced users. Also, it is difficult to give complex commands using a direct manipulation interface. For example, if one has to drag an icon representing the file to a trash box icon for deleting a file, then in order to delete all the files in the directory one has to perform this operation individually for all files – which could be very easily done by issuing a command like delete *.*.

Menu-based Interfaces

When the menu choices are large, they can be structured as the following way:

Scrolling Menu

When a full choice list can not be displayed within the menu area, scrolling of the menu items is required. This would enable the user to view and select the menu items that cannot be accommodated on the screen. However, in a scrolling menu all the commands should be highly correlated, so that the user can easily locate a command that he needs. This is important since the user cannot see all the commands at any one time. An example situation where a scrolling menu is frequently used is font size selection in a document processor. Here, the user knows that the command list contains only the font sizes that are arranged in some order and he can scroll up and down to find the size he is looking for. However, if the commands do not have any definite ordering relation, then the user would have to in the worst case, scroll through all the commands to find the exact command he is looking for, making this organization inefficient.

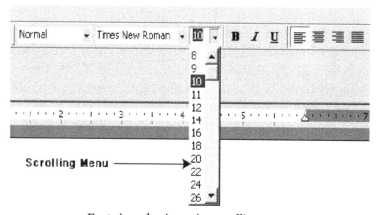

Font size selection using scrolling menu

Walking Menu

Walking menu is very commonly used to structure a large collection of menu items. In this technique, when a menu item is selected, it causes further menu items to be displayed adjacent to it in a sub-menu. An example of a walking menu is shown in figure. A walking menu can successfully be used to structure commands only if there are tens rather than hundreds of choices since each adjacently displayed menu does take up screen space and the total screen area is after limited.

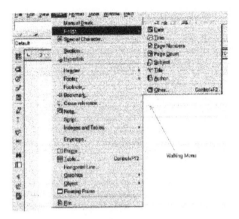

Example of walking menu

Hierarchical Menu

In this technique, the menu items are organized in a hierarchy or tree structure. Selecting a menu item causes the current menu display to be replaced by an appropriate sub-menu. Thus in this case, one can consider the menu and its various sub-menus to form a hierarchical tree-like structure. Walking menu can be considered to be a form of hierarchical menu which is practicable when the tree is shallow. Hierarchical menu can be used to manage large number of choices, but the users are likely to face navigational problems because they might lose track of where they are in the menu tree. This probably is the main reason why this type of interface is very rarely used.

Characteristics of Command Language-based Interface

Characteristics of command language-based interface have been discussed earlier.

Disadvantages of Command Language-based Interface

Command language-based interfaces suffer from several drawbacks. Usually, command language-based interfaces are difficult to learn and require the user to memorize the set of primitive commands. Also, most users make errors while formulating commands in the command language and also while typing them in. Further, in a command language-based interface, all interactions with the system is through a key-board and can not take advantage of effective interaction devices such as a mouse. Obviously, for casual and inexperienced users, command language-based interfaces are not suitable.

Issues in Designing a Command Language-based Interface

Two overbearing command design issues are to reduce the number of primitive commands that a user has to remember and to minimize the total typing required while issuing commands. These can be elaborated as follows:

- The designer has to decide what mnemonics are to be used for the different commands. The designer should try to develop meaningful mnemonics and yet be concise to minimize the amount of typing required. For example, the shortest mnemonic should be assigned to the most frequently used commands.

- The designer has to decide whether the users will be allowed to redefine the command names to suit their own preferences. Letting a user define his own mnemonics for various commands is a useful feature, but it increases the complexity of user interface development.

- The designer has to decide whether it should be possible to compose primitive commands to form more complex commands. A sophisticated command composition facility would require the syntax and semantics of the various command composition options to be clearly and unambiguously specified. The ability to combine commands is a powerful facility in the hands of experienced users, but quite unnecessary for inexperienced users.

Types of Menus and their Features

Three main types of menus are scrolling menu, walking menu, and hierarchical menu. The features of scrolling menu, walking menu, and hierarchical menu have been discussed earlier.

Iconic Interface

Direct manipulation interfaces present the interface to the user in the form of visual models (i.e. icons or objects). For this reason, direct manipulation interfaces are sometimes called iconic interfaces. In this type of interface, the user issues commands by performing actions on the visual representations of the objects, e.g. pull an icon representing a file into an icon representing a trash box, for deleting the file.

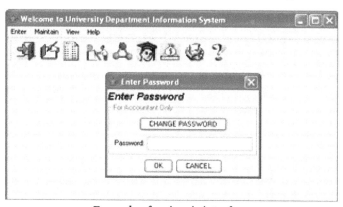

Example of an iconic interface

Figure shows an iconic interface. Here, the user is presented with a set of icons at the top of the frame for performing various activities. On clicking on any of the icons, either the user is prompted with a sub menu or the desired activity is performed.

Component-based GUI Development

A development style based on widgets (window objects) is called component- based (or widget-based) GUI development style. There are several important advantages of using a widget-based design style. One of the most important reasons to use widgets as building blocks is because they help users learn an interface fast. In this style of development, the user interfaces for different applications are built from the same basic components. Therefore, the user can extend his knowledge of the behavior of the standard components from one application to the other. Also, the component-based user interface development style reduces the application programmer's work significantly as he is more of a user interface component integrator than a programmer in the traditional sense.

Need for Component-based GUI Development

The current style of user interface development is component-based. It recognizes that every user interface can easily be built from a handful of predefined components such as menus, dialog boxes, forms, etc. Besides the standard components, and the facilities to create good interfaces from them, one of the basic support available to the user interface developers is the window system. The window system lets the application programmer create and manipulate windows without having to write the basic windowing functions.

Command-line Interface

Screenshot of a sample bash session in GNOME Terminal 3, Fedora 15

Screenshot of Windows PowerShell 1.0, running on Windows Vista

A command-line user interface (CLI), also known as a console user interface, and character user interface (CUI), is a means of interacting with a computer program where the user (or client) issues commands to the program in the form of successive lines of text (command lines). A program which handles the interface is called a command language interpreter or shell.

The CLI was the primary means of interaction with most computer systems until the introduction of the video display terminal in the mid-1960s, and continued to be used throughout the 1970s and 1980s on OpenVMS, Unix systems and personal computer systems including MS-DOS, CP/M and Apple DOS. The interface is usually implemented with a command line shell, which is a program that accepts commands as text input and converts commands into appropriate operating system functions.

Command-line interfaces to computer operating systems are less widely used by casual computer users, who favor graphical user interfaces or menu-driven interaction.

Alternatives to the command line include, but are not limited to text user interface menus, keyboard shortcuts, and various other desktop metaphors centered on the pointer (usually controlled with a mouse). Examples of this include the Windows versions 1, 2, 3, 3.1, and 3.11 (an OS shell that runs in DOS), DosShell, and Mouse Systems PowerPanel.

Command-line interfaces are often preferred by more advanced computer users, as they often provide a more concise and powerful means to control a program or operating system.

Programs with command-line interfaces are generally easier to automate via scripting.

Command line interfaces for software other than operating systems include a number of programming languages such as Tcl/Tk, PHP and others, as well as utilities such as the compression utilities WinZip and UltimateZip, and some FTP and ssh/telnet clients.

Advantages

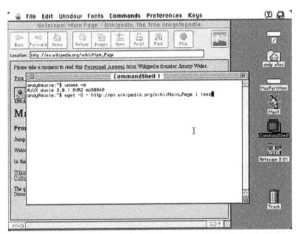

Screenshot of Apple Computer's CommandShell in A/UX 3.0.1

- Requires fewer resources
- Concise access to options
- *Expert*-friendly
- Easier to automate via scripting or batch files
- Commands can be logged to review or repeat
- Easy to add special sub-options
- Shorter to show multi-step actions

Disadvantages

- Requires help guide for commands
- Commands can foster complex options
- Not visually rich, results might scroll off-screen
- *Beginner*-unfriendly

Operating System Command-line Interfaces

Operating system (OS) command line interfaces are usually distinct programs supplied with the operating system.

A program that implements such a text interface is often called a command-line interpreter, command processor or shell.

Examples of command-line interpreters include DEC's DIGITAL Command Language (DCL) in OpenVMS and RSX-11, the various Unix shells (sh, ksh, csh, tcsh, bash, etc.), the historical CP/M CCP, and MS-DOS/IBM-DOS/DR-DOS's COMMAND.COM, as well as the OS/2 and the Windows CMD.EXE programs, the latter groups being based heavily on DEC's RSX-11 and RSTS CLIs. Under most operating systems, it is possible to replace the default shell program with alternatives; examples include 4DOS for DOS, 4OS2 for OS/2, and 4NT or Take Command for Windows.

Although the term 'shell' is often used to describe a command-line interpreter, strictly speaking a 'shell' can be any program that constitutes the user-interface, including fully graphically oriented ones. For example, the default Windows GUI is a shell program named EXPLORER.EXE, as defined in the SHELL=EXPLORER.EXE line in the WIN. INI configuration file. These programs are shells, but not CLIs.

Application Command-line Interfaces

Application programs (as opposed to operating systems) may also have command line interfaces.

An application program may support none, any, or all of these three major types of command line interface mechanisms:

1. Parameters: Most operating systems support a means to pass additional information to a program when it is launched. When a program is launched from an OS command line shell, additional text provided along with the program name is passed to the launched program.

2. Interactive command line sessions: After launch, a program may provide an operator with an independent means to enter commands in the form of text.

3. OS inter-process communication: Most operating systems support means of inter-process communication (for example; standard streams or named pipes). Command lines from client processes may be redirected to a CLI program by one of these methods.

CLI Software

Some applications support only a CLI, presenting a CLI prompt to the user and acting upon command lines as they are entered. Some examples of CLI-only applications are:

- DEBUG

- Diskpart

- Ed

- Edlin

- Fdisk

- Ping

Hybrid Software

Some computer programs support both a CLI and a GUI. In some cases, a GUI is simply a wrapper around a separate CLI executable file. In other cases, a program may provide a CLI as an optional alternative to its GUI. CLIs and GUIs often support different functionality. For example, all features of MATLAB, a numerical analysis computer program, are available via the CLI, whereas the MATLAB GUI exposes only a subset of features.

The early Sierra games, like the first three King's Quest games (1984–1986), used commands from an internal command line to move the character around in the graphic window.

History

The command-line interface evolved from a form of dialog once conducted by humans over teleprinter (TTY) machines, in which human operators remotely exchanged information, usually one line of text at a time. Early computer systems often used teleprinter machines as the means of interaction with a human operator. The computer became one end of the human-to-human teleprinter model. So instead of a human communicating with another human over a teleprinter, a human communicated with a computer.

In time, the actual mechanical teleprinter was replaced by a "glass tty" (keyboard and screen, but emulating the teleprinter), and then by a "smart" terminal (where a microprocessor in the terminal could address all of the screen, rather than only print successive lines). As the microcomputer revolution replaced the traditional – minicomputer + terminals – time sharing architecture, hardware terminals were replaced by terminal emulators — PC software that interpreted terminal signals sent through the PC›s serial ports. These were typically used to interface an organization's new PC's with their existing mini- or mainframe computers, or to connect PC to PC. Some of these PCs were running Bulletin Board System software.

Early operating system CLIs were implemented as part of resident monitor programs, and could not easily be replaced. The concept of implementing the shell as a replaceable component is usually attributed to Multics.

Early microcomputers themselves were based on a command-line interface such as CP/M, MS-DOS or AppleSoft BASIC. Throughout the 1980s and 1990s—especially after the introduction of the Apple Macintosh and Microsoft Windows—command line interfaces were replaced in popular usage by the Graphical User Interface. The command line remains in use, however, by system administrators and other advanced users for system administration, computer programming, and batch processing.

In November 2006, Microsoft released version 1.0 of Windows PowerShell (formerly codenamed *Monad*), which combined features of traditional Unix shells with their proprietary object-oriented .NET Framework. MinGW and Cygwin are open-source packages for Windows that offer a Unix-like CLI. Microsoft provides MKS Inc.'s ksh implementation *MKS Korn shell* for Windows through their Services for UNIX add-on.

Since 2001, the Macintosh operating system is based on a variation of Unix called Darwin. On these computers, users can access a Unix-like command-line interface called Terminal found in the Applications Utilities folder. This terminal uses bash by default.

Screenshot of the MATLAB 7.4 command-line interface and GUI

Usage

A CLI is used whenever a large vocabulary of commands or queries, coupled with a wide (or arbitrary) range of options, can be entered more rapidly as text than with a pure GUI. This is typically the case with operating system command shells. CLIs are also used by systems with insufficient resources to support a graphical user interface. Some computer language systems (such as Python, Forth, LISP, Rexx, and many dialects of BASIC) provide an interactive command-line mode to allow for rapid evaluation of code.

CLIs are often used by programmers and system administrators, in engineering and scientific environments, and by technically advanced personal computer users. CLIs are also popular among people with visual disability, since the commands and responses can be displayed using Refreshable Braille displays.

Anatomy of a Shell CLI

The general pattern of an OS command line interface is:

Prompt command param1 param2 param3 ... paramN

- Prompt - generated by the program to provide context for the client.

- Command — provided by the client. Commands are usually one of three classes:

    1. Internal — recognized and processed by the command line interpreter itself and not dependent upon any external executable file.

    2. Included — A separate executable file generally considered part of the operating environment and always included with the OS.

    3. External — External executable files not part of the basic OS, but added by other parties for specific purposes and applications.

- param1 ...paramN — Optional parameters provided by the client. The format and meaning of the parameters depends upon the command issued. In the case of Included or External commands, the values of the parameters are delivered to the program (specified by the Command) as it is launched by the OS. Parameters may be either Arguments or Options.

In this example, the delimiters between command line elements are whitespace characters and the end-of-line delimiter is the newline delimiter. This is a widely used (but not universal) convention for command-line interfaces.

A CLI can generally be considered as consisting of syntax and semantics. The *syntax* is the grammar that all commands must follow. In the case of operating systems (OS), MS-DOS and Unix each define their own set of rules that all commands must follow. In the case of embedded systems, each vendor, such as Nortel, Juniper Networks or Cisco Systems, defines their own proprietary set of rules that all commands within their CLI conform to. These rules also dictate how a user navigates through the system of commands. The *semantics* define what sort of operations are possible, on what sort of data these operations can be performed, and how the grammar represents these operations and data—the symbolic meaning in the syntax.

Two different CLIs may agree on either syntax or semantics, but it is only when they agree on both that they can be considered sufficiently similar to allow users to use both CLIs without needing to learn anything, as well as to enable re-use of scripts.

A simple CLI will display a prompt, accept a "command line" typed by the user terminated by the Enter key, then execute the specified command and provide textual display of results or error messages. Advanced CLIs will validate, interpret and parameter-expand the command line before executing the specified command, and optionally capture or redirect its output.

Unlike a button or menu item in a GUI, a command line is typically self-documenting, stating exactly what the user wants done. In addition, command lines usually include many defaults that can be changed to customize the results. Useful command lines can be saved by assigning a character string or alias to represent the full command, or several commands can be grouped to perform a more complex sequence – for instance, compile the program, install it, and run it — creating a single entity, called a command procedure or script which itself can be treated as a command. These advantages mean that a user must figure out a complex command or series of commands only once, because they can be saved, to be used again.

The commands given to a CLI shell are often in one of the following forms:

- *doSomething how toFiles*

- *doSomething how sourceFile destinationFile*

- *doSomething how < inputFile > outputFile*

- *doSomething how | doSomething how | doSomething how > outputFile*

where *doSomething* is, in effect, a verb, *how* an adverb (for example, should the command be executed "verbosely" or "quietly") and *toFiles* an object or objects (typically one or more files) on which the command should act. The > in the third example is a redirection operator, telling the command-line interpreter to send the output of the command not to its own standard output (the screen) but to the named file. This will overwrite the file. Using >> will redirect the output and append it to the file. Another redirection operator is the vertical bar (|), which creates a pipeline where the output of one command becomes the input to the next command.

CLI and Resource Protection

One can modify the set of available commands by modifying which paths appear in the PATH environment variable. Under Unix, commands also need be marked as executable files. The directories in the path variable are searched in the order they are given. By re-ordering the path, one can run e.g. \OS2\MDOS\E.EXE instead of \OS2\E.EXE, when the default is the opposite. Renaming of the executables also works: people often rename their favourite editor to EDIT, for example.

The command line allows one to restrict available commands, such as access to advanced internal commands. The Windows CMD.EXE does this. Often, shareware programs will limit the range of commands, including printing a command 'your administrator has disabled running batch files' from the prompt.

Some CLIs, such as those in network routers, have a hierarchy of modes, with a different set of commands supported in each mode. The set of commands are grouped by association with security, system, interface, etc. In these systems the user might traverse through a series of sub-modes. For example, if the CLI had two modes called *interface* and *system*, the user might use the command *interface* to enter the interface mode. At this point, commands from the system mode may not be accessible and the user exits the interface mode and enters the system mode.

Command Prompt

A command prompt (or just *prompt*) is a sequence of (one or more) characters used in a command-line interface to indicate readiness to accept commands. It literally prompts the user to take action. A prompt usually ends with one of the characters $, %, #, :, > and often includes other information, such as the path of the current working directory and the hostname.

On many Unix and derivative systems, the prompt commonly ends in $ or % if the user is a normal user, but in # if the user is a superuser ("root" in Unix terminology).

End-users can often modify prompts. Depending on the environment, they may include colors, special characters, and other elements (like variables and functions for the current time, user, shell number or working directory) in order, for instance, to make the prompt more informative or visually pleasing, to distinguish sessions on various machines, or to indicate the current level of nesting of commands. On some systems, special tokens in the definition of the prompt can be used to cause external programs to be called by the command-line interpreter while displaying the prompt.

In DOS's COMMAND.COM and in Windows NT's cmd.exe users can modify the prompt by issuing a `prompt` command or by directly changing the value of the corresponding `%PROMPT%` environment variable. The default of most modern systems, the `C:\>` style is obtained, for instance, with `prompt $P$G`. The default of older DOS systems, `C>` is obtained by just prompt, although on some systems this produces the newer `C:\>` style, unless used on floppy drives A: or B:; on those systems `prompt $N$G` can be used to override the automatic default and explicitly switch to the older style.

Many Unix systems feature the `$PS1` variable (Prompt String 1), although other variables also may affect the prompt (depending on the shell used). In the bash shell, a prompt of the form:

```
[time] user@host: work_dir $
```

could be set by issuing the command

```
export PS1=' [\t] \u@\H: \W $'
```

In zsh the `$RPROMPT` variable controls an optional "prompt" on the right-hand side of the display. It is not a real prompt in that the location of text entry does not change. It is used to display information on the same line as the prompt, but right-justified.

In RISC OS the command prompt is a * symbol, and thus (OS)CLI commands are often referred to as "star commands". One can also access the same commands from other command lines (such as the BBC BASIC command line), by preceding the command with a *.

Arguments

An MS DOS command line, illustrating parsing into command and arguments

A command-line argument or parameter is an item of information provided to a program when it is started. A program can have many command-line arguments that identify sources or destinations of information, or that alter the operation of the program.

When a command processor is active a program is typically invoked by typing its name followed by command-line arguments (if any). For example, in Unix and Unix-like environments, an example of a command-line argument is:

```
rm file.s
```

"file.s" is a command-line argument which tells the program rm to remove the file "file.s".

Some programming languages, such as C, C++ and Java, allow a program to interpret the command-line arguments by handling them as string parameters in the main function. Other languages, such as Python, expose these arguments as global variables.

In Unix-like operating systems, a single hyphen-minus by itself is usually a special value specifying that a program should handle data coming from the standard input or send data to the standard output.

Command-line Option

A command-line option or simply option (also known as a flag or switch) modifies the operation of a command; the effect is determined by the command's program. Options follow the command name on the command line, separated by spaces. A space before the first option is not always required, for example Dir/? and DIR /? have the same effect in DOS (list the DIR command's options) whereas dir --help (in many versions of Unix) *does* require the option to be preceded by at least one space (and is case-sensitive).

The format of options varies widely between operating systems. In most cases the syntax is by convention rather than an operating system requirement; the entire command line is simply a string passed to a program, which can process it in any way the programmer wants, so long as the interpreter can tell where the command name ends and its arguments and options begin.

A few representative samples of command-line options, all relating to listing files in a directory, to illustrate some conventions:

Operating system	Command	Valid alternative	Notes
OpenVMS	directory/owner	Dir /Owner	instruct the *directory* command to also display the ownership of the files. *Note the Directory command name is not case sensitive, and can be abbreviated to as few letters as required to remain unique.*
DOS	dir/Q/O:S d*	diR /q d* /o:s	display ownership of files whose names begin with "D", sorted by size, smallest first. *Note spaces around argument d* are required.*
Unix-like systems	ls -lS D*	ls -S -l D*	display in long format files and directories beginning with "D" (but not "d"), sorted by size (largest first). *Note spaces are required around all arguments and options, but some can be run together, e.g. -lS is the same as -l -S.*
Data General RDOS CLI	list/e/s 04-26-80/b	List /S/E 4-26-80/B	list every attribute for files created before 26 April 1980. *Note the /B at the end of the date argument is a **local switch**, that modifies the meaning of that argument, while /S and /E are **global switches**, i.e. apply to the whole command.*

Abbreviating Commands

In Multics, command-line options and subsystem keywords may be abbreviated. This idea appears to derive from the PL/I programming language, with its shortened keywords (e.g., STRG for STRINGRANGE and DCL for DECLARE). For example, in the Multics "forum" subsystem, the *-long_subject* parameter can be abbreviated *-lgsj*. It is also common for Multics commands to be abbreviated, typically corresponding to the initial letters of the words that are strung together with underscores to form command names, such as the use of *did* for *delete_iacl_dir*.

In some other systems abbreviations are automatic, such as permitting enough of the first characters of a command name to uniquely identify it (such as SU as an abbreviation for SUPERUSER) while others may have some specific abbreviations pre-programmed (e.g. MD for MKDIR in COMMAND.COM) or user-defined via batch scripts and aliases (e.g. alias md mkdir in tcsh).

Option Conventions in DOS, Windows, OS/2

On DOS, OS/2 and Windows, different programs called from their COMMAND.COM or CMD.EXE (or internal their commands) may use different syntax within the same operating system. For example:

- Options may be indicated by either of the "switch characters": -, /, or either may be allowed.

- They may or may not be case-sensitive.

- Sometimes options and their arguments are run together, sometimes separated by whitespace, and sometimes by a character, typically : or =; thus `Prog -fFilename`, `Prog -f Filename`, `Prog -f:Filename`, `Prog -f=-Filename`.

- Some programs allow single-character options to be combined; others do not. The switch `-fA` may mean the same as `-f -A`, or it may be incorrect, or it may even be a valid but different parameter.

In DOS, OS/2 and Windows, the forward slash (/) is most prevalent, although the hyphen-minus is also sometimes used. In many versions of DOS (MS-DOS/PC DOS 2.xx and higher, all versions of DR-DOS since 5.0, as well as PTS-DOS, Embedded DOS, FreeDOS and RxDOS) the switch character (sometimes abbreviated switchar or switchchar) to be used is defined by a value returned from a system call (INT 21h/AH=37h). The default character returned by this API is /, but can be changed to a hyphen-minus on the above-mentioned systems, except for Datalight ROM-DOS and MS-DOS/PC DOS 5.0 and higher, which always return / from this call (unless one of many available TSRs to reenable the SwitChar feature is loaded). In some of these systems (MS-DOS/PC DOS 2.xx, DOS Plus 2.1, DR-DOS 7.02 and higher, PTS-DOS, Embedded DOS, FreeDOS and RxDOS), the setting can also be pre-configured by a SWITCHAR directive in CONFIG.SYS. Embedded DOS provides a SWITCH command for the same purpose, whereas 4DOS allows the setting to be changed via `SETDOS /W:n`. Under DR-DOS, if the setting has been changed from /, the first directory separator \ in the display of the PROMPT parameter `$G` will change to a forward slash / (which is also a valid directory separator in DOS, FlexOS, 4680 OS, 4690 OS, OS/2 and Windows) thereby serving as a visual clue to indicate the change. Some versions of DR-DOS COMMAND.COM also support a PROMPT token `$/` to display the current setting. COMMAND.COM since DR-DOS 7.02 and 4DOS also provide a pseudo-environment variable named `%/%` to allow portable batchjobs to be written. Several external DR-DOS commands additionally support an environment variable `%SWITCHAR%` to override the system setting.

However, many programs are hardwired to use / only, rather than retrieving the switch setting before parsing command line arguments. A very small number, mainly ports from Unix-like systems, are programmed to accept "-" even if the switch character is not set to it (for example netstat and ping, supplied with Windows, will accept the /? option to list available options, and yet the list will specify the "-" convention).

Option Conventions in Unix-like Systems

In Unix-like systems, the ASCII hyphen-minus begins options; the new (and GNU) convention is to use *two* hyphens then a word (e.g. `--create`) to identify the option's use while the old convention (and still available as an option for frequently-used options) is to use one hyphen then one letter (e.g. -c); if one hyphen is followed by two or more letters it may mean two options are being specified, or it may mean the second and subsequent letters are a parameter (such as filename or date) for the first option.

Two hyphen-minus characters without following letters (--) may indicate that the remaining arguments should not be treated as options, which is useful for example if a file name itself begins with a hyphen, or if further arguments are meant for an inner command (e.g. sudo). Double hyphen-minuses are also sometimes used to prefix "long options" where more descriptive option names are used. This is a common feature of GNU software. The *getopt* function and program, and the *getopts* command are usually used for parsing command-line options.

Unix command names, arguments and options are case-sensitive (except in a few examples, mainly where popular commands from other operating systems have been ported to Unix).

Options Conventions in other Systems

FlexOS, 4680 OS and 4690 OS use - .

CP/M typically used [.

Conversational Monitor System (CMS) uses a single left parenthesis to separate options at the end of the command from the other arguments. For example, in the following command the options indicate that the target file should be replaced if it exists, and the date and time of the source file should be retained on the copy: COPY source file a target file b (REPLACE OLDDATE)

Data General's CLI under their RDOS, AOS, etc. operating systems, as well as the version of CLI that came with their Business Basic, uses only / as the switch character, is case-insensitive, and allows "local switches" on some arguments to control the way they are interpreted, such as MAC/U LIB/S A B C $LPT/L has the global option "U" to the macro assembler command to appemd user symbols, but two local switches, one to specify LIB should be skipped on pass 2 and the other to direct listing to the printer, $LPT.

Built-in usage Help

One of the criticisms of a CLI is the lack of cues to the user as to the available actions. In contrast, GUIs usually inform the user of available actions with menus, icons, or other visual cues. To overcome this limitation, many CLI programs display a brief summary of its valid parameters, typically when invoked with no arguments or one of ?, -?, -h, -H, /?, /h, /H, -help, or --help.

However, entering a program name without parameters in the hope that it will display usage help can be hazardous, as some programs and scripts execute without further notice.

Although desirable at least for the help parameter, programs may not support all option lead-in characters exemplified above. Under DOS, where the default command line option character can be changed from / to -, programs may query the SwitChar API in order to determine the current setting. So, if a program is not hard-wired to support them all, a user may need to know the current setting even to be able to reliably request help. If the SwitChar has been changed to - and therefore the / character is accepted as alternative path delimiter also at the DOS command line, programs may misinterpret options like /h or /H as paths rather than help parameters. However, if given as first or only parameter, most DOS programs will, by convention, accept it as request for help regardless of the current SwitChar setting.

In some cases, different levels of help can be selected for a program. Some programs supporting this allow to give a verbosity level as an optional argument to the help parameter (as in /H:1, /H:2, etc.) or they give just a short help on help parameters with question mark and a longer help screen for the other help options.

Depending on the program, additional or more specific help on accepted parameters is sometimes available by either providing the parameter in question as an argument to the help parameter or vice versa (as in /H:W or in /W:? (assuming /W would be another parameter supported by the program)).

In a similar fashion to the help parameter, but much less common, some programs provide additional information about themselves (like mode, status, version, author, license or contact information) when invoked with an "about" parameter like -!, /!, -about, or --about.

Since the ? and ! characters typically also serve other purposes at the command line, they may not be available in all scenarios, therefore, they should not be the only options to access the corresponding help information.

If more detailed help is necessary than provided by a program's built-in internal help, many systems support a dedicated external "HELP command" command (or similar), which accepts a command name as calling parameter and will invoke an external help system.

In the DR-DOS family, typing /? or /H at the COMMAND.COM prompt instead of a command itself will display a dynamically generated list of available internal commands; 4DOS and NDOS support the same feature by typing ? at the prompt (which is also accepted by newer versions of DR-DOS COMMAND.COM); internal commands can be individually disabled or reenabled via SETDOS /I. In addition to this, some newer versions of DR-DOS COMMAND.COM also accept a ?% command to display a list of available built-in pseudo-environment variables. Besides their purpose as quick help reference this can be used in batchjobs to query the facilities of the underlying command line processor.

Command Description Syntax

Built-in usage help and man pages commonly employ a small syntax to describe the valid command form:

- angle brackets for *required* parameters: `ping <hostname>`

- square brackets for *optional* parameters: `mkdir [-p] <dirname>`

- ellipses for *repeated* items: `cp <source1> [source2...] <dest>`

- vertical bars for *choice* of items: `netstat {-t|-u}`

Notice that these characters have different meanings than when used directly in the shell. Angle brackets may be omitted when confusing the parameter name with a literal string is not likely.

The Space Character

In many areas of computing, but particularly in the command line, the space character can cause problems as it has two distinct and incompatible functions: as part of a command or parameter, or as a parameter or name separator. Ambiguity can be prevented either by prohibiting embedded spaces in file and directory names in the first place (for example, by substituting them with underscores _), or by enclosing a name with embedded spaces between quote characters or using an escape character before the space, usually a backslash (\). For example

```
Long path/Long program name Parameter one Parameter two ...
```

is ambiguous (is "program name" part of the program name, or two parameters?); however

```
Long_path/Long_program_name  Parameter_one   Parameter_two
...,
```

```
LongPath/LongProgramName ParameterOne ParameterTwo ...,
```

```
"Long path/Long program name" "Parameter one" "Parameter
two" ...
```

and

```
Long\ path/Long\ program\ name Parameter\ one Parameter\
two ...
```

are not ambiguous. Unix-based operating systems minimize the use of embedded spaces to minimize the need for quotes. In Microsoft Windows, one often has to use quotes because embedded spaces (such as in directory names) are common.

Command-line Interpreter

"Although most users think of the shell as an interactive command interpreter, it is really a programming language in which each statement runs a command. Because it must satisfy both the interactive and programming aspects of command execution, it is a strange language, shaped as much by history as by design."

—Brian Kernighan & Rob Pike

The terms command-line interpreter, command line shell, command language interpreter, or identical abbreviation CLI, are applied to computer programs designed to interpret a sequence of lines of text which may be entered by a user, read from a file or another kind of data stream. The context of interpretation is usually one of a given operating system or programming language.

Command-line interpreters allow users to issue various commands in a very efficient (and often terse) way. This requires the user to know the names of the commands and their parameters, and the syntax of the language that is interpreted.

The Unix #! mechanism and OS/2 EXTPROC command facilitate the passing of batch files to external processors. One can use these mechanisms to write specific command processors for dedicated uses, and process external data files which reside in batch files.

Many graphical interfaces, such as the OS/2 Presentation Manager and early versions of Microsoft Windows use command-lines to call helper programs to open documents and programs. The commands are stored in the graphical shell or in files like the registry or the OS/2 `os2user.ini` file.

Early History

The earliest computers did not support interactive input/output devices, often relying on sense switches and lights to communicate with the computer operator. This was adequate for batch systems that ran one program at a time, often with the programmer acting as operator. This also had the advantage of low overhead, since lights and switches could be tested and set with one machine instruction. Later a single system console was added to allow the operator to communicate with the system.

From the 1960s onwards, user interaction with computers was primarily by means of command-line interfaces, initially on machines like the Teletype Model 33 ASR, but then on early CRT-based computer terminals such as the VT52.

All of these devices were purely text based, with no ability to display graphic or pictures. For business application programs, text-based menus were used, but for more general interaction the command line was the interface.

Around 1964 Louis Pouzin introduced the concept and the name *shell* in Multics, building on earlier, simpler facilities in the Compatible Time-Sharing System (CTSS).

From the early 1970s the Unix operating system adapted the concept of a powerful command-line environment, and introduced the ability to *pipe* the output of one command in as input to another. Unix also had the capability to save and re-run strings of commands as "shell scripts" which acted like custom commands.

The command-line was also the main interface for the early home computers such as the Commodore PET, Apple II and BBC Micro – almost always in the form of a BASIC interpreter. When more powerful business oriented microcomputers arrived with CP/M and later MS-DOS computers such as the IBM PC, the command-line began to borrow some of the syntax and features of the Unix shells such as globbing and piping of output.

The command-line was first seriously challenged by the PARC GUI approach used in the 1983 Apple Lisa and the 1984 Apple Macintosh. A few computer users used GUIs such as GEOS and Windows 3.1 but the majority of IBM PC users did not replace their command.com shell with a GUI until Windows 95 was released in 1995.

Modern usage as an Operating System Shell

While most non-expert computer users now use a GUI almost exclusively, more advanced users have access to powerful command-line environments:

- The default VAX/VMS command shell, using the DCL language, has been ported to Windows systems at least three times, including PC-DCL and Accel-er8 DCL Lite. MS-DOS 6.22 has been ported to Linux type systems, Unix command shells have been ported to VMS and MS-DOS/Windows 95 and Windows NT types of operating systems. Command.com and Windows NT cmd.exe have been ported to Windows CE and presumably works on Microsoft Windows NT Embedded 4.0

- Windows Resource Kit and Windows Services for Unix include Korn and the Bourne shells along with a Perl interpreter (Services of Unix contains Active State ActivePerl in later versions and Interix for versions 1 and 2 and a shell compiled by Microsoft)

- IBM OS/2 has the cmd.exe processor. This copies the command.com commands, with extensions to REXX.

- Cmd.exe and Command.com are part of the Windows NT stream operating systems.

- Yet another Cmd.exe is a stripped-down shell for Windows CE 3.0

- An MS-DOS type interpreter called PocketDOS has been ported to Windows CE machines; the most recent release is almost identical to MS-DOS 6.22 and can also run Windows 1, 2, and 3.0, QBasic and other development tools, 4NT and

4DOS. The latest release includes several shells, namely MS-DOS 6.22, PC-DOS 7, DR DOS 3, and others.

- PocketConsole is a Windows NT 4.0 shell for Windows CE that is much like 4NT.

- Windows users have a CLI environment named Windows Command Prompt, which might use the CScript interface to alternate programs. PowerShell provides a command-line interface, but its applets are not written in Shell script. Implementations of the Unix shell are also available as part of the POSIX sub-system, Cygwin, MKS Toolkit, UWIN, Hamilton C shell and other software packages. Available shells for these interoperability tools include csh, ksh, sh, bash, rsh, tclsh and less commonly zsh, ysh, psh.

- Command.com (4DOS), Windows NT cmd.exe (4NT, TCC), and OS/2 cmd.exe (4OS2) and others based on them are enhanced shells which can be a replacement for the native shell or a means of enhancement of the default shell.

- Implementations of PHP have a shell for interactive use called php-cli.

- Standard Tcl/Tk has two interactive shells, Tclsh and Wish, the latter being the GUI version.

- Python, Ruby, Lua, XLNT, and other interpreters also have command shells for interactive use.

- FreeBSD uses tcsh as its default interactive shell for the superuser.

- Apple macOS and many Linux distributions have the Bash implementation of the Unix shell. Early versions of macOS used tcsh as the default shell.

- Embedded Linux (and other embedded Unix-like) devices often use the Ash implementation of the Unix shell, as part of Busybox.

- Android uses the mksh shell, which replaces a shell derived from ash that was used in older Android versions, supplemented with commands from the separate *toolbox* binary.

- Routers with Cisco IOS, Junos and many others are commonly configured from the command line.

Scripting

Most command-line interpreters support scripting, to various extents. (They are, after all, interpreters of an interpreted programming language, albeit in many cases the language is unique to the particular command-line interpreter.) They will interpret scripts (variously termed shell scripts or batch files) written in the language that they interpret. Some command-line interpreters also incorporate the interpreter engines of other languages, such as REXX, in addition to their own, allowing the executing of scripts, in those languages, directly within the command-line interpreter itself.

Conversely, scripting programming languages, in particular those with an eval function (such as REXX, Perl, Python, Ruby or Jython), can be used to implement command-line interpreters and filters. For a few operating systems, most notably DOS, such a command interpreter provides a more flexible command line interface than the one supplied. In other cases, such a command interpreter can present a highly customised user interface employing the user interface and input/output facilities of the language.

Other Command-line Interfaces

The command line provides an interface between programs as well as the user. In this sense, a command line is an alternative to a dialog box. Editors and data-bases present a command line, in which alternate command processors might run. On the other hand, one might have options on the command line which opens a dialog box. The latest version of 'Take Command' has this feature. DBase used a dialog box to construct command lines, which could be further edited before use.

Programs like Basic, Diskpart, Edlin, and QBasic all provide command-line interfaces, some of which use the system shell. Basic is modeled on the default interface for 8-bit Intel computers. Calculators can be run as command-line or dialog interfaces.

Emacs provides a command line interface in the form of its minibuffer. Commands and arguments can be entered using Emacs standard text editing support, and output is displayed in another buffer.

There are a number of pre-mouse games, like *Adventure* or *King's Quest 1-3*, which relied on the user typing commands at the bottom of the screen. One controls the character by typing commands like 'get ring' or 'look'. The program returns a text which describes how the character sees it, or makes the action happen. The text adventure *The Hitchhiker's Guide to the Galaxy*, a piece of interactive fiction based on Douglas Adam's book of the same name, is a teletype-style command-line game.

The most notable of these interfaces is the standard streams interface, which allows the output of one command to be passed to the input of another. Text files can serve either purpose as well. This provides the interfaces of piping, filters and redirection. Under Unix, devices are files too, so the normal type of file for the shell used for stdin,stdout and stderr is a tty device file.

Another command-line interface allows a shell program to launch helper programs, either to launch documents or start a program. The command is processed internally by the shell, and then passed on to another program to launch the document. The graphical interface of Windows and OS/2 rely heavily on command-lines passed through to other programs – console or graphical, which then usually process the command line without presenting a user-console.

Programs like the OS/2 E editor and some other IBM editors, can process command-lines normally meant for the shell, the output being placed directly in the document window.

A web browser's URL input field can be used as a command line. It can be used to "launch" web apps, access browser configuration, as well as perform a search. Google, which has been called "the command line of the internet" will perform a domain-specific search when it detects search parameters in a known format. This functionality is present whether the search is triggered from a browser field or one on Google's web site.

Direct Manipulation Interface

In computer science, direct manipulation is a human–computer interaction style which involves continuous representation of objects of interest and rapid, reversible, and incremental actions and feedback. As opposed to other interaction styles, for example, a command language, the intention of direct manipulation is to allow a user to manipulate objects presented to them, using actions that correspond at least loosely to manipulation of physical objects. An example of direct-manipulation is resizing a graphical shape, such as a rectangle, by dragging its corners or edges with a mouse.

Having real-world metaphors for objects and actions can make it easier for a user to learn and use an interface (some might say that the interface is more natural or intuitive), and rapid, incremental feedback allows a user to make fewer errors and complete tasks in less time, because they can see the results of an action before completing the action, thus evaluating the output and compensating for mistakes.

The term was introduced by Ben Shneiderman in 1982 within the context of office applications and the desktop metaphor. Individuals in academia and computer scientists doing research on future user interfaces often put as much or even more stress on tactile control and feedback, or sonic control and feedback than on the visual feedback given by most GUIs. As a result, the term has been more widespread in these environments.

In Contrast to WIMP/GUI Interfaces

Direct manipulation is closely associated with interfaces that use windows, icons, menus, and a pointing device (WIMP GUI) as these almost always incorporate direct manipulation to at least some degree. However, direct manipulation should not be confused with these other terms, as it does not imply the use of windows or even graphical output. For example, direct manipulation concepts can be applied to interfaces for blind or vision-impaired users, using a combination of tactile and sonic devices and software.

Compromises to the degree to which an interface implements direct manipulation are frequently seen. For example, most versions of windowing interfaces allow users to reposition a window by dragging it with the mouse. In early systems, redrawing the window while dragging was not feasible due to computational limitations. Instead, a rectangular outline of the window was drawn while dragging. The complete window contents were redrawn once the user released the mouse button.

In Computer Graphics

Because of the difficulty of visualizing and manipulating various aspects of computer graphics, including geometry creation and editing, animation, layout of objects and cameras, light placement, and other effects, direct manipulation is an extremely important part of 3D computer graphics. There are standard direct manipulation widgets as well as many unique widgets that are developed either as a better solution to an old problem or as a solution for a new and/or unique problem. The widgets attempt to allow the user to modify an object in any possible direction while also providing easy guides or constraints to allow the user to easily modify an object in the most common directions, while also attempting to be as intuitive as to the function of the widget as possible. The three most ubiquitous transformation widgets are mostly standardized and are:

- The translation widget, which usually consists of three arrows aligned with the orthogonal axes centered on the object to be translated. Dragging the center of the widget translates the object directly underneath the mouse pointer in the plane parallel to the camera plane, while dragging any of the three arrows translates the object along the appropriate axis. The axes may be aligned with the world-space axes, the object-space axes, or some other space.

- The rotation widget, which usually consists of three circles aligned with the three orthogonal axes, and one circle aligned with the camera plane. Dragging any of the circles rotates the object around the appropriate axis, while dragging elsewhere will freely rotate the object (virtual trackball rotation).

- The scale widget, which usually consists of three short lines aligned with the orthogonal axes terminating in boxes, and one box in the center of the widget. Dragging any of the three axis-aligned boxes effects a non-uniform scale along solely that axis, while dragging the center box effects a uniform scale on all three axes at once.

Depending on the specific common uses of an object, different kinds of widgets may be used. For example, a light in computer graphics is, like any other object, also defined by a transformation (translation and rotation), but it is sometimes positioned and directed simply with its endpoint positions because it may be more intuitive to define the position of the light source and then define the light's target, rather than rotating it around the coordinate axes in order to point it at a known position.

Other widgets may be unique for a particular tool, such as edge controls to change the cone of a spotlight, points and handles to define the position and tangent vector for a spline control point, circles of variable size to define a blur filter width or paintbrush size, IK targets for hands and feet, or color wheels and swatches for quickly choosing colors. Complex widgets may even incorporate some from scientific visualization to efficiently present relevant data (such as vector fields for particle effects or false color images to display vertex maps).

Direct manipulation, as well as user interface design in general, for 3D computer graphics tasks, is still an active area of invention and innovation, as the process of generating CG images is generally not considered to be intuitive or easy in comparison to the difficulty of what the user wants to do, especially for complex tasks. The user interface for word processing, for example, is easy to learn for new users and is sufficient for most word processing purposes, so it is a mostly solved and standardized UI, while the user interfaces for 3D computer graphics are usually either difficult to learn and use and not sufficiently powerful for complex tasks, or sufficiently powerful but difficult to learn and use, so direct manipulation and user interfaces will vary wildly from application to application.

Graphical user Interface

The Xerox Alto was the first device to use a graphical user interface.

Example of GUI in macOS Sierra

The graphical user interface, is a type of user interface that allows users to interact with electronic devices through graphical icons and visual indicators such as secondary notation, instead of text-based user interfaces, typed command labels or text navigation. GUIs were introduced in reaction to the perceived steep learning curve of command-line interfaces (CLIs), which require commands to be typed on a computer keyboard.

The actions in a GUI are usually performed through direct manipulation of the graphical elements. Beyond computers, GUIs are used in many handheld mobile devices such as MP3 players, portable media players, gaming devices, smartphones and smaller household, office and industrial controls. The term *GUI* tends not to be applied to other lower-display resolution types of interfaces, such as video games (where *heads-up display* (HUD) is preferred), or not including flat screens, like volumetric displays because the term is restricted to the scope of two-dimensional display screens able to describe generic information, in the tradition of the computer science research at the Xerox Palo Alto Research Center (PARC).

User Interface and Interaction Design

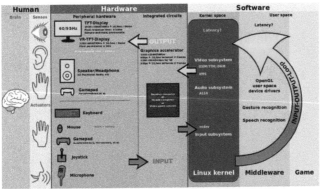

The graphical user interface is presented (displayed) on the computer screen. It is the result of processed user input and usually the main interface for human-machine interaction. The touch user interfaces popular on small mobile devices are an overlay of the visual output to the visual input.

Designing the visual composition and temporal behavior of a GUI is an important part of software application programming in the area of human–computer interaction. Its goal is to enhance the efficiency and ease of use for the underlying logical design of a stored program, a design discipline named *usability*. Methods of user-centered design are used to ensure that the visual language introduced in the design is well-tailored to the tasks.

The visible graphical interface features of an application are sometimes referred to as *chrome* or *GUI* (pronounced *gooey*). Typically, users interact with information by manipulating visual widgets that allow for interactions appropriate to the kind of data they hold. The widgets of a well-designed interface are selected to support the actions necessary to achieve the goals of users. A model–view–controller allows a flexible structure in which the interface is independent from and indirectly linked to application functions, so the GUI can be customized easily. This allows users to select or design a different *skin* at will, and eases the designer's work to change the interface as user needs evolve. Good user interface design relates to users more, and to system architecture less.

Large widgets, such as windows, usually provide a frame or container for the main presentation content such as a web page, email message or drawing. Smaller ones usually act as a user-input tool.

A GUI may be designed for the requirements of a vertical market as application-specific graphical user interfaces. Examples include automated teller machines (ATM), point of sale (POS) touchscreens at restaurants, self-service checkouts used in a retail store, airline self-ticketing and check-in, information kiosks in a public space, like a train station or a museum, and monitors or control screens in an embedded industrial application which employ a real-time operating system (RTOS).

By the 1990s, cell phones and handheld game systems also employed application specific touchscreen GUIs. Newer automobiles use GUIs in their navigation systems and multimedia centers, or navigation multimedia center combinations.

Examples

- Sample graphical desktop environments

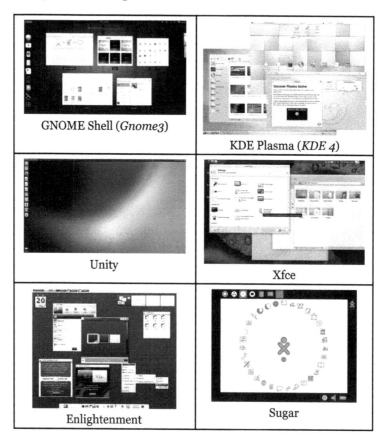

GNOME Shell (*Gnome3*)

KDE Plasma (*KDE 4*)

Unity

Xfce

Enlightenment

Sugar

Components

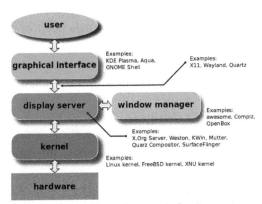

Layers of a GUI based on a windowing system

A GUI uses a combination of technologies and devices to provide a platform that users can interact with, for the tasks of gathering and producing information.

A series of elements conforming a visual language have evolved to represent information stored in computers. This makes it easier for people with few computer skills to work with and use computer software. The most common combination of such elements in GUIs is the *windows, icons, menus, pointer* (WIMP) paradigm, especially in personal computers.

The WIMP style of interaction uses a virtual input device to represent the position of a pointing device, most often a mouse, and presents information organized in windows and represented with icons. Available commands are compiled together in menus, and actions are performed making gestures with the pointing device. A window manager facilitates the interactions between windows, applications, and the windowing system. The windowing system handles hardware devices such as pointing devices, graphics hardware, and positioning of the pointer.

In personal computers, all these elements are modeled through a desktop metaphor to produce a simulation called a desktop environment in which the display represents a desktop, on which documents and folders of documents can be placed. Window managers and other software combine to simulate the desktop environment with varying degrees of realism.

Post-WIMP Interfaces

Smaller mobile devices such as personal digital assistants (PDAs) and smartphones typically use the WIMP elements with different unifying metaphors, due to constraints in space and available input devices. Applications for which WIMP is not well suited may use newer interaction techniques, collectively termed *post-WIMP* user interfaces.

As of 2011, some touchscreen-based operating systems such as Apple's iOS (iPhone) and Android use the class of GUIs named post-WIMP. These support styles of interaction using more than one finger in contact with a display, which allows actions such as pinching and rotating, which are unsupported by one pointer and mouse.

Interaction

Human interface devices, for the efficient interaction with a GUI include a computer keyboard, especially used together with keyboard shortcuts, pointing devices for the cursor (or rather pointer) control: mouse, pointing stick, touchpad, trackball, joystick, virtual keyboards, and head-up displays (translucent information devices at the eye level).

There are also actions performed by programs that affect the GUI. For example, there are components like inotify or D-Bus to facilitate communication between computer programs.

History

Early Efforts

Ivan Sutherland developed Sketchpad in 1963, widely held as the first graphical computer-aided design program. It used a light pen to creating and manipulate objects in engineering drawings in realtime with coordinated graphics. In the late 1960s, researchers at the Stanford Research Institute, led by Douglas Engelbart, developed the On-Line System (NLS), which used text-based hyperlinks manipulated with a then new device: the mouse. In the 1970s, Engelbart's ideas were further refined and extended to graphics by researchers at Xerox PARC and specifically Alan Kay, who went beyond text-based hyperlinks and used a GUI as the main interface for the Xerox Alto computer, released in 1973. Most modern general-purpose GUIs are derived from this system.

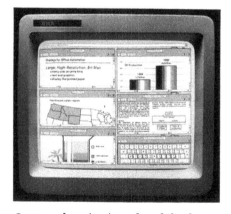

The Xerox Star 8010 workstation introduced the first commercial GUI.

The Xerox PARC user interface consisted of graphical elements such as windows, menus, radio buttons, and check boxes. The concept of icons was later introduced by David

Canfield Smith, who had written a thesis on the subject under the guidance of Kay. The PARC user interface employs a pointing device along with a keyboard. These aspects can be emphasized by using the alternative term and acronym for *windows, icons, menus, pointing device* (WIMP). This effort culminated in the 1973 Xerox Alto, the first computer with a GUI, though the system never reached commercial production.

The first commercially available computer with a GUI was the 1979 PERQ workstation, manufactured by Three Rivers Computer Corporation. In 1981, Xerox eventually commercialized the Alto in the form of a new and enhanced system – the Xerox 8010 Information System – more commonly known as the Xerox Star. These early systems spurred many other GUI efforts, including the Apple Lisa (which presented the concept of menu bar and window controls) in 1983, the Apple Macintosh 128K in 1984, and the Atari ST with Digital Research's GEM, and Commodore Amiga in 1985. Visi On was released in 1983 for the IBM PC compatible computers, but was never popular due to its high hardware demands. Nevertheless, it was a crucial influence on the contemporary development of Microsoft Windows.

Apple, Digital Research, IBM and Microsoft used many of Xerox's ideas to develop products, and IBM's Common User Access specifications formed the basis of the user interfaces used in Microsoft Windows, IBM OS/2 Presentation Manager, and the Unix Motif toolkit and window manager. These ideas evolved to create the interface found in current versions of Microsoft Windows, and in various desktop environments for Unix-like operating systems, such as macOS and Linux. Thus most current GUIs have largely common idioms.

Macintosh 128K, the first Macintosh (1984)

Popularization

GUIs were a hot topic in the early 1980s. The Apple Lisa was released in 1983, and various windowing systems existed for DOS operating systems (including PC GEM and PC/GEOS). Individual applications for many platforms presented their own GUI variants. Despite the GUIs advantages, many reviewers questioned the value of the entire concept, citing hardware limits, and problems in finding compatible software.

In 1984, Apple released a television commercial which introduced the Apple Macintosh during the telecast of Super Bowl XVIII by CBS, with allusions to George Orwell's noted novel, *Nineteen Eighty-Four*. The goal of the commercial was to make people think about computers, identifying the user-friendly interface as a personal computer which departed from prior business-oriented systems, and becoming a signature representation of Apple products.

Accompanied by an extensive marketing campaign, Windows 95 was a major success in the marketplace at launch and shortly became the most popular desktop operating system.

In 2007, with the iPhone and later in 2010 with the introduction of the iPad, Apple popularized the post-WIMP style of interaction for multi-touch screens, and those devices were considered to be milestones in the development of mobile devices.

The GUIs familiar to most people as of the mid-2010s are Microsoft Windows, macOS, and the X Window System interfaces for desktop and laptop computers, and Android, Apple's iOS, Symbian, BlackBerry OS, Windows Phone/Windows 10 Mobile, Palm OS-WebOS, and Firefox OS for handheld (smartphone) devices.

Comparison to Other Interfaces

Command-line Interfaces

A modern CLI

Since the commands available in command line interfaces can be many, complex operations can be performed using a short sequence of words and symbols. This allows greater efficiency and productivity once many commands are learned, but reaching this level takes some time because the command words may not be easily discoverable or mnemonic. Also, using the command line can become slow and error-prone when users must enter long commands comprising many parameters or several different filenames at once. However, *windows, icons, menus, pointer* (WIMP) interfaces present users with many widgets that represent and can trigger some of the system's available commands.

GUIs can be made quite hard when dialogs are buried deep in a system, or moved about to different places during redesigns. Also, icons and dialog boxes are usually harder for users to script.

WIMPs extensively use modes, as the meaning of all keys and clicks on specific positions on the screen are redefined all the time. Command line interfaces use modes only in limited forms, such as for current directory and environment variables.

Most modern operating systems provide both a GUI and some level of a CLI, although the GUIs usually receive more attention. The GUI is usually WIMP-based, although occasionally other metaphors surface, such as those used in Microsoft Bob, 3dwm, or File System Visualizer (FSV).

GUI Wrappers

Graphical user interface (GUI) wrappers circumvent the command-line interface versions (CLI) of (typically) Linux and Unix-like software applications and their text-based user interfaces or typed command labels. While command-line or text-based application allow users to run a program non-interactively, GUI wrappers atop them avoid the steep learning curve of the command-line, which requires commands to be typed on the keyboard. By starting a GUI wrapper, users can intuitively interact with, start, stop, and change its working parameters, through graphical icons and visual indicators of a desktop environment, for example. Applications may also provide both interfaces, and when they do the GUI is usually a WIMP wrapper around the command-line version. This is especially common with applications designed for Unix-like operating systems. The latter used to be implemented first because it allowed the developers to focus exclusively on their product's functionality without bothering about interface details such as designing icons and placing buttons. Designing programs this way also allows users to run the program in a shell script.

Three-dimensional user Interfaces

For typical computer displays, *three-dimensional* is a misnomer—their displays are two-dimensional. Semantically, however, most graphical user interfaces use three dimensions. With height and width, they offer a third dimension of layering or stacking screen elements over one another. This may be represented visually on screen through an illusionary transparent effect, which offers the advantage that information in background windows may still be read, if not interacted with. Or the environment may simply hide the background information, possibly making the distinction apparent by drawing a drop shadow effect over it.

Some environments use the methods of 3D graphics to project virtual three dimensional user interface objects onto the screen. These are often shown in use in science fiction films. As the processing power of computer graphics hardware increases, this becomes less of an obstacle to a smooth user experience.

Three-dimensional graphics are currently mostly used in computer games, art, and computer-aided design (CAD). A three-dimensional computing environment can also be useful in other uses, like molecular graphics and aircraft design.

Several attempts have been made to create a multi-user three-dimensional environment, including the Croquet Project and Sun's Project Looking Glass.

Technologies

The use of three-dimensional graphics has become increasingly common in mainstream operating systems, from creating attractive interfaces, termed eye candy, to functional purposes only possible using three dimensions. For example, user switching is represented by rotating a cube which faces are each user's workspace, and window management is represented via a Rolodex-style flipping mechanism in Windows Vista. In both cases, the operating system transforms windows on-the-fly while continuing to update the content of those windows.

Interfaces for the X Window System have also implemented advanced three-dimensional user interfaces through compositing window managers such as Beryl, Compiz and KWin using the AIGLX or XGL architectures, allowing use of OpenGL to animate user interactions with the desktop.

Another branch in the three-dimensional desktop environment is the three-dimensional GUIs that take the desktop metaphor a step further, like the BumpTop, where users can manipulate documents and windows as if they were physical documents, with realistic movement and physics.

The zooming user interface (ZUI) is a related technology that promises to deliver the representation benefits of 3D environments without their usability drawbacks of orientation problems and hidden objects. It is a logical advance on the GUI, blending some three-dimensional movement with two-dimensional or 2.5D vector objects. In 2006, Hillcrest Labs introduced the first zooming user interface for television, literature and films before they were technically feasible or in common use. For example; the 1993 American film *Jurassic Park* features Silicon Graphics' three-dimensional file manager File System Navigator, a real-life file manager for Unix operating systems. The film Minority Report has scenes of police officers using specialized 3d data systems. In prose fiction, three-dimensional user interfaces have been portrayed as immersible environments like William Gibson's Cyberspace or Neal Stephenson's Metaverse. Many futuristic imaginings of user interfaces rely heavily on object-oriented user interface (OOUI) style and especially object-oriented graphical user interface (OOGUI) style.

Touch user Interface

A touch user interface (TUI) is a computer-pointing technology based upon the sense of touch (haptics). Whereas a graphical user interface (GUI) relies upon the sense of sight, a TUI enables not only the sense of touch to innervate and activate computer-based functions, it also allows the user, particularly those with visual impairments, an added level of interaction based upon tactile or Braille input.

Technology

Generally, the TUI requires pressure or presence with a switch located outside of the printed paper. Electronic paper endeavors, the TUI requires the printed pages to act as a template or overlay to a switch array. By interacting with the switch through touch or presence, an action is innervated. The switching sensor cross-references with a database. The database retains the correct pathway to retrieve the associated digital content or launch the appropriate application.

TUI icons may be used to indicate to the reader of the printed page what action will occur upon interacting with a particular position on the printed page.

Turning pages and interacting with new pages that may have the same touch points as previous or subsequent pages, a z-axis may be used to indicate the plane of activity. Z-axis can be offset around the boundary of the page. When the unique z-axis is interacted with, x,y-axis can have identical touch points as other pages. For example, 1,1,1 indicates a z-axis of 1 (page 1) and the x,y-axis is 1,1. However, turning the page and pressing a new z-axis, say page 2, and then the same x,y-axis content position as page 1, gains the following coordinate structure: 2,1,1.

An integrated circuit (IC) is located either within the printed material or within an enclosure that cradles the printed material. This IC receives a signal when a switch is innervated. The firmware located within the IC communicates via Universal Serial Bus (USB) either connected to a cable, or using a wireless protocol adapter to a reference database that can reside on media within a computer or appliance. Upon receipt of the coordinate structure from the firmware, the database correlates the position with a pre-determined link or pathway to digital content or execution command for an application. After correlating the link with the pathway, a signal is sent to retrieve and render the terminal of the path.

Implications for use

Those with special requirements can use touch with fingers or pointer to gain access to the digital environment. Typing, currently a traditional method for accessing the digital world, can be replaced for users who are missing fingers or are not capable of typing. Touching a link on printed paper takes advantage of the ubiquitous presence of printed paper while it removes barriers of entry to the digital world. Further, removing the need to type pathways removes errors from the entry process, potentially protecting companies and organizations that have potential users going to a cybersquatting site due to a misspelling. Typing is also time consuming. A touch interface provides a reduction in time to get where the reader wants to go in the digital world.

The coupling of printed advertising with online advertising is promising. A reader can touch a printed advertisement and connect directly to the online experience provided by the advertiser. This can include initiating a Voice over Internet Protocol (VoIP), Instant Messaging (IM), or Electronic Mail (e-mail) by simply touching the page. Further, electronic commerce (e-commerce) transactions can be initiated and completed with the TUI. This type of interaction can also exist in the Television Commerce (tcommerce) space with a magazine, catalog, or television guide.

The TUI technology applied to the printed world serves to converge the printed world with the digital world. This provides an alternative to the either print or digital paradigm shift currently experienced by today's users. It also serves to facilitate the vast majority of the world's peoples to a linguistic and culturally non-specific experience that can provide an on-ramp to the digital world.

Educational Mandate

In the United States, legislation took effect in December 2006, that requires educational publishers in the K-12 education industry to provide a National Instructional Materials Accessibility Standard (NIMAS). In essence, educational publishers must provide an inclusive experience to those students who are blind. If they are unable to provide this experience, they are required to provide the digital content source files to a clearing house that will convert the materials into an accessible experience for the student. The TUI has the promise of enabling the publishers to maintain control of their content while providing an inclusive, tactile, or Braille experience to students who are visually impaired. Further, using a Braille approach may serve to help enhance Braille literacy while meeting the mandates of NIMAS.

Characteristics of a user Interface

It is very important to identify the characteristics desired of a good user interface. Because unless we are aware of these, it is very much difficult to design a good user interface. A few important characteristics of a good user interface are the following:

- Speed of learning: A good user interface should be easy to learn. Speed of learning is hampered by complex syntax and semantics of the command issue procedures. A good user interface should not require its users to memorize commands. Neither should the user be asked to remember information from one screen to another while performing various tasks using the interface. Besides, the following three issues are crucial to enhance the speed of learning:

- Use of Metaphors and intuitive command names: Speed of learning an interface is greatly facilitated if these are based on some day-to-day real-life examples or some physical objects with which the users are familiar. The abstractions of real-life objects or concepts used in user interface design are called metaphors. If the user interface of a text editor uses concepts similar to the tools used by a writer for text editing such as cutting lines and paragraphs and pasting it at other places, users can immediately relate to it. Another popular metaphor is a shopping cart. Everyone knows how a shopping cart is used to make choices while purchasing items in a supermarket. If a user interface uses the shopping cart metaphor for designing the interaction style for a situation where similar types of choices have to be made, then the users can easily understand and learn to use the interface. Yet another example of a metaphor is the trashcan. To delete a file, the user may drag it to the trashcan. Also, learning is facilitated by intuitive command names and symbolic command issue procedures.

- Consistency: Once a user learns about a command, he should be able to use the similar commands in different circumstances for carrying out similar actions. This makes it easier to learn the interface since the user can extend his knowledge about one part of the interface to the other parts. For example, in a word processor, "Control-b" is the short-cut key to embolden the selected text. The same short-cut should be used on the other parts of the interface, for example, to embolden text in graphic objects also - circle, rectangle, polygon, etc. Thus, the different commands supported by an interface should be consistent.

- Component-based interface: Users can learn an interface faster if the interaction style of the interface is very similar to the interface of other applications with which the user is already familiar. This can be achieved if the interfaces of different applications are developed using some standard user interface components. This, in fact, is the theme of the component-based user interface. Examples of standard user interface components are: radio button, check box, text field, slider, progress bar, etc.

The speed of learning characteristic of a user interface can be determined by measuring the training time and practice that users require before they can effectively use the software.

- Speed of use: Speed of use of a user interface is determined by the time and user effort necessary to initiate and execute different commands. This characteristic of the interface is some times referred to as productivity support of the interface. It indicates how fast the users can perform their intended tasks. The time and user effort necessary to initiate and execute different commands should be minimal. This can be achieved through careful design of the interface. For example, an interface that requires users to type in lengthy commands or involves mouse movements to different areas of the screen that are wide apart for issuing commands can slow down the operating speed of users. The most frequently used commands should have the smallest length or be available at the top of the menu to minimize the mouse movements necessary to issue commands.

- Speed of recall: Once users learn how to use an interface, the speed with which they can recall the command issue procedure should be maximized. This characteristic is very important for intermittent users. Speed of recall is improved if the interface is based on some metaphors, symbolic command issue procedures, and intuitive command names.

- Error prevention: A good user interface should minimize the scope of committing errors while initiating different commands. The error rate of an interface can be easily determined by monitoring the errors committed by average users while using the interface. This monitoring can be automated by instrumenting the user interface code with monitoring code which can record the frequency and types of user error and later display the statistics of various kinds of errors committed by different users.

Moreover, errors can be prevented by asking the users to confirm any potentially destructive actions specified by them, for example, deleting a group of files.

Consistency of names, issue procedures, and behavior of similar commands and the simplicity of the command issue procedures minimize error possibilities. Also, the interface should prevent the user from entering wrong values.

- Attractiveness: A good user interface should be attractive to use. An attractive user interface catches user attention and fancy. In this respect, graphics-based user interfaces have a definite advantage over text-based interfaces.

- Consistency: The commands supported by a user interface should be consistent. The basic purpose of consistency is to allow users to generalize the knowledge about aspects of the interface from one part to another. Thus, consistency facilitates speed of learning, speed of recall, and also helps in reduction of error rate.

- Feedback: A good user interface must provide feedback to various user actions. Especially, if any user request takes more than few seconds to process, the user should be informed about the state of the processing of his request. In the absence of any response from the computer for a long time, a novice user might even start recovery/shutdown procedures in panic. If required, the user should be periodically informed about the progress made in processing his command.

For example, if the user specifies a file copy/file download operation, a progress bar can be displayed to display the status. This will help the user to monitor the status of the action initiated.

- Support for multiple skill levels: A good user interface should support multiple levels of sophistication of command issue procedure for different categories of users. This is necessary because users with different levels of experience in using an application prefer different types of user interfaces. Experienced users are more concerned about the efficiency of the command issue procedure, whereas novice users pay importance to usability aspects. Very cryptic and complex commands discourage a novice, whereas elaborate command sequences make the command issue procedure very slow and therefore put off experienced users. When someone uses an application for the first time, his primary concern is speed of learning. After using an application for extended periods of time, he becomes familiar with the operation of the software. As a user becomes more and more familiar with an interface, his focus shifts from usability aspects to speed of command issue aspects. Experienced users look for options such as "hot-keys", "macros", etc. Thus, the skill level of users improves as they keep using a software product and they look for commands to suit their skill levels.

- Error recovery (undo facility): While issuing commands, even the expert users can commit errors. Therefore, a good user interface should allow a user to undo a mistake committed by him while using the interface. Users are put to inconvenience, if they cannot recover from the errors they commit while using the software.

- User guidance and on-line help: Users seek guidance and on-line help when they either forget a command or are unaware of some features of the software. Whenever users need guidance or seek help from the system, they should be provided with the appropriate guidance and help.

User Guidance and Online Help

Users may seek help about the operation of the software any time while using the software. This is provided by the on-line help system. This is different from the guidance and error messages which are flashed automatically without the user asking for them. The guidance messages prompt the user regarding the options he has regarding the next command, and the status of the last command, etc.

On-line Help System. Users expect the on-line help messages to be tailored to the context in which they invoke the "help system". Therefore, a good on-line help system should keep track of what a user is doing while invoking the help system and provide the output message in a context- dependent way. Also, the help messages should be tailored to the user's experience level. Further, a good on-line help system should take advantage of any graphics and animation characteristics of the screen and should not just be a copy of the user's manual. Figure gives a snapshot of a typical on-line help provided by a user interface.

Example of an on-line help interface

Guidance Messages: The guidance messages should be carefully designed to prompt the user about the next actions he might purse, the current status of the system, the progress made so far in processing his last command, etc. A good guidance system should have different levels of sophistication for different categories of users. For example, a user using a command language interface might need a different type of guidance compared to a user using a menu or iconic interface. Also, users should have an option to turn off detailed messages.

Mode-based Interface Vs. Modeless Interface

A mode is a state or collection of states in which only a subset of all user interaction tasks can be performed. In a modeless interface, the same set of commands can be invoked at any time during the running of the software. Thus, a modeless interface has only a single mode and all the commands are available all the time during the operation of the software. On the other hand, in a mode-based interface, different set of commands can be invoked depending on the mode in which the system is, i.e. the mode at any instant is determined by the sequence of commands already issued by the user.

A mode-based interface can be represented using a state transition diagram, where each node of the state transition diagram would represent a mode. Each state of the state transition diagram can be annotated with the commands that are meaningful in that state.

An example of mode-based interface

Figure shows the interface of a word processing program. The top-level menu provides the user with a gamut of operations like file open, close, save, etc. When the user chooses the open option, another frame is popped up which limits the user to select a name from one of the folders.

Graphical user Interface Vs. Text-based user Interface

The following comparisons are based on various characteristics of a GUI with those of a text-based user interface.

- In a GUI multiple windows with different information can simultaneously be displayed on the user screen. This is perhaps one of the biggest advantages of GUI over text- based interfaces since the user has the flexibility to simultaneously interact with several related items at any time and can have access to different system information displayed in different windows.

- Iconic information representation and symbolic information manipulation is possible in a GUI. Symbolic information manipulation such as dragging an icon representing a file to a trash can be deleting is intuitively very appealing and the user can instantly remember it.

- A GUI usually supports command selection using an attractive and user-friendly menu selection system.

- In a GUI, a pointing device such as a mouse or a light pen can be used for issuing commands. The use of a pointing device increases the efficacy issue procedure.

- On the flip side, a GUI requires special terminals with graphics capabilities for running and also requires special input devices such a mouse. On the other hand, a text-based user interface can be implemented even on a cheap alphanumeric display terminal. Graphics terminals are usually much more expensive than alphanumeric terminals. However, display terminals with graphics capability with bit-mapped high-resolution displays and significant amount of local processing power have become affordable and over the years have replaced text-based terminals on all desktops. Therefore, the emphasis of this lesson is on GUI design rather than text- based user interface design.

User Interface Design

User interface design (UI) or user interface engineering is the design of user interfaces for machines and software, such as computers, home appliances, mobile devices, and other electronic devices, with the focus on maximizing usability and the user experience. The goal of user interface design is to make the user's interaction as simple and efficient as possible, in terms of accomplishing user goals (user-centered design).

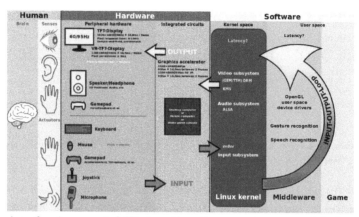

The graphical user interface is presented (displayed) on the computer screen. It is the result of processed user input and usually the primary interface for human-machine interaction. The touch user interfaces popular on small mobile devices are an overlay of the visual output to the visual input.

Good user interface design facilitates finishing the task at hand without drawing unnecessary attention to itself. Graphic design and typography are utilized to support its usability, influencing how the user performs certain interactions and improving the aesthetic appeal of the design; design aesthetics may enhance or detract from the ability of users to use the functions of the interface. The design process must balance technical functionality and visual elements (e.g., mental model) to create a system that is not only operational but also usable and adaptable to changing user needs.

Interface design is involved in a wide range of projects from computer systems, to cars, to commercial planes; all of these projects involve much of the same basic human interactions yet also require some unique skills and knowledge. As a result, designers tend to specialize in certain types of projects and have skills centered on their expertise, whether that be software design, user research, web design, or industrial design.

Processes

User interface design requires a good understanding of user needs. There are several phases and processes in the user interface design, some of which are more demanded upon than others, depending on the project. (Note: for the remainder of this section, the word *system* is used to denote any project whether it is a website, application, or device.)

- Functionality requirements gathering – assembling a list of the functionality required by the system to accomplish the goals of the project and the potential needs of the users.

- User and task analysis – a form of field research, it's the analysis of the potential users of the system by studying how they perform the tasks that the design must support, and conducting interviews to elucidate their goals. Typical questions involve:

o   What would the user want the system to do?

o   How would the system fit in with the user's normal workflow or daily activities?

o   How technically savvy is the user and what similar systems does the user already use?

o   What interface look & feel styles appeal to the user?

- Information architecture – development of the process and/or information flow of the system (i.e. for phone tree systems, this would be an option tree flowchart and for web sites this would be a site flow that shows the hierarchy of the pages).

- Prototyping – development of wire-frames, either in the form of paper proto-types or simple interactive screens. These prototypes are stripped of all look & feel elements and most content in order to concentrate on the interface.

- Usability inspection – letting an evaluator inspect a user interface. This is gener-ally considered to be cheaper to implement than usability testing, and can be used early on in the development process since it can be used to evaluate prototypes or specifications for the system, which usually cannot be tested on users. Some common usability inspection methods include cognitive walkthrough, which fo-cuses the simplicity to accomplish tasks with the system for new users, heuristic evaluation, in which a set of heuristics are used to identify usability problems in the UI design, and pluralistic walkthrough, in which a selected group of people step through a task scenario and discuss usability issues.

- Usability testing – testing of the prototypes on an actual user—often using a technique called think aloud protocol where you ask the user to talk about their thoughts during the experience. User interface design testing allows the design-er to understand the reception of the design from the viewer's standpoint, and thus facilitates creating successful applications.

- Graphical user interface design – actual look and feel design of the final graph-ical user interface (GUI). It may be based on the findings developed during the user research, and refined to fix any usability problems found through the re-sults of testing.Depending on the type of interface being created, this process typically involves some computer programming in order to validate forms, es-tablish links or perform a desired action.

- Software Maintenance - After the deployment of a new interface, occasional maintenance may be required to fix software bugs, change features, or com-pletely upgrade the system. Once a decision is made to upgrade the interface, the legacy system will undergo another version of the design process, and will begin to repeat the stages of the interface life cycle.

Requirements

The dynamic characteristics of a system are described in terms of the dialogue requirements contained in seven principles of part 10 of the ergonomics standard, the ISO 9241. This standard establishes a framework of ergonomic "principles" for the dialogue techniques with high-level definitions and illustrative applications and examples of the principles. The principles of the dialogue represent the dynamic aspects of the interface and can be mostly regarded as the "feel" of the interface. The seven dialogue principles are:

- Suitability for the task: the dialogue is suitable for a task when it supports the user in the effective and efficient completion of the task.

- Self-descriptiveness: the dialogue is self-descriptive when each dialogue step is immediately comprehensible through feedback from the system or is explained to the user on request.

- Controllability: the dialogue is controllable when the user is able to initiate and control the direction and pace of the interaction until the point at which the goal has been met.

- Conformity with user expectations: the dialogue conforms with user expectations when it is consistent and corresponds to the user characteristics, such as task knowledge, education, experience, and to commonly accepted conventions.

- Error tolerance: the dialogue is error tolerant if despite evident errors in input, the intended result may be achieved with either no or minimal action by the user.

- Suitability for individualization: the dialogue is capable of individualization when the interface software can be modified to suit the task needs, individual preferences, and skills of the user.

- Suitability for learning: the dialogue is suitable for learning when it supports and guides the user in learning to use the system.

The concept of usability is defined of the ISO 9241 standard by effectiveness, efficiency, and satisfaction of the user. Part 11 gives the following definition of usability:

- Usability is measured by the extent to which the intended goals of use of the overall system are achieved (effectiveness).

- The resources that have to be expended to achieve the intended goals (efficiency).

- The extent to which the user finds the overall system acceptable (satisfaction).

Effectiveness, efficiency, and satisfaction can be seen as quality factors of usability. To evaluate these factors, they need to be decomposed into sub-factors, and finally, into usability measures.

The information presentation is described in Part 12 of the ISO 9241 standard for the organization of information (arrangement, alignment, grouping, labels, location), for the display of graphical objects, and for the coding of information (abbreviation, color, size, shape, visual cues) by seven attributes. The "attributes of presented information" represent the static aspects of the interface and can be generally regarded as the "look" of the interface. The attributes are detailed in the recommendations given in the standard. Each of the recommendations supports one or more of the seven attributes. The seven presentation attributes are:

- Clarity: the information content is conveyed quickly and accurately.

- Discriminability: the displayed information can be distinguished accurately.

- Conciseness: users are not overloaded with extraneous information.

- Consistency: a unique design, conformity with user's expectation.

- Detectability: the user's attention is directed towards information required.

- Legibility: information is easy to read.

- Comprehensibility: the meaning is clearly understandable, unambiguous, interpretable, and recognizable.

The user guidance in Part 13 of the ISO 9241 standard describes that the user guidance information should be readily distinguishable from other displayed information and should be specific for the current context of use. User guidance can be given by the following five means:

- Prompts indicating explicitly (specific prompts) or implicitly (generic prompts) that the system is available for input.

- Feedback informing about the user's input timely, perceptible, and non-intrusive.

- Status information indicating the continuing state of the application, the system's hardware and software components, and the user's activities.

- Error management including error prevention, error correction, user support for error management, and error messages.

- On-line help for system-initiated and user initiated requests with specific information for the current context of use.

Research

User interface design has been a topic of considerable research, including on its aesthetics. Standards have been developed as far back as the 1980s for defining the usability of software products. One of the structural bases has become the IFIP user interface reference model. The model proposes four dimensions to structure the user interface:

- The input/output dimension (the look)

- The dialogue dimension (the feel)

- The technical or functional dimension (the access to tools and services)

- The organizational dimension (the communication and co-operation support)

This model has greatly influenced the development of the international standard ISO 9241 describing the interface design requirements for usability. The desire to understand application-specific UI issues early in software development, even as an application was being developed, led to research on GUI rapid prototyping tools that might offer convincing simulations of how an actual application might behave in production use. Some of this research has shown that a wide variety of programming tasks for GUI-based software can, in fact, be specified through means other than writing program code.

Research in recent years is strongly motivated by the increasing variety of devices that can, by virtue of Moore's law, host very complex interfaces.

Research has also been conducted on generating user interfaces automatically, to match a user's level of ability for different levels of interaction.

At the moment, in addition to traditional prototypes, the literature proposes new solutions, such as an experimental mixed prototype based on a configurable physical prototype that allow to achieve a complete sense of touch, thanks to the physical mock-up, and a realistic visual experience, thanks to the superimposition of the virtual interface on the physical prototype with Augmented Reality techniques.

References

- Greg Wilson (2006). "Off with Their HUDs!: Rethinking the Heads-Up Display in Console Game Design". Gamasutra. Retrieved February 14, 2006

- "Introduction Section". Recent advances in business administration. [S.l.]: Wseas. 2010. p. 190. ISBN 978-960-474-161-8. Other terms used are operator interface console (OIC) and operator interface terminal (OIT)

- Citi, Luca (2009). "Development of a neural interface for the control of a robotic hand" (PDF). Scuola Superiore Sant'Anna, Pisa, Italy: IMT Institute for Advanced Studies Lucca: 5. Retrieved 7 June 2014

- John W. Satzinger; Lorne Olfman (March 1998). "User interface consistency across end-user applications: the effects on mental models". Journal of Management Information Systems. Managing virtual workplaces and teleworking with information technology. Armonk, NY. 14 (4): 167–193

- Raskin, Jef (2000). The human interface : new directions for designing interactive systems (1. printing. ed.). Reading, Mass. [u.a.]: Addison Wesley. ISBN 0-201-37937-6

- Sweet, David (October 2001). "9 - Constructing A Responsive User Interface". KDE 2.0 Development. Sams Publishing. Retrieved 13 June 2014

- "The role of context in perceptions of the aesthetics of web pages over time". International Journal of Human–Computer Studies. 2009-01-05. Retrieved 2009-04-02

- Kernighan, Brian W.; Pike, Rob (1984). The UNIX Programming Environment. Englewood Cliffs: Prentice-Hall. ISBN 0-13-937699-2

- Shneiderman, Ben (August 1983). "Direct Manipulation. A Step Beyond Programming Languages". IEEE Computer. 1 (8): 57–69. Archived from the original on 8 Feb 2012. Retrieved 2010-12-28

- Friedman, Ted (2005). "Chapter 5: 1984". Electric Dreams: Computers in American Culture. New York University Press. ISBN 0-8147-2740-9. Retrieved October 6, 2011

- Washington Post (August 24, 1995). "With Windows 95's Debut, Microsoft Scales Heights of Hype". Washington Post. Retrieved November 8, 2013

Permissions

All chapters in this book are published with permission under the Creative Commons Attribution Share Alike License or equivalent. Every chapter published in this book has been scrutinized by our experts. Their significance has been extensively debated. The topics covered herein carry significant information for a comprehensive understanding. They may even be implemented as practical applications or may be referred to as a beginning point for further studies.

We would like to thank the editorial team for lending their expertise to make the book truly unique. They have played a crucial role in the development of this book. Without their invaluable contributions this book wouldn't have been possible. They have made vital efforts to compile up to date information on the varied aspects of this subject to make this book a valuable addition to the collection of many professionals and students.

This book was conceptualized with the vision of imparting up-to-date and integrated information in this field. To ensure the same, a matchless editorial board was set up. Every individual on the board went through rigorous rounds of assessment to prove their worth. After which they invested a large part of their time researching and compiling the most relevant data for our readers.

The editorial board has been involved in producing this book since its inception. They have spent rigorous hours researching and exploring the diverse topics which have resulted in the successful publishing of this book. They have passed on their knowledge of decades through this book. To expedite this challenging task, the publisher supported the team at every step. A small team of assistant editors was also appointed to further simplify the editing procedure and attain best results for the readers.

Apart from the editorial board, the designing team has also invested a significant amount of their time in understanding the subject and creating the most relevant covers. They scrutinized every image to scout for the most suitable representation of the subject and create an appropriate cover for the book.

The publishing team has been an ardent support to the editorial, designing and production team. Their endless efforts to recruit the best for this project, has resulted in the accomplishment of this book. They are a veteran in the field of academics and their pool of knowledge is as vast as their experience in printing. Their expertise and guidance has proved useful at every step. Their uncompromising quality standards have made this book an exceptional effort. Their encouragement from time to time has been an inspiration for everyone.

The publisher and the editorial board hope that this book will prove to be a valuable piece of knowledge for students, practitioners and scholars across the globe.

Index

Printed in the USA
CPSIA information can be obtained
at www.ICGtesting.com
JSHW051407221024
72173JS00006B/1318

9 781632 407047